LIFE
STORIES

LIFE STORIES

D. C. Reardon

CROSSWAY BOOKS • WHEATON, ILLINOIS
A DIVISION OF GOOD NEWS PUBLISHERS

Life Stories.

Copyright © 1992 by D. C. Reardon.

Published by Crossway Books, a division of
Good News Publishers, 1300 Crescent St., Wheaton, Illinois 60187.

Excerpted from *Aborted Women: Silent No More,* © 1987 by David C. Reardon;
published by Crossway Books and Loyola University Press.

First printing, 1992

Printed in the United States of America

ISBN 0-89107-693-X

Library of Congress Catalog Card Number 92-073373

00		99		98		97		96		95		94		93		92
15	14	13	12	11	10	9	8	7	6	5	4	3	2	1

*To Mary
and her children
of tears*

CONTENTS

FOREWORD

"And when Pandora lifted the lid of the gift she had coveted for so long, out flew plagues and sorrows for all humankind."

—Pandora's box

In 1973, the United States Supreme Court legalized abortion on demand throughout the nation. Many hailed it as a great step forward for women. Others called it a terrible crime against unborn children. Since that time, the nation has been torn by the political debate and civil strife between these two opposing groups. Both sides speak in terms of high ideals. Those who defend abortion speak of "freedom of choice." Those who denounce it emphasize the "right to life."

Between these polarized groups lies a third group, a group largely ignored in this battle of ideals and rhetoric. This third group is made up of the women who have actually had abortions. These women do not speak of abortion in terms of political or ideological philosophies. They do not cherish abortion as a utopian freedom, nor do they condemn it as the ultimate vice. They have no patience with such abstract mindgames, because to them, abortion is very real.

These women have confronted the harsh circumstances which demand abortion, and they have struggled with its painful decisions. They have experienced abortion in all its realities, in its relief and in its shame. Theirs is a voice that needs to be heard—indeed, has a right to be heard. For above all others, theirs is the voice of experience.

This book is based on the experiences of women who have had abortions. The hundreds of women who have joined together here to share their stories and insights have done so in order to separate the realities of abortion from the myths and the slogans. They come from all parts of the country, from all walks of life. Some are rich, others poor. Some aborted for reasons of health, some because they could not afford a child. A few aborted because their pregnancies were the result of rape, others because the child they carried might have been deformed. Others aborted purely for the sake of convenience.

But despite their many differences, all these women feel that they were deceived and manipulated. Together, they are determined to save other women from the same fate. For these women, abortion is not some great "privilege" which has been granted to their gender. Instead, they see abortion as a tool by which women have been *abandoned* and *exploited*.

Contrary to the popular slogan "freedom of choice," women who have experienced it know that abortion is seldom, if ever, a "free choice." Instead, legalized abortion has become a tool for the manipulation and exploitation of women. As will be seen, many of these women were forced to abort by boyfriends and husbands who begged and threatened them to "do the sensible thing." Some were forced to abort by insistent parents. Others were intimidated into abortion by physicians who were afraid of malpractice suits, or by social workers seeking to reduce the welfare rolls. Still others felt forced to abort because of the social prejudice against unwed mothers, or because of a social insistence that they handle their problems alone. But whatever the pressures they faced, all of these women felt backed into a corner and saw abortion as the only way out. They were made to feel trapped and isolated. For nearly all women, abortion is experienced not as an act of "choice," but as an act of despair—their *only* choice.

The price which women pay for being abandoned and exploited by the "privilege" of abortion is extremely high. Women who have abortions quickly learn that it is not nearly as "safe and easy" as pro-abortionists would have us believe. Instead, *abortion is dangerous to both the physical and mental health of women*. In fact, as we will see, half of all aborted women experience some immediate or long-term physical complications, and almost all suffer emotional or psychological aftershocks.

Finally, instead of being a giant step forward for women's rights, *legal abortion is the most destructive manifestation of discrimination against women today*. The abortion mentality is sexism incarnate. This sexism is apparent in four ways.

First, with abortions easily and legally available, as well as socially acceptable, it is easier than ever for men to sexually exploit women. When their promises of love end in pregnancy, these uncommitted and selfish men are free to manipulate women into abortions so as to free themselves of unwanted commitments. They whine and pout about "doing the sensible thing," or resort to threats—"If you don't have an abortion, I'll leave you." In either case, the end result is the same: the women face the risks and guilt of abortion alone. And if a woman resists such coercion, her exploiter can simply deny all personal and financial responsibility for *his* "unwanted" child, saying, "You're stuck with it now, baby. After all, you could have had an abortion." Thus, the abortion "choice" is just one more arena in which men condition their love and respect on the basis of women's obedience to their desires.

Second, beyond subjecting women to manipulation and threats of abandonment, the abortion mentality attacks the unique value of female sexuality. This is a result of the pro-abortion rhetoric (generally promulgated by population control zealots) which portrays abortion not as an *alternative* to childbirth, but as *preferable* to childbirth. This attempt to de-sex women, to separate them from their reproductive potentials, has eroded the natural pride which women enjoy in being able to conceive and bear children—a creative wonder which no man can duplicate. Instead of praising this unique potential of women, the abortion mentality belittles it, or at best dismisses it as commonplace. No other public policy has ever attempted to undermine a creative capacity of one half of its populace.

Third, women are being abandoned by a society which has no patience for a problem unique to women—an unplanned pregnancy. Rather than receiving the love and support needed to cope with this challenge, women are offered the easy way out, the "quick fix," the cover-up—abortion. They are seen as second-rate citizens with second-rate problems, and so they are handed a make-shift solution. They themselves are "socially aborted." Abortion is a superficial and potentially dangerous answer to the problems of a pregnant woman. Abortion is the "cheap love" which society offers as a substitute for costly care and honest commitment. Though offered superficial support in making their abortion decisions, women must always face the consequences alone. Abortion, unlike childbirth, is always a lonely process.

Lastly, while feminists have won women the right to both family and career, the abortion mentality tells women that one must be sacrificed for the other. Women are made to feel that they must "plan" children around their careers, because "unplanned" children will ruin their lives. Thus, abortion is defended with the argument that women are restricted by the limits of their careers, their education, or their finances. Faced with these limits, the sexist abortion mentality says, women are not "strong" enough to survive an unplanned pregnancy, much less raise an "unwanted" child or endure giving it up for adoption. Instead of helping women to be strong, independent, and capable of handling their lives in spite of the social prejudices against "problem" pregnancies, the expediency of abortion encourages women to be weak, dependent, and incapable of dealing with unexpected challenges. This mentality tells women that they must depend on the technology of abortion to solve their problems for them. Just as in the traditional, male-dominated social order, the abortion mentality dictates to women what they *cannot* do, what they *cannot* handle.

In the simplest of terms, abortion has been sold to women under false premises. We have been lied to, manipulated, and exploited. For too long we have remained silent, too ashamed to speak out, too ashamed to admit our errors. Now this has changed. Those who have experienced abortion firsthand are no longer willing to be silent.

My name is Nancyjo Mann. I am one of the sixteen million women who has had an abortion since 1973. I've seen this from all angles; from the pro-choice side, the pro-life side, and most importantly, from the side of a woman who has experienced abortion. I exercised my "right to choose," and I became a victim of this Pandora's Box. It was a pretty, tempting treasure. It promised to solve all my problems and restore full control over my life. But instead this "right," this "gift," was filled with sufferings and regret which I could never have anticipated or imagined. What follows here is my story. It is not a unique one. Millions of others have been seduced by the same false promises. Mine is but one example of the abortion reality.

Abortion is the result of pressures on a woman's life. The pressures leading up to my abortion began in high school where, like many careless, impatient, and short-sighted teens, my boyfriend and I were sexually active. In my junior year, I became pregnant.

My mother was terribly upset. "Oh, what are the neighbors going to say?" she worried. "You'll shame the family. You've got to have an abortion."

This was in 1970. We lived in Iowa where abortion was still illegal except when necessary to save a woman's life. This fact, however, did not deter my insistent mother, since abortions were easily available under the "progressive" laws of New York and California. My mother only wanted what she thought was best for me, but I *didn't* want an abortion. I wanted to get married. Fortunately, my father stood by me and my mother learned to accept my decision. This was the first time that abortion was ever in my thoughts.

Being a wife, raising a daughter, and finishing school is rough, especially for a seventeen-year-old. No one goes out of their way to make it easier, either. Instead, it seemed like everyone figured I wanted to face all those pressures alone. After all, I could have had an abortion and saved everyone the hassle.

But I survived. I graduated. And I was happy. Two years later I had my second child, a son. Not long after that, my husband left me. The responsibilities of being a father and a husband had become more than he was willing to handle. The joys of our young married life were no longer worth the pressures of adjustment. He wanted out, and so he left.

No sooner were we divorced than I fell right back into trouble. I was still on the Pill, and so when I began dating a new guy, I figured there was nothing to worry about. After all, I was being "responsible." But despite the wonders of modern contraception, I became pregnant with my third child. Four months later we were married.

Though there was a superficial happiness in this second marriage, it didn't last more than ten weeks. On October 30, 1974, he walked out the front door. My strong, "dependable" husband just couldn't handle the prospect of being responsible for another child. It was too much for him.

I was absolutely stunned by the suddenness of his departure. I was left five and a half months pregnant, with my two young children and no source of income. I didn't know what to do. Finally, I took the kids and drove over to my parents' house. My mother and one of my brothers were there. I was at a loss. "What am I going to do? He left!" I said. They talked to me for a while and finally my mother said, "Nancy, you're never going to amount to a hill of beans. What man is ever going to want you with three children, let alone the two you already have? With all those kids, you'll probably end up on welfare for the rest of your life. You're never going to be anybody. It's obvious that you'll just have to have an abortion."

If I wasn't upset and depressed enough already, this type of "practical" advice made me feel even worse. I felt totally helpless. I was a failure. . . . How could I resist when everyone was just trying to "do the best thing" for me? They were sincerely trying to help me and they were the only source of support I had. Upset, depressed, tired, desperate, I took the path of least resistance. I adopted the attitudes of those around me. I accepted their decisions as my own. I simply floated along with "what had to be done." Besides, I thought, maybe if I get rid of this "problem pregnancy," my husband will come back to me.

My mother made all the arrangements. She called my ob/gyn and he said he wouldn't do an abortion, much less a second trimester. He told her that the only one in town that would do it was Dr. Paulino Fong, a prominent doctor in that area. Without losing a moment of time for reflection or doubts, my mother and I went over to see him. When he learned that I was seeking an abortion, he immediately had me brought into an examination room.

After a quick examination, my abortionist told me that I would have to have the abortion done within the next twenty-four hours or I would be outside the limit of the law. Of course this wasn't true, but I didn't know that then. Abortions are legal throughout all three trimesters, right up to the day before birth, and I was still well within the second trimester. He just used this little lie to pressure me into making a quick decision.

But that was only the first lie he told me. The second lie came during my "counseling session," when I asked, "What are you going to do to me if I have this abortion?" All he did was look at my stomach and say, "I'm going to take a little fluid out, put a little fluid in, you'll have severe cramps and expel the fetus." "Is that all?" I asked. "That's it." "O.K.," I said. It was only later, after the abortion had begun, that I was to learn that what he described as "cramps" was actually the labor process. These "severe cramps" were not just going to make my pregnancy magically disappear. Instead, I was going to go through all the motions of normal childbirth—water breaking, labor pains, etc. The only difference was that the baby I would deliver would be dead.

After telling me I had to have the abortion within the next twenty-four hours, Dr. Fong scheduled me for a saline abortion in the hospital that same afternoon. Ironically, a little while after my abortion a nurse who worked at the hospital told me that Fong always scheduled his abortions for the same day that the patient contacted him. At one time he had admitted patients to the hospital the night before the surgery so that they could be observed and their food intake limited. But when some of his patients had changed their minds during the night, sometimes after questioning nurses about what actually would happen, he began to insist on doing the abortions immediately. Too many patients, and profits, were slipping out the front door.

The third lie in my "counseling" was a lie of omission. He never told me any of the risks involved. Only later did I find out that if he had hit a vein, the saline solution could have made me violently ill or caused any number of other complications, including death. He told me none of this. Instead he made it sound like a simple and relatively painless procedure.

I was so naive. I trusted him. After all, he was a doctor. A respected and educated man. And like everyone else, I had always heard that legal abortion was "safe and easy." It wasn't until he had me on the table that I began to question these illusions. It wasn't until he pulled out an enormous syringe that I became scared. The needle alone was four inches long. Suddenly I realized that this was not going to be as easy as he had implied.

The first thing he did was withdraw 60 cc's of amniotic fluid. At that point I started to feel afraid for my baby. I could feel her thrashing about, scared by this intrusion. I wanted to scream out, "Please, stop. Don't do this to me!" But I just couldn't get it out. I was petrified with fear.

After the fluid was withdrawn, he injected 200 cc's of the saline solution—half a pint of concentrated salt solution. From then on, it was terrible. My baby began thrashing about—it was like a regular boxing match in there. She was in pain. The saline was burning her skin, her eyes, her throat. It was choking her, making her sick. She was in agony, trying to escape. She was scared and confused at how her wonderful little home had suddenly been turned into a death trap.

For some reason it had never entered my mind that with an abortion she would have to die. I had never wanted my baby to die; I only wanted to get rid of my "problem." But it was too late to turn back now. There was no way to save her. So instead I talked to her. I tried to comfort her. I tried to ease her pain. I told her I didn't want to do this to her, but it was too late to stop it. I didn't want her to die. I begged her not to die. I told her I was sorry, to forgive me, that I was wrong, that I didn't want to kill her.

For two hours I could feel her struggling inside me. But then, as suddenly as it began, she stopped. Even today, I remember her very last kick on my left side. She had no strength left. She gave up and died. Despite my grief and guilt, I was relieved that her pain was finally over. But I was never the same again. The abortion killed not only my daughter; it killed a part of me.

Before that needle had entered my abdomen I had liked myself. Though I may have had my share of problems, I had seen myself as basically a good person. I wasn't into any wild scenes. I was a good housewife and a loving mother. I was happy to be me. But when that needle entered my womb, when it pulled out the nurturing fluid of motherhood and replaced it with that venom of death, when the child I had abandoned suddenly began its struggle within me, I hated myself. It was that fast. Every bit of self-esteem, every value I held dear, every hope of which I had ever dreamed—all were stripped away by the poison of that one vain act. Every memory of joy was now tainted by the stench of death. That moment of desperation which had led me to this "healer's table" had now positioned itself as ruler of my life. I had abandoned myself to despair and despair was my future. There was no way to stop it. There was no way to put everything back the way it had been. I no longer had any control, any choice. I was powerless. I was weak. I was a murderer.

A little while after my baby stopped moving they gave me an intravenous injection to help stimulate labor. I was in hard labor for twelve hours, all through the night. When finally I delivered, the nurses didn't make it to my room in time. I delivered my daughter myself at 5:30 the next morning, October 31st. After I delivered her, I held her in my hands. I looked her over from top to bottom. She had a head of hair, and her eyes had begun to open. I looked at her little tiny feet and hands. Her fingers and toes even had little fingernails and swirls of fingerprints. Everything was perfect. She was not a "fetus." She was not a "product of conception." She was a tiny human being. The pathology report listed her as more than seven inches from head to rump. With her legs extended, she was over a foot long. She weighed a pound and a half, more than many of the premature babies being saved in incubators in every hospital in the country. But these vital statistics did not mention her most striking trait: She was my daughter. Twisted with agony. Silent and still. Dead.

It seemed like I held her for ten minutes or more, but it was probably only thirty seconds because as soon as the nurses came rushing in, they grabbed her from my hands and threw her—literally threw her—into a bedpan and carried her away.

To add insult to injury, after my daughter was taken away, they brought another woman into the room to finish the last hour of her labor. But this woman wasn't having an abortion. No, she had a beautiful, healthy baby boy. No words can describe how rough that was on me.

I was released from the hospital eight hours after the delivery. The official report filled out by my abortionist stated that the procedure had been completed with "no complications." Three days later I went back into what felt like labor again, and I passed a piece of placenta about the size of my hand. It had been an incomplete abortion, a fact which had been missed by the pathology lab which had reported that the placenta had been delivered "intact."

Soon afterwards I began to withdraw from those who loved me, especially from my family since they had supported and encouraged me to have the abortion. There was a part of me that didn't want to be loved, especially by those who had known me before. I was filled with guilt and sorrow. I felt empty, and I lived under a constant feeling of dread. Newborn infants caught my eye and filled me with longing, but I was afraid to touch them. Whenever a friend would offer to let me hold her baby, I would always refuse. I was too afraid of my own destructiveness. I was terrified that I might somehow hurt another child.

Three weeks after my abortion, I chose to be sterilized by tubal ligation. I couldn't cope with the idea that I could ever possibly kill again. It was too devastating. Too mind-boggling. My body which had the potential of creating life was now too easily a host of death.

I became preoccupied with thoughts of death. I fantasized about how I would die. My baby had struggled for two hours. I've tried to imagine myself dying a similar kind of death. If a pillow was put over my face to suffocate me, I would struggle for a bit, but in less than four minutes I would pass out. But she had suffered for *two hours*. Would I be so tormented?

Four months after my abortion, the bleeding and infection were still persistent. Too ashamed to go to my own ob/gyn, I returned to Dr. Fong and he performed a D&C to clean out the uterus. He cut off my cervix and left the packing inside of me. Three weeks later I was grossly rotted out inside. Seven months later, at twenty-two years of age, I was forced to undergo a total hysterectomy—all because of that "safe and easy," legal abortion.

By this time, I didn't care if I lived or died anymore. I was going through a radical personality change and was becoming increasingly self-destructive. Though I had been shy as a teenager, now I forced myself to become bold and aggressive. If I could only become tough and callous, I reasoned, I would be protected from the hurt. So I began to hang around the tough crowd, imitating their ways, taking on their attitudes. What attracted me to them was their destructiveness—their contempt for the world. Soon I was carrying guns and knives, and biking around with motorcycle gangs and worse. The people I ran with were out to destroy, steal, and maim, and that is what I wanted to do to both others and *myself.*

The desire to destroy is a double-edged weapon. It is both a sword of wrath and a ritual suicide knife of *hari-kari.* I hated the world only as much as I hated myself. By becoming destructive I was able to release my growing hatred towards this world that had abandoned me, abused me, and exploited me. At the same time, by running outside of the law, by attacking others, I opened myself up to attack. I signaled the world that I was ready to be punished and even killed. It didn't matter. Anger, defiance, self-punishment and self-destructiveness—all were one, and they were me.

I tried to immerse myself in destruction. I wanted to prove to myself that destroying others didn't hurt. After all, once you've killed you should be able to do anything. By doing every conceivable wrong, I hoped to strip myself of my conscience. I hoped to destroy all the values I had ever held. If only I could prove to myself that everything was meaningless, including the innocent daughter I had killed through abortion, then perhaps I could have the peace of total meaninglessness.

The natural center of this destructive, escapist world in which I lived, of course, was drugs. I began to fire up on heroin, cocaine—anything and everything I could find. I took acid every day for a year and a half. I smoked an ounce of pot every day. Drugs were my refuge, my comfort, my slow fuse to self-obliteration. Whenever I was stoned, I didn't have to think. If I couldn't think, I couldn't feel, and if I couldn't feel that was almost as good as being dead. It was a lot better than facing myself.

To earn my living during this time, I became a country pop singer for a small band that played the bars. But singing didn't provide enough to cover my drug expenses, so I began dealing drugs across the state line. Whenever that wasn't enough, I would join a few friends and burgle houses. The extra cash from our "discount sales" helped to tide me over.

On top of all of this, I swiftly became promiscuous. Sleeping around was a way to degrade myself while at the same time feeding on the false comforts of a sexual embrace. Through these quick and desperate intimacies, I secretly hoped I would someday find the love I so desperately needed, but all I found was sex. Soon this turned into prostituting myself to any man who could supply me with the drugs I needed. The promise of forgetfulness was worth any price.

I lived a life like this for four and a half years. It was a hell that can't be described. During this time, I was constantly pushing my abortion out of my mind. I never talked about it. I never dared to let myself even think about it. But it was never far away. In fact, a boyfriend of mine at that time later told me that almost every time I was stoned (which was every day) I would confess to him in a daze: "I had an abortion. You know, I had an abortion." No more than that. I would just keep telling him I had had an abortion, and he just kept telling me, "That's alright. It's in the past. Just forget about it." But I never remembered telling anyone, especially him. To me it was the deepest, darkest secret. It was only when all my conscious barriers were dropped that it came tumbling out.

The subconscious rumblings of my abortion revealed themselves in other ways, too. For example, after my abortion I became deathly afraid of the night. I would *never* go to sleep when it was dark. The night was the time during which I had labored for death. Only at 5 in the morning, when the new dawn was breaking, the time when my labor had ended and my daughter had been released, did I finally settle down and prepare myself for sleep. Never knowing why, my nights had become a time for escape, a time for restless fear.

Four years after my abortion, my self-destructive attitudes turned into an open desire for death. Suicide beckoned me, and I had no place to turn.

My suicidal desires climaxed on one bitter night in January of 1978. After putting the children to bed I sat dazed and despondent. What reason did I have to live? My two children were the only people I loved and valued. But did I really even deserve them? I wasn't worthy of their love. And the only love I was capable of giving to them was shriveled and distant. I took more than I gave. They would be better off with someone else. If anything, love for my children was a reason to die, not live. There were no reasons to live. Life was only pain and loneliness.

I was so low. There was no place lower to go. No place to hide. There were no more scraps of comfort to be found in the beds of strangers or the lines of coke. There was nothing. I was nothing.

I cried and I cried. My longing for death had become so overwhelming that I was scared that I was really going to do it. There was no reason *not to* die. Suddenly, I jumped up and ran into the bathroom and flushed my bottle of sleeping pills down the toilet.

Everything in me wanted to die, but I was scared of death. What was on the other side? Where would I go? I felt like I *needed* to die, but I was afraid to.

This long, dark night was filled with the bitter tears and taste of salt: Wanting to die. Afraid to die. My only escape was filled with unknown terrors.

In that brief sort of faith born of desperation, I cried out: "God, You've got to give me a reason to live." But even as the words left my lips, I was certain that it could not be. Even if there was a God, He could never love me after all that I had done. All my life I had ignored Him and mocked Him. Why should He come to my aid? My life was worth nothing.

I finally found sleep that night in the weakness brought by tears. Early the next morning, as if in answer to my faithless plea, hope came to me in the form of a phone call. It was Mark, a friend who seemed to have a knack for always popping into my life when I was in trouble. At first I was mad at him for calling so early in the morning, but it was worth it. His news was great. "Nancy," he said, "I'm down here in Kansas City and there is a studio here that wants to record you!"

"Baby, I've got it made," I yelled. "Kansas, here I come."

The recording date was set for April 28th. For four months I lived on that promise of fame. I practiced eight hours a day and took drugs all night.

Months later, after my recording date in Kansas turned out to be fictitious and my friend Mark dropped out of sight, never to be heard from again, I decided to take my career into my own hands. Leaving my children with my mother, I headed off to Golfport, Illinois. There I hoped I would find the big break which would get me a recording opportunity in Nashville.

Those were my plans, but they were scattered like straw when I was involved in a nearly fatal motorcycle accident. The front wheel simply popped off the bike, and I went skidding down the highway at full speed. Instead of Nashville, I found myself in the hospital with second and third degree burns covering approximately 50 percent of my body. In some areas, asphalt and gravel were imbedded up to three inches in my flesh. The pain was unbelievable. My vain dreams of glory were gone. I was back into the state of desperation from which I had first called out to God.

I was at the bottom of the barrel. This time I was certain that I was going to die. I had nothing to lose and everything to gain, so I prayed, "God, please be with me. I need You." And again He answered my prayer. After having resisted for so long, I allowed Him to become my Lord and Savior. The void in my heart that I had been trying to fill with everything else was finally filled with faith in God. From that moment on, I knew I wasn't going to die.

About nine months after leaving the hospital, I finally started to face the abortion I had tried so hard to bury. It was a very, very painful process. The wounds of abortion run deep, especially when they have been pushed down for so long. I nearly went through an emotional breakdown. I had to relive it all, to sort it all out. But this time the Lord was with me offering support and forgiveness. Step by step we went. But He was patient. It took three years, but finally I was able to forgive myself. That's the hardest part. God's forgiveness is ready and waiting. It's forgiving yourself that's hard.

By 1981, I had not only found peace with my abortion experience but felt drawn to help other women to overcome their pain and hurt. I knew that if I had hurt so much, surely there must be at least one other woman who felt the same. In early 1982, I founded Women Exploited By Abortion (WEBA) to minister to the needs of aborted women, to help them heal their pains. It immediately began to grow on its own. A newspaper article was written, then another and another, followed by radio and television appearances. Women from around the country began contacting me. As it turned out, there was a pent-up demand for a place of refuge, a place where women could share their abortion experiences, share their pain, share their strengths, and rebuild their lives.

With the founding of WEBA, the aftermath of abortion was no longer to be ignored. Women were no longer to be abandoned to silently suffer alone. It was time for this "evil necessity" to be purged in the open light. It was time for people to learn that abortion does not solve problems; instead, it changes them, warps them, and creates new problems. It was time for society to learn that abortion was no favor which women had the "right" to enjoy. It was a trap. A curse. A cheap substitute for love and support. A tool for the manipulation and exploitation of the women society has abandoned. We are its victims, the aborted women of an unwanting society.

Nancy Jo Mann
Founder, Women Exploited by Abortion (WEBA)

O N E

A Survey of Women Who Aborted

Since the mid-1960s, abortion has been a major national issue, the subject of state and Congressional investigations, thousands of articles, and hundreds of books. But most of this attention has been focused on the ideological aspects of abortion: "freedom of choice" versus the "right to life." While those on both sides of the issue have published reams of material investigating whether or not the aborted fetus is a "person," comparatively little has been done to identify and understand the *women* who have abortions—until now.

Who are the women who abort? This is a question which should be answered with more than government statistics of age, race, and marital status. Instead, women who abort must be understood as *people*, a group of women faced with a common problem, seeking a common solution. To understand their needs and to empathize with their lives, we must understand their feelings, their dreams, their joys, and their sorrows. We need to know *who* these women are, *why* they choose abortion, and perhaps most importantly, *how* abortion changes their lives. Knowing the answer to these questions, other women who are faced with unplanned pregnancies will be better prepared to decide when abortion is their best choice, and when it is their worst.

There are two possible approaches to understanding the who, how, and why of the abortion experience. The first method is a *subjective* approach which looks at the personal stories and reflections of aborted women. The second method is an *objective* approach based on surveys and statistical analyses. Each approach has its own particular strengths and weaknesses. The subjective approach is more detailed and more intimate, but its personal nature makes it more difficult to reach general conclusions. If left to stand alone, one could never be sure whether a particular woman's subjective experiences are typical of aborted women, or whether her experience is a rare exception. Objective data, on the other hand, is better suited for drawing general conclusions: but it is so impersonal that it is good *only* for drawing generalities.

While subjective testimonies and objective surveys each have their weaknesses, when used together they can give us a complete view of the abortion experience. The objective data serves as the foundation, or skeleton, for identifying "typical" patterns, while the subjective testimony adds personal details and "fleshes out" the skeleton, providing it with depth and perspective.

To provide a complete picture of the abortion experience, therefore, this book includes both objective data and subjective testimonies.

LIMITATIONS OF THE SURVEY

Up to this time, there has been very little quantifiable information about women's experiences before, during, and after their abortions. Many studies have been done, but most have been severely limited in scope, concentrating on the demographic characteristics of aborting women, or only on their immediate, short-term reactions.

Detailed studies of the abortion experience are often blocked by practical and political difficulties. First, many pro-choice groups, such as the National Organization for Women (NOW), have long opposed any survey of aborted women. To these pro-choice advocates, it is not necessary to know *why* women abort or *how* abortion affects their lives, it is only important that their *choice* to abort is respected. Investigations into *why* women abort, they argue, are a violation of the aborted woman's right to privacy.[1] While NOW's position is intended to prevent probing into the private and pain-filled memories of aborted women, the lack of such information has prevented other women from being warned about the potential physical and psychological risks they face if they, too, choose abortion.

A second major obstacle to surveying aborted women is that access to these women is generally controlled by abortion providers. While a few abortion clinics have performed minor surveys of their clients, these surveys are generally superficial and are always limited to only the patients' short-term reactions to their experiences. Most abortion providers have little or no motivation to perform a five- or ten-year post-abortion follow-up study; yet they are the only ones with the names and addresses necessary to perform this research. On the other hand, even if there were a desire on the part of clinics to participate in such a study, there are legal obstacles which would probably prevent them from contacting previous patients for such purposes, since such an outreach effort might violate the former clients' rights of privacy.

Furthermore, even if abortion clinics were willing and able to cooperate in a long-range follow-up survey, the sample obtained would still be distorted by many factors. First, it is known that many women give false names and addresses to abortion clinics in order to protect their anonymity. Second, many women would have moved or married (and thus changed their names) during the course of the five to ten years between the abortion and the survey. Third, many of those who could be reached might refuse to "stir up" their abortion memories in order to answer a survey. Any and all of these factors might bias the results of the survey, since the few who would respond might not be fully representative of aborters in general.

The third limiting factor which has plagued all previous surveys is one of geographical constraints. Over 1.5 million elective abortions are performed each year in the United States. From one-fourth to one-third of all pregnancies are terminated by abortion. The abortion rate, however, is not uniform across the nation. Regional attitudes towards abortion play a major influence on the attractiveness of the abortion option. In more rural states, such as Missouri and Wyoming, less than one-tenth of all pregnancies are aborted. But in such major metropolitan areas as New York City and Washington, D. C., abortions outnumber live births.

The differences in abortion rates around the country seem to be directly related to regional values and social "sophistication." In most rural areas, attitudes toward abortion are generally negative, while urban areas tend to reflect more laissez-faire attitudes. In some large urban areas, however, lax standards are beginning to be replaced by a "social obligation to have an abortion if the conditions for carrying a baby to term are not perfect."[2]

Because all previous studies of aborted women have been performed out of a single clinic or abortion hospital, the results of all prior studies are limited by these regional attitudes and biases. With the creation of WEBA, however, a national, independent, long-range follow-up study of aborted women finally became possible. For the first time an identifiable group of aborted women was finally obtainable, without the need to rely on the cooperation (or face the interference) of an abortion clinic. Thus, in order to perform a long-range evaluation of the abortion experience, a survey was prepared and distributed through WEBA chapters in forty-two states to 252 previously aborted women. (The complete results of the survey are reproduced in the Appendix.)

COMPARING STATISTICS

Before evaluating the survey responses dealing with the abortion experience, however, it is necessary to see whether or not WEBA members are typical of a random sample of aborting women. This can be done by comparing the demographic characteristics of the WEBA women surveyed with the national abortion statistics which describe the "typical" aborter.

Age

National Statistics: The majority of all aborters, 55 percent, are between the ages of twenty and twenty-nine. Approximately 16 percent of aborting women are thirty years of age or over. The remaining 30 percent of abortions are performed on teenagers, with most teenage aborters in the range of seventeen to nineteen years of age. Less than one percent of all abortions are performed on girls under the age of fifteen.[3]

WEBA Sample: At the time of their abortions, 3 percent of the WEBA members sampled were fifteen years old or under, 42 percent were between fifteen and nineteen years old, 47 percent were between twenty and twenty-nine years old, and 8 percent were thirty years old or more. The youngest aborter in the sample was twelve years old, the oldest aborter was forty. The average age at the time of their abortions was 21.2 years old.

This sample suggests that WEBA members are a relatively close match to the national pattern discussed above, though WEBA's membership tends slightly towards younger aborters. This small variation from national averages might be an insignificant "blip" caused by the sampling process, or it may indicate that younger aborters are more likely to suffer traumatic abortion experiences and therefore be more likely to be attracted to contact an organization like WEBA. Since the evidence to be presented later shows that young women are more likely to be vulnerable to manipulation and exploitation by their boyfriends or parents, we are inclined to believe the latter hypothesis.

Marital Status

National Statistics: Approximately 80 percent of all aborters are reported as being unmarried. Most studies agree that the fear of single parenthood is a primary factor, if not the leading one, in the choice for most abortions.[4]

WEBA Sample: At the time of their abortions, 67 percent of the WEBA members surveyed were single and not engaged, 9 percent were single but engaged to be married, 6 percent were divorced or separated, and 18 percent were married. Again, WEBA members are a close match to the typical pattern of aborters described by national statistics.

Family Size

National Statistics: Approximately 58 percent of aborting women had no children at the time of their abortions. Of the rest, 19 percent already had one child, 14 percent had two, and the remaining 10 percent had three or more children.[5]

In terms of family planning, abortion is seldom used to avoid excess children. In fact, national statistics indicate that the more children a woman has, the less likely she is to abort a later child. Instead, most aborting women desire to have children at a later date, under more controlled circumstances. By aborting their first pregnancies, these women seek to delay their wanted children until some time when they have better marital and/or financial security.

WEBA Sample: Of the women surveyed, 73 percent were childless at the time of their abortion, 14 percent had one child, 9 percent had two children, and 5 percent had three or more children. In terms of family planning, only 7 percent indicated that concern over limiting their family size was an important factor in their abortion decisions.

Race

National Statistics: More than two-thirds of all abortions are done on white women. But the remaining one-third which are performed on non-white women is a comparatively high figure, since non-whites constitute only about 13 percent of the total American population. When measured on a per capita basis, non-white women are subjected to twice as many abortions as white women.[6]

This disproportionate concentration of abortions among non-whites stands in stark contrast to the situation prior to 1973, when the rate of abortion (both legal and illegal) among whites was twice as high as that found among non-whites. Before it was elevated to the status of a social right, or even a "social duty," abortion was primarily a middle- and upper-class vice associated with "saving face" or "status climbing." Racial minorities, and the poor in particular, were (and are) generally more accepting of unplanned pregnancies, and are more likely to be opposed to abortion on ethical grounds than is the population as a whole.[7] As we will see, however, minorities today are facing increased social and financial pressures to abort against their wills.[8] The rapid rise of abortion among non-whites, therefore, should be taken as evidence that the pressures which compel non-white women to abort are increasing, not that it has become a more "desirable" alternative among minorities.

WEBA Sample: Of the WEBA members surveyed, 87 percent were white and 13 percent were non-white. This percentage of non-whites is very close to the national percentage of non-whites in the population as a whole, but is only half of what should be expected in a perfect sample of "typical" aborters.

There are two possible explanations for this variance. First, the sampling technique used for this survey was geared towards maximizing input from a wide variety of geographical areas. This sampling method may not have included a proportionate representation of major population centers where there are high concentrations of non-whites. Second, the WEBA network is only four years old and may not have yet reached all segments of the aborting community in proportion to their need. Its public speakers, the majority of whom are white, may be concentrating on reaching out to predominantly white groups with whom they are already familiar and have easy access.

Repeat Abortions

National Statistics: Approximately 33 percent of all abortions are performed for repeat aborters. About 70 percent of repeat aborters have had one previous abortion, 16 percent have had two previous abortions, and the remainder have had three or more previous abortions. The number of women resorting to repeat abortions is increasing at a rate of about 3 percent yearly.[9]

WEBA Sample: Of the WEBA members sampled, 24 percent have had more than one abortion. This rate is approximately equivalent to the average national rate of repeat aborters in 1977, which is consistent with the fact that most of the WEBA women surveyed aborted from eight to twelve years ago.

When compared to the national demographic characteristics of the "typical" aborting women, WEBA members roughly fit into the same "typical" pattern. In other words, the WEBA women sampled in our survey are a fair, but not perfect, representation of aborting women in general. Therefore, in their answers to objective questions such as "What circumstances led to your abortions?" or "How long did it take you to make your decision?," the answers of the WEBA members sample are representative of aborting women in general.

When it comes to more subjective questions, however, such as "Are you satisfied with your abortion choice today?," it is uncertain how accurately the answers of WEBA members reflect those of aborting women in general. It cannot be forgotten that WEBA members are women who today regret their abortions, and this regret is clearly reflected in many of their answers. On the other hand, many WEBA members were once very much satisfied with their abortion decisions. If any one point is made clear by this survey and the interviews which follow, it is the fact that *dissatisfaction and regrets over abortion grow with time.*

In general, then, WEBA members represent a matured, reflective point of view of their abortion experiences. The average time between having their abortions and answering this survey is 10.0 years. While most short-term studies, performed only a few months after the abortion, reveal a seesawing ambivalence, a reluctant satisfaction with their choice, this study reflects the long-term view of aborted women. With the privilege of hindsight, the thoughts and feelings of the WEBA women surveyed are endowed with years of self-examination, learning, and change.

In short, because of the nature of the organization, the WEBA members who answered this survey generally represent a more settled and mature view of their abortion experience—a view which is primarily negative. How deeply this bias influences their answers to a specific question depends on the nature of the question. How accurately their answers reflect the long-term reactions of the general population of aborting women must be judged on whether or not WEBA women represent the attitudes of aborting women in general.

We maintain that WEBA is representative of the aborting population as a whole. This point will be further substantiated in Chapter Three, where we will see that most pro-choice studies have found the same doubts, the same complaints, and the same negative experiences among most aborting women. For now, it is sufficient for the reader to remember that as with all surveys, the following results are approximations based on a selected sample of persons. The results are more valuable for drawing general conclusions than specific ones.

CIRCUMSTANCES LEADING TO THE ABORTION

Age and Marital Status

As indicated earlier, 83 percent of the WEBA members surveyed were single, engaged, or separated when they discovered they were pregnant. Their average age at the time of their abortions was 21.2 years; the oldest was forty and the youngest was twelve. Nearly half were under the age of twenty.

Use of Birth Control

More than three-quarters of all those surveyed were not using any form of birth control at the time of conception. Lack of contraceptive protection, however, was *not* due to lack of knowledge or lack of access to birth control devices. Over 70 percent of these women were highly informed about birth control alternatives, and an additional 15 percent considered themselves to be moderately well informed. Only 15 percent claimed that they had had little or no knowledge of contraceptive practices. As we will see, these findings are consistent with other studies which have shown that most aborters tend to be highly informed about contraceptives but failed to use them at the time they became pregnant.

A significant number of abortions, however, do occur because of contraceptive failure. In this sample of aborting women, 23 percent were using a form of birth control at the time of conception. The method which failed most often for these aborters was the birth control pill. Forty-four percent of those using contraceptives were on the Pill, 22 percent were using a spermicide, 16 percent were using a diaphragm, 9 percent had an IUD in place, and 9 percent were using condoms. In addition, one woman became pregnant even though she had had a tubal ligation, and another became pregnant despite her mate's vasectomy.

After relying on the promises of these "responsible" birth control methods, many of these women felt betrayed by the technology they had trusted to keep them from becoming pregnant in the first place. In general, they felt that the pregnancy was not their fault but rather the fault of a contraceptive failure which they were now "forced" to correct through abortion.

FACTORS INFLUENCING THE ABORTION DECISION

Situational Factors

The aborted women who were surveyed were given a list of common reasons for aborting and asked to indicate to what degree each of these factors influenced their final decision. The following table summarizes the results from the most frequently cited reason to the least:

Was your decision made for reasons of:	
social acceptance?	57%
short-term needs?	37%
financial limits?	28%
long-term needs?	24%
career goals?	18%
mental health?	17%
family size?	7%
physical health?	7%

In addition to these reasons, 41 percent reported "other" reasons that played a primary role in their abortion decisions. The "other" reason most often listed was the result of some interpersonal problems, such as "pressure from boyfriend," or "fear of telling parents." (The influence of other people in the abortion decision was dealt with more thoroughly in a later part of the survey—"Interpersonal Influences.") Several women described the "other" major reasons in their abortion decision in terms of their own immaturity, claiming that the decision was motivated by "selfishness," "embarrassment," "ignorance," "shame," "fright," "aloneness," or because it was the "easy way out." One woman noted that the major reason for choosing abortion was because "I didn't know I had options," while another stated that there was "no other place to go." Three women reported that the major reason for their abortions was the fact they were pregnant by men other than their husbands.

A surprising finding in the "other" category was that approximately 8 percent of the WEBA women surveyed aborted for the "hard" reasons. Half of these "hard case" aborters felt "forced" to abort because their pregnancies were the result of rape, and the other half aborted because of the possibility that the child they carried might be handicapped. This number of "hard case" aborters is from five to twenty times greater than that found among the general population of aborting women. The explanation for such a high concentration of "hard case" aborters in this sample lies in the fact that abortion in these "hard cases" is generally more traumatic than in "common case" abortions. "Hard case" aborters, therefore, are more likely to need and be attracted to a support group like WEBA.

Altogether, fully 64 percent of the aborted women surveyed described themselves as "forced" into abortion because of their particular circumstances at that time. Most of these women also indicated that during the time between discovering they were pregnant and having the abortion there was such a high level of emotional trauma that they were unable to thoughtfully and cautiously consider their alternatives. Abortion was simply the most obvious and fastest way to escape from their dilemmas. Over 84 percent state that they would have kept their babies "under better circumstances."

Personal Influences

Presented with a list of persons who may have played a role in their abortion decision, the women were asked to indicate to what degree each of these persons influenced their final decisions. The following table summarizes the results in the order from the most frequently cited interpersonal influence to the least:

Were you encouraged to have an abortion by:	
husband or boyfriend?	51%
abortion counselor?	35%
friends?	24%
parents?	23%
doctor?	23%
social worker?	14%
other family members?	14%

Other persons reported to have played a major role in the abortion decisions were "school authorities" and "boyfriend's parents." A few women made other notes at this point such as: "Would have been kicked out if not aborted," "Forced by mother; father opposed," "No other option given," "Lack of support from society," and "Planned Parenthood counselor said under my situation abortion was my best choice."

The opinions and pressures of others plays a major role in the final decision of most aborting women. Asked "Would your choice have been different if any or all of the above had encouraged you differently?," more than 83 percent indicated that they definitely would have chosen *against* abortion.

For the majority of those surveyed, these "significant others" played more than advisory roles in determining the women's final decisions. *Nearly 55 percent of the respondents felt they had been very much "forced" to abort by others.* Another 10 percent felt moderate pressure from others to "do the sensible thing," and only 33 percent felt free to make their own decisions.

In another series of questions, approximately 73 percent indicated they did not feel in control of their own lives when making their abortion decisions. Sixty-one percent said that their lives at that time were very much "controlled by others," and another 12 percent indicated their lives were moderately "controlled by others."

Attitudes Toward Pregnancy

The fact that all of these women chose abortion does not mean that they were all equally opposed to pregnancy and parenthood. Instead, many actually desired to keep the baby but felt that abortion was their "only" alternative, given the pressures of their situations and the demands of those around them.

A majority of those surveyed, 53 percent, described themselves as having felt very "good or excited" about being pregnant. Another 6 percent were moderately pleased, and 31 percent were not at all pleased when they first learned of their pregnancy. In general, it might be concluded, an unplanned pregnancy conjures up mixed emotions. While pleasure is experienced from feeling the creative power of fertility and from imagining the beauties and joys of a newborn child, this pleasure is muted by the distressful realization that responsibility for the child will force changes in future plans and expectations.

The pleasurable side of being pregnant was significant for most of these women. Over 85 percent hoped to bear children at some time in their lives. The problem was that this unplanned pregnancy occurred at an undesirable time. Despite this problem, however, 50 percent of those surveyed gave much consideration to carrying the pregnancy to term, 15 percent gave moderate consideration to childbirth, and 12 percent gave it small consideration. Only 19 percent gave no thought to childbirth, apparently certain of their abortion choice from the first moment they found out they were pregnant.

Most aborters tend to equate childbirth with parenthood. Only 14 percent gave much thought to the option of placing the child up for adoption. For many the possibility of adoption was surrounded by ignorance and myths. For most, there seemed to be only two alternatives: raising the child themselves or having an abortion. Fear of raising the child themselves was also compounded by a general ignorance of the support groups and financial aid programs which might have been available.

Despite the hardships they faced, 59 percent gave strong consideration to keeping the baby, and another 13 percent gave it moderate consideration. Most of the women in this category very much *wanted* to keep the baby but felt "forced" to abort by the demands of those around them.

Perhaps the most revealing discovery was that over 84 percent said they would have been very willing to keep the child "under better circumstances." Less than 2 percent indicated they would not have kept the child under any circumstances. This finding suggests that positive programs to improve the circumstances of women faced with unplanned pregnancies would have a major impact on the abortion rate in America. Most women do not desire abortion and would do almost anything to avoid it, but they need support and help to improve their circumstances and to make parenting (and/or adoption) a reasonable alternative.

Prior Attitudes Toward Abortion

Many studies have shown that before becoming pregnant themselves, most aborted women have "definite moral opinions but little factual knowledge about abortion." These studies have found that until placed in a situation where they themselves are "forced" into an abortion, the majority of aborting women disapprove of it. Compelled by their circumstances, most aborting women feel "forced" to compromise their moral values or compelled to rationalize themselves as being "exceptions" to the rule.[10]

This survey found the same trend, and even the same approximate percentages, as recorded by other researchers. Asked "What were your feelings about abortion prior to becoming pregnant?," 21 percent of the WEBA women responded "unsure." Besides the passage of time which might make it difficult to recall one's earlier attitudes, this high percentage of "unsure" responses suggests that many of these young women simply had never given abortion much thought before they became pregnant. They had no clear opinion to guide them once pregnancy did occur.

Looking at those with a definite opinion, 41 percent indicated a very negative attitude toward abortion, compared to 15 percent who had a very positive view of abortion. The remaining 44 percent were somewhere in between the extremes, indicating limited approval of abortion under "special" circumstances.

Given their doubts about the morality of abortion, most aborting women are strongly influenced by the legal status of the abortion option. Asked "Did the knowledge that abortion was legal influence your opinion about the morality of choosing abortion?," 70 percent said that the law had played a major role in their moral perception of abortion, 6 percent stated that it played a moderate role, and 13 percent said it played little or no role. Taken in context with the above information, this suggests that while most aborting women have a negative moral view of abortion before their own abortions, they find comfort (and grounds for rationalization) in the socio-legal view of abortion. Some, perhaps, even doubt their own moral values, thinking, "If it's legal, it must be all right. I just have to get over my own stupid hang-ups."

MAKING THE ABORTION DECISION

The period before a woman's abortion is a time of personal crisis. For the vast majority of aborters, external pressures and internal needs demand a quick resolution to the crisis situation. Of the aborted women surveyed, 81 percent felt extremely rushed to make the abortion decision.

For most, the amount of time taken to make the decision was amazingly short. Fifty-one percent decided to abort in less than four days after learning they were pregnant. Several noted that the decision was made within hours. Twenty-four percent took a week to make their decisions, 12 percent took two to three weeks, 6 percent waited four to six weeks before deciding, and 7 percent waited seven weeks or more before deciding to abort. It should be noted that many of these late decisions were not due to indecisiveness so much as changing circumstances. For example, a few women learned only several weeks after becoming pregnant with a wanted pregnancy that there was a risk that the child they carried might be handicapped, and so, usually after the urging of a physician, chose abortion.

Asked "Do you feel you had all of the necessary information to make the decision [to abort]?," 93 percent insisted that they had little or none of the necessary information. Only 3 percent believed they had most or all of the pertinent information. This, however, is one of the questions which is strongly affected by the fact that all of the women surveyed are members of WEBA. It is probable that at the time of their abortions, many or even most of these women felt they had all the information necessary—though many may have felt ignorant of what would be done or about what risks they would face. But looking back on their abortions from an average of ten years later, most of these women acquired information and experiences that were not available to them at that time. What might have seemed like an informed choice then is later seen as ignorant, foolish, and hasty.

Similarly, over 82 percent of the WEBA women stated that their abortion decision was not at all "thought out." Only 9 percent felt it was moderately well thought out, and only 8 percent believed that their decision had been "well thought out" under the circumstances.

Degree of Certainty about the Decision

Given the crisis situations in which they were forced to make their decisions, most of the women were *not* content with their decisions even at the time of their abortions. Approximately 56 percent of those surveyed said they had been extremely dissatisfied with their "only" option, 13 percent were moderately satisfied with their choice to abort, and only 24 percent were happy with their decision and secure in their choice.

For most, then, the decision to abort was filled with ambivalence. Any slight change in circumstances or encouragement from significant persons in their lives (especially husbands and boyfriends) could have brought about a reversal of their choice. In fact, even by the time they committed themselves to go to the clinic, only 39 percent felt very firm in their decision to abort. In contrast, 41 percent felt very uncertain about their decision, and the remainder were somewhere in between. Because of this uncertainty, 44 percent said they were still very actively looking for another option up to the final moments before their abortions.

The low degree of commitment to securing an abortion was also evident in answers to questions relating to illegal abortion. Asked whether or not they would have sought an illegal abortion if a legal abortion had not been available, 75 percent said they definitely would not have sought an illegal abortion, 4 percent said there was a moderate chance they would have sought an illegal abortion, 6 percent stated it was very likely they would have sought an illegal abortion, and 16 percent were unsure.[11] Asked whether or not they would have considered self-induced abortion as a desperate last resort, 89 percent totally rejected that alternative, and only 5 percent said self-abortion would have been strongly considered.

What is clear from all these responses is that the vast majority of aborting women are extremely uncertain about and uncommitted to their abortion decisions. Abortion is a "marginal good" at best. Any minor barrier to securing an abortion, or any perception that there are physical risks to the abortion, or any reasonable hope that her circumstances might be improved so as to make childbearing a reasonable possibility might alter the final decision away from abortion and towards accepting the pregnancy, childbirth, and parenting.

ABORTION COUNSELING AND CLINIC SERVICES

At most abortion clinics it is assumed that once a woman enters and begins to inquire about abortion, her decision to abort has already been firmly made. Abortion counselors believe it is their role to reassure the woman and ease her through the abortion, not to provide her with information or help her review her decision. The weaknesses of this approach are readily apparent in the survey responses of aborted women.

Rather than being certain of their abortion decisions, 40 to 50 percent of the women surveyed were wavering in their choice and were actually hoping for another option when they first went to speak with the counselor. But instead, 91 percent reported that their abortion counselors offered little or no help in exploring their decision and options. Only 4 percent of the women gave their abortion counselors high grades for being informative and helpful. Overall, 66 percent believed that their abortion counselors were strongly biased toward selling them an abortion as the "best solution." Only 9 percent felt that their counselors had been relatively free of a pro-abortion bias, with another 23 percent saying they were uncertain whether any bias existed.

Adequacy of Information

Even pro-choice surveys agree that most aborting women have little or no prior knowledge about what is technically involved in an abortion, what its risks are, or how developed the fetus is that they are thinking to abort.[12] Over 90 percent of the women surveyed felt that they did not have enough information to make an informed abortion choice. In almost all cases this ignorance was not corrected during abortion counseling.

Having been through their abortions and having learned more about abortion since that time, the WEBA women are almost unanimous in their complaint that abortion clinics did not provide them with enough information to make an informed choice. Even basic information about how the abortion would be performed was generally weak, with 76 percent complaining that they were not given an accurate description of the procedure during their pre-abortion counseling session. While at least "watered-down" descriptions of the abortion procedure are almost always given, many of the women complained that there was no mention of the physical pain involved. Only 16 percent felt that the counseling session had adequately informed them about the technical aspects of the abortion procedure.

In the vast majority of counseling sessions, discussion of the health risks of abortion was also absent. Over 80 percent reported that little or no discussion of risks had taken place, and only 8 percent believed their counselors had adequately discussed the surgical risks of the procedure.

But the worst marks for counseling occurred for failure to provide information about the fetus's stage of development, information which many believed would have been a crucial factor in their final decisions. Over 90 percent of the women stated that the biological nature of the fetus had not been discussed during their counseling session. Only 2 percent said that fetal development had been thoroughly or even moderately discussed.

Some abortion counselors maintain that discussion of the abortion procedure and fetal development are not necessary because women have enough information before coming to the clinic, presumably from high school biology courses. This belief is not supported by the evidence, however. Asked whether or not they had felt "well informed about the procedure and fetus through other sources before seeking an abortion," 90 percent claimed they had little or no prior knowledge, and 5 percent stated they had had only moderate prior knowledge. Only 4 percent claimed to have been well informed about abortion and fetal development through prior knowledge.

While the need for information in all three major areas is not being met, the evidence shows that most clinics do not even want to ensure informed consent. Fully 80 percent of the women surveyed felt their counselors had not encouraged—or had even attempted to discourage—questions about the abortion. Only 5 to 13 percent believed that their counselors were open and willing to answer their questions. When questions were asked, only 8 percent felt that their questions were thoroughly answered, 8 percent believed they received moderately complete answers, and 52 to 71 percent felt that their questions were trivialized or avoided.

In sum, nearly 80 percent of the women surveyed believed that they had been denied pertinent information or had been actively misinformed by their counselors prior to their abortions. Asked what were the most important facts they felt misinformed about, nearly 50 percent complained they had not been told about fetal development. The second most common complaint, mentioned by approximately one-fourth of those surveyed, was that they had not been adequately warned about the physical risks of the procedure. Many also complained that they had not been warned about the pain or about the nature of the procedure in general. The third most common complaint was that there had been no warning about the "psychological aftereffects," or the "emotional pain," which would follow their abortion. Finally, several women felt that their counseling had been totally inadequate, stating that "nothing was discussed" or that they had been misinformed about "everything." One woman charged that her counselor had led her to believe that she had "no other choice." Another felt lied to by her doctor when he told her that "saline abortion [is] easier than childbirth." And yet another felt that the entire counseling system was a sham of "prejudice and conspiracy against [the] weak and poor," designed to seduce the poor into aborting their children so as to save the rich from the costs of welfare support.

Asked the general question of whether they were "satisfied with the abortion services you received," 18 percent registered high to very high satisfaction, 18 percent were moderately well satisfied, 52 percent were very dissatisfied, and 10 percent were "unsure."

Services at Planned Parenthood Clinics

Some might question whether the poor counseling and abortion services WEBA women received is not, in fact, atypical. It is at least a possibility that WEBA women were the victims of poorly run clinics, and thus were more likely to feel misinformed and exploited. Defenders of abortion might insist that most clinics are in fact better than these.

In Chapter Eight we will examine what most typical abortion clinics are like. But for now, it is useful to compare the possibly "atypical" clinics described above with the nationally respected clinics operated by the Planned Parenthood Federation of America.

Planned Parenthood is the self-proclaimed leader in providing quality family planning and abortion services. Even clinics not affiliated with Planned Parenthood generally agree that Planned Parenthood clinics are the closest thing to the abortion industry's standard. Thus, in order to compare the general results on abortion clinic performance described above with this standard, we separately evaluated those WEBA surveys in which abortion counseling and/or the abortion procedure were performed at a Planned Parenthood clinic.

Of the 252 women surveyed, 21 percent received their counseling and/or their abortions at a Planned Parenthood facility. Sixty percent stated that their Planned Parenthood counselor had very strongly encouraged them to choose abortion as the "best" solution to their problems. This is especially significant when over 90 percent of those encouraged to abort by their Planned Parenthood counselor said that there was a strong chance they would have chosen against the abortion if they had not been so strongly encouraged to abort by others, *including their counselor.*

Of the Planned Parenthood patients, over 60 percent were still hoping to find an alternative to abortion when they went in for counseling.[13] Only 25 percent were already firm in their abortion choice before counseling, and all felt that their Planned Parenthood counselor did little or nothing to help them explore their decisions. Instead, 89 percent felt that the Planned Parenthood counselor was strongly biased in favor of the abortion option.

In terms of describing the abortion procedure, Planned Parenthood counselors scored slightly higher than their counterparts at other clinics. Almost 17 percent of the Planned Parenthood clients stated that the abortion procedure was thoroughly described to them, 23 percent said it was moderately well described, while 68 percent still felt that the procedure was not described with any degree of depth or clarity. In the task of describing fetal development and the health risks of abortion, however, Planned Parenthood counselors were scored as being no better than abortion counselors in general. Ninety-five percent of the Planned Parenthood counselors gave little or no biological information about the fetus which the abortion would destroy, and over 80 percent of the Planned Parenthood counselors gave little or no information about the potential health risks which might follow the surgery.

Planned Parenthood counselors were scored slightly higher for encouraging their clients to ask questions; but when questions were asked, over 64 percent of these women felt their questions were not adequately answered or were trivialized. In fact, over three-fourths of the Planned Parenthood patients felt that they had been misled by their counselors and had been denied information which might have influenced their final decisions. Only 13 percent felt adequately prepared for the abortion and forewarned of its risks after receiving counseling at a Planned Parenthood facility.

Overall, only 19 percent of the women who were served by Planned Parenthood clinics or referrals registered high to very high satisfaction with the abortion services they received there, as compared to an 18 percent high satisfaction rate of those going to abortion clinics in general. Another 13 percent were moderately satisfied with Planned Parenthood abortion services, while the majority, 56 percent, were very dissatisfied.

THE PHYSICAL AFTEREFFECTS OF ABORTION

The physical aftereffects of abortion range from those which are minor (e. g., headaches and nausea), to those which are very severe (e. g., chronic infections or a punctured uterus). But not all complications, particularly severe ones, are readily apparent. While some physical aftereffects show up immediately after the abortion and others a short time later, many complications may not appear until several years later (e. g., a slightly damaged uterus may cause miscarriages in later pregnancies, or a small infection may cause scarring of the fallopian tube and permanent infertility).

Of the 252 women surveyed, approximately one-half complained of suffering from at least one type of physical complication following their abortions. Moreover, at least 18 percent of those surveyed reported having suffered permanent physical damage traceable to the procedure.

Of the 47 percent who reported suffering from a complication, 40 percent said it was a very minor problem, 26 percent said it was moderately severe, and 35 percent claimed that it was very severe. Judging by the complications which were listed, it would seem that immediate and short-term complications were generally listed as the least severe type. Delayed or long-term complications, often involving a reduced or a total fertility loss, were most likely to be listed by the respondents as being very severe. This trend, which subjectively evaluates delayed and permanent damage as being more severe than immediate compli-cations, suggests that aborting women are able and willing to tolerate correctable mistakes. But when unforeseen and irreversible damage is done to their reproductive lives, this damage is more unforgivable and is therefore subjectively rated as being more severe.

Of the short-term complications, the most frequently identified was post-operative hemorrhage, noted by 15 percent of all the women surveyed. Infection was the second most likely complication, reported by 9 percent of those surveyed. Incomplete abortions were also fre-quently noted, which though correctable by a second abortion, carried additional risks, especially of infection. Other relatively minor prob-lems included: clotting, cramps, irregular periods, chronic bleeding, chronic infections, exhaustion, loss of weight, pelvic inflammatory dis-ease, and endometriosis.

Long-term complications were generally more severe and more permanent. Of the aborted women surveyed, approximately 6 percent were forced to undergo a total hysterectomy to remove a uterus that had been damaged or infected by the abortion procedure. Another 8 percent reported that post-abortion infection had left them sterile by blocking their fallopian tubes or through some other means. Yet another 4 percent contracted cervical cancer, which they attribute to the abortion.[14]

Besides suffering sterility from the above causes, many aborted women suffer a reduced ability to carry a later wanted pregnancy to term. Of the women surveyed, approximately 20 percent later suffered miscarriage of a wanted child. In addition, no less than 8 percent were diagnosed as suffering from cervical incompetence after their abor-tions. Other birthing problems and reproductive damage were also fre-quently reported.

Finally, several women reported that a fear of needing another abortion "forced" them to undergo tubal ligations, which they later regretted. In these cases, sterility was not directly caused by way of a post-abortion physical complication. Rather, post-abortion psycho-logical trauma indirectly "forced" these women to submit to "volun-tary sterilizations" which were often irreversible.

In Chapter Five we will examine the physical complications of abortion in greater detail. We will see that the complication rates reported by WEBA members are well within the rates reported by independent sources. In other words, WEBA members are not more likely to have suffered from abortion-related physical complications than is any other sample of aborting women in general.

THE PSYCHOLOGICAL AFTERMATH

As with the physical complications, the psychological traumas caused by abortion vary from mild to severe, may occur immediately or may be delayed, and may take many forms. The main difference is that while physical complications affect only about 50 percent of all aborted women, psychological problems occur in the lives of almost all aborted women. This impact is not always readily apparent and may even be denied by many aborted women, but most psychiatrists agree that it is always there.

Of the 252 women surveyed, 94 percent said they had experienced negative psychological effects attributable to their abortions. This response rate is certainly higher than what would be reported from the general population of aborting women. One reason for this lies in the fact that by joining WEBA the women surveyed in this study have already recognized the problems they had following their abortions. Over 70 percent of the WEBA women reported that there was a time when they would have denied the existence of any negative reactions after their abortions. For some this denial stage lasted only a few months, for others it lasted over ten or fifteen years.

The evidence shows that denial is an almost universal reaction to post-abortion trauma. Just as most alcoholics are unable or unwilling to recognize their affliction, so it is with aborted women. But similarly, just as the ability to join Alcoholics Anonymous signals that an alcoholic has finally recognized his or her problem, so too aborted women do not join WEBA until they have stopped denying their problems and have begun to face them head-on. Furthermore, many of the psychological aftereffects of abortion are not obviously linked to that experience. A woman may be suffering from chronic depression, anger, bitterness, loneliness, or low self-esteem, yet never realize until undergoing psychotherapy that these problems stem back to her repressed abortion experience.[15] In fact, one of the most significant findings of this survey and of the testimonies which follow is that abortion is *typically* followed by a long period of denial and unrecognized negative reactions.

Because they are more actively coping with their abortion experiences than are the "average" aborters, WEBA members are more keenly aware of the emotional and psychological effects of their abortions. Rating the severity of their post-abortion problems, 73 percent said the negative impact was severe, 14 percent said it was moderate, 7 percent said it was minor, and 6 percent were unsure.

Asked to list what they felt were their most significant psychological reactions, over forty different reactions were reported. The most frequently listed reactions were guilt, depression, a lowered sense of self-worth, and self-hatred.

Depression and loss of self-esteem often lead to self-destructive behavior. Of the aborted women surveyed, 62 percent described themselves as having become "suicidal" as a direct or indirect result of their abortions. Approximately 20 percent reported that they actually made one or more suicide attempts.

Self-destructive behavior was also displayed in other ways. Nearly one-third of the women surveyed described themselves as drinking more heavily after their abortions, while 15 percent admitted that they became alcoholics. Allowing for overlap, 40 percent said that after their abortions they began to use or increased their use of drugs. Eleven percent described themselves as having become drug addicts.

Many of those surveyed reported that their abortion left them feeling extreme and chronic anger or rage at others. Short-fused, over 5 percent admitted engaging in "child abuse" or "child neglect," and several others reported "parenting difficulties."

For some of the aborted women, interpersonal relationships became difficult or impossible to handle. Anger, resentment, and even hatred was directed at the husbands or boyfriends who had been involved in the abortion. No less than 50 percent experienced "sexual coldness" or a "revulsion of sex" following their abortions. For some, this sexual coldness was directed toward the father of the aborted child; for others it was due to a fear of becoming pregnant and being "forced" into another abortion. Many women also reported becoming "promiscuous" after their abortions, even though they might also have experienced a loss of pleasure from intercourse.

Many reported that they had been unable to put the abortion out of their minds. These women struggled with constant thoughts about the abortion and were particularly distressed on the anniversary of the abortion and the would-have-been due date for the child.

Many others had frequent thoughts about the child, wondering what he or she would have been like, what mother and child would have been doing together now, and so on. About 30 percent of those surveyed indicated a strong desire to conceive a "replacement" or "atonement baby." One woman described herself as being under the "compulsion to be a perfect mother," in order to atone for the child she had destroyed in her abortion. Another woman felt a constant need to touch babies, while others were afraid to touch babies and would even break into tears whenever they saw one.

Over 40 percent of the women surveyed noted that they had experienced nightmares related to the abortion, and about the same number said they suffered from insomnia. Another 20 percent claimed to have undergone a "nervous breakdown" or a "complete mental breakdown."

Two women suffered from anorexia nervosa, the onset of which they attributed to their abortions. In contrast, at least one woman suffered from excessive weight gain after her abortion, as she tried to bury her guilt in food.

Other frequently reported symptoms were profound remorse, regret, grief, a sense of murder, fear of punishment, and a general sense of loss. Miscellaneous responses included bitterness, unforgiveness of others, unforgiveness of self, anxiety, fear of others finding out, loneliness, isolation, feelings of having been exploited, a feeling of helplessness, indecisiveness, and the inability to make decisions.

It should be noted that the list of psychological aftereffects to abortion discussed in this section was based on short, written responses—not a checklist of possible reactions. Therefore, most responses simply indicated what was at the top of each woman's mind, or what seemed to her to be the most severe problem she faced. If they had been given a checklist on which to mark off the aftereffects they experienced, it is probable that most would have indicated a broader pattern of reactions. With this in mind, it is clear that the percentages given above cannot be projected onto the population of aborting women as a whole. Instead, these percentages can best be described as minimum rates useful for understanding the range and severity of post-abortion sequelae, but not its scope.

With regard to their post-abortion psychological conditions, the women surveyed were asked, "Did you require professional counseling and/or treatment?" In response, 37 percent felt a very strong need for psychological counseling. Another 6 percent felt a moderate need for counseling, and 49 percent said they did not "require" counseling. Eight percent answered with an "unsure" response. Several women, however, added a comment to this question, saying something like "I needed counseling, but none was available." Because of confusion as to whether the question asked if they actually *had* received counseling or whether they had *needed* counseling, some of these women answered negatively and others positively.

The duration of psychological aftereffects, regardless of severity, was almost always long. Approximately 82 percent said their post-abortion emotional and psychological aftereffects lasted for three years or longer. Eight percent began to feel "normal" again one to two years after their abortions, and another 8 percent felt relief only one to six months after their abortions.

For most of those surveyed, participation in WEBA seemed to have played a significant role in easing their post-abortion trauma. Approximately 48 percent stated that they have almost completely reconciled themselves to their abortion experience, 19 percent are still moderately troubled, and 26 percent are still faced with persistent post-abortion emotional problems.

LOOKING BACK

Hindsight is always clearer than foresight. Thus, in retrospect, after facing the physical and psychological aftereffects, after struggling with ambivalence and doubts, after seeing their lives unimproved or even worsened, it is no surprise that the vast majority of the women surveyed rejected their original choice for abortion.

As we saw earlier, for most of those surveyed the choice to abort was unfirm, marginal, and filled with doubts. The vast majority were unsatisfied with the choice they had been "forced" to make, and many were looking for options, hoping for a better way out, even up to the final hour before their abortions. Afterwards, 93 percent felt that their self-images had been very much worsened by their abortion experience.

If they had known where their lives would have been today, over 95 percent of those surveyed said they would not have chosen abortion. Asked if their lives now are better or worse because of their choice, 66 percent said that their lives are worse because of their abortions, 8 percent said their lives were about the same, and only 5 percent said their lives were better. It should be noted, however, that those who said their lives are better almost always added a qualifying note. For these women, it was not the abortion which had improved their lives, but rather the realization of how wrong their abortion had been. After "hitting the bottom," they had "found God" or had otherwise "grown" to greater personal maturity. Thus, it was by repudiating their abortions that these women felt their lives had been indirectly improved by their abortion experiences. For them, evil had been turned into good.

Nearly all of those surveyed are no longer ambivalent about abortion. Instead, they all have a clear and negative view of abortion, but this view was seldom quickly achieved. For most, there was a long period of denial and rationalization. For almost 25 percent, their first abortion was followed by a second abortion, or even a third or fourth, until at last they were able to free themselves from the self-destructive, self-punishing cycle of repeat abortions.

Obviously, not all aborted women have yet reached this level of insight, this level of inner peace. Most have yet to cope with how they have been manipulated, exploited, and deceived for the convenience of others. That type of self-examination takes time, patience, and often requires help and support from others. In the stories which follow, we will see what several of the women who participated in this survey actually experienced and how they finally found the inner peace they so desperately needed.

Each story describes the situation leading up to the abortion, how the decision was made, what feelings were experienced afterwards, and how the feelings of guilt and remorse were finally resolved. This last point, the self-reconciliation of aborted women, is unique to this collection of abortion testimonies. For most of these WEBA members, the discovery or renewal of religious faith became the cornerstone around which they rebuilt their lives and their self-images. Particularly for those who have publicly revealed their identities, it is from their religious faiths that they draw the strength to make this public "confession" in the hope that other women will be forewarned.

Before their abortions, very few of these women had strong religious beliefs. Most were religiously apathetic, if not agnostic. But in the years that followed, most felt increasingly isolated from others by the pain and doubts associated with their abortion experiences. The depth of this isolation is demonstrated by the need of so many to turn to the solace of religion. In descovering a religious faith, these women found a constructive way to deal with their abortion experience by placing it in a spiritual context. Thus, just as Alcoholics Anonymous encourages members to draw on the strength of a Higher Power outside themselves, so WEBA also encourages aborted women to draw on that same Higher Power, rebuilding their lives around the spiritual message of forgiveness, hope, and eternal life. For many WEBA members their greatest comfort comes from the belief that the children they aborted were not truly destroyed, but instead are waiting with forgiveness to be reunited with their mothers in the afterlife.

One last note: unless set off in quotes, all of the names used in these stories are real. Many have publicly testified about their abortion experiences before; for others, this is the first time they have placed themselves under public scrutiny. For those who preferred to remain anonymous, the reader will quickly see that anonymity was most often retained to preserve the privacy of others, often their parents or children, rather than to protect themselves. Whether they have gone public or remain anonymous, all these women deserve our utmost respect and admiration for bravely sharing their painful stories.

TWO

Women Who Face Coercion

As will become increasingly clear throughout this book, women faced with problem pregnancies often face coercion from loved ones or civil authorities who insist that abortion is "the best solution" to their problems. Usually this pressure to do the "practical" thing is exerted out of sincere love for the woman and with the sincere belief that such paternalistic care will be appreciated later. At other times, loved ones will push abortion on a woman not out of concern for her so much as out concern for themselves. In either case, the woman who gives in to such pressures suffers because her abortion is not the result of *her* free choice. Instead, she feels compelled to compromise her own values in order to please others, and this compromise always involves a loss of self-respect.

Perhaps the most powerful form of coercion which women face is the threat that families and boyfriends will withdraw their love and support. For example, WEBA member Sandra Morean was forced to choose between her husband and her unborn child:

> The more I thought about being pregnant, I realized there was a life in me, and I wanted to give birth to it. But my husband told me, "Either you have an abortion, or I'll leave you. You can raise it by yourself, because I don't want any more children." Not being strong enough to do what was right, and too afraid to go it alone, I gave in.

Another survey respondent describes the pressures she faced as coming from all directions:

> My family would not support my decision to keep my baby. My boyfriend said he would give me no emotional or financial help whatsoever. All the people that mattered told me to abort. When I said I didn't want to they started listing reasons why I should. They said it

would be detrimental to my career, and my health, and that I would have no social life and no future with men. Could I actually do it alone? I started feeling like maybe I was crazy to want to keep it. I finally told everyone that I would have the abortion just to get them off my back. But inside I still didn't want to have the abortion. Unfortunately, when the abortion day came I shut off my inside feelings. I was scared to not do it because of how my family and boyfriend felt. I'm so angry at myself for giving in to the pressure of others. I just felt so alone in my feelings to have my baby.

Two days later this same woman attempted suicide. Seven months later, at the time she responded to the survey, she was attempting to deceive her boyfriend into making her pregnant again in the belief that a second pregnancy could somehow make up for the first.

These two examples, and the profile which follows, demonstrate some of the forces which pressure women into having abortions. Coercion may come from the woman's family, the baby's father, physicians, welfare workers, or some other person with a measure of power and authority over their lives. Whatever the source of this pressure, these women feel that abortion was not really *their* choice. It was a choice which they accepted because they were scared, because they trusted others, because they wanted to please others, or even because they were made to feel that they "owed" it to others to "do the right thing." Abortion was chosen by these women not with a bold step of strength, but because they were unable to find a way to defend their own desires.

GAYLENE "HAYES"

Gaylene was forced into an abortion when she was fourteen years old. Her California high school authorities and the local Planned Parenthood chapter worked closely together. Together, they made Gaylene feel that she had no choice in "the matter." When she tried to ask questions about what they would do to her and her baby, they refused to answer. This loss of choice about her life led her to drugs, alcoholism, suicide attempts, jail, a probation farm, and a religious cult.

In my case, I was fourteen years old and somewhat serious over a young man. When I thought I was pregnant, I talked to the high school counselors, who said I should go to Planned Parenthood for a pregnancy test.

This was easy to do. I lived in a town with a high school population of 2,400. In addition, there were five other high schools within a thirty-mile radius. So Planned Parenthood had a well-organized operation for all of these schools. Every Tuesday, a scheduled bus picked up students from all the area high schools and took them to the Planned Parenthood clinic. The bus had posters extolling the virtues and ideals of Planned Parenthood—have small families, intelligent people only have two children, etc. School counselors arranged for the visits, and provided the students with passes to be excused from school for the entire day.

So on that Tuesday, I took the bus to the large, modern Planned Parenthood clinic. All of us students were greeted by a pleasant receptionist, who sent us to our designated areas: boys with V.D. to one room, girls for pregnancy tests to another, etc. After we were seated, we were instructed to move to the adjacent chair whenever the person occupying the first chair went into the examining room—it was all so organized.

When it was my turn to go in, I was greeted by a doctor and nurse, who told me that my urine would be tested for pregnancy and then they would phone me with the results. They were all particularly careful to find out when my parents would not be home, so as not to "embarrass" me or cause me any kind of "family problems."

So I returned to school and then rode my regular bus home. I sat by the phone for the entire hour that they were to call me. When they called and told me I was pregnant, they said I could return to the clinic the following week and that they would "go from there." The word "abortion" was *never* used, nor was any reference made to abortion.

Two days later, I finally had enough courage to see the counselor. He was sympathetic and understanding—he felt there was no need to worry my family. He also explained about having a child, how tough it would be on me and that I wouldn't be able to do what I wanted to do. He said the child would suffer because I was much too young to be a parent. He pointed out that the best thing for me to do was to abort the fetus at this stage so that no one would be hurt. No mention was made of talking to my parents about this or of carrying my baby to term. He indicated that adoption would be difficult and not an option for me. The cost (thanks to Planned Parenthood) was only $35, as opposed to thousands of dollars for raising a child. He said he would even pay the $35 if I couldn't.

So I took the bus again the following week, on a different day. Then there were college-age girls as well as women in their twenties and thirties. Looking back, I realized that there must have been a particular day of the week on the bus for abortions, for all of these women were taken to Planned Parenthood for that purpose. On the bus, I felt as though I had no control over what was happening to me. I started to question what I was doing, but in my logic I'd refer back to what the counselor had told me and then I would think he was right. But still today, I feel like *I* did not decide to have the abortion.

At the clinic we were ushered into a different room than the one we came in for pregnancy tests. The chairs were lined up in the organized way, though. We were given pamphlets which showed a uterus with a pink blob in it. The aide matter of factly told us that they would remove the "pink blob." She said that then we would no longer be pregnant, and that it was a simple surgical procedure. That's all she said.

Upon entering the surgery room I was told to go behind a curtain, put on a hospital gown, and fold my clothes into a neat pile. When I climbed up on the surgery table, the nurse instructed me to move my hips down on the table. Since I was only fourteen, I really didn't know what she meant. So she grabbed my hips roughly and pulled my body down to the end of the table, and fastened the straps around my feet. I asked what was going on, and she snapped that I had already been given that information. She said this was not the time to be asking questions, that I should have asked them sooner.

The nurse and doctor then acted angry with me. I had the feeling that I had done something wrong or that I wasn't cooperating. I was confused because I thought these people were the answer to my problems, but they weren't treating me with the consideration that they had the other day when I'd had my pregnancy test. I didn't even know what they were going to do to me or my baby.

I was given no anesthetic. There was a needle nearby, but they told me that by the time the anesthetic took effect the procedure would be over. They gave me an option, but they made me feel as though it was unnecessary. The vacuum was very noisy. The doctor and nurse went about their work as a routine—almost as though I weren't there. It was very painful. I know it was only a short time, but when you're in pain it seems like an eternity.

When they were finished they rolled me out into a recovery room, where ten or fifteen other girls were lying on surgical beds. Some were sitting up, but most were lying down. A couple were crying, and I was sniffling because it hurt. I wanted to get back to school and put all this behind me, because the school counselor had said that everything would be alright after it was over. I just kept repeating to myself what the counselor had said.

After two to three hours of lying there and juice and cookies, we boarded the bus and were taken back to our schools. We went to the school counselor and he gave us all a school pass for classes the next day. He asked how we felt, and joked about how we shouldn't let this happen again.

My regular bus had already left, so I had to phone my mother. The counselor filled out a detention slip stating that I'd had to stay after school, and that was why I'd missed my bus. My mom asked me what I had done to be detained and I said that I had mouthed off to a teacher. This was the beginning of a major barrier with my family.

The nurse from the clinic phoned me at home at the hour I had said that my parents wouldn't be there. She asked how I was feeling and if there were any problems. I was just glad it was over, and would just as soon have not heard from them again. They told me to get on contraceptives right away.

After the abortion, I turned to drugs. Before the abortion, I had tried pot, but only to the point of getting buzzed. But after it, I always tried to get bombed—totally loaded. On a few occasions I tried the needle—LSD. I continued with school but was kicked out after a series of being busted: for skipping school, drug dealing, and as an accomplice to robbery. I was sent to a probationary farm for nine months and had classes there. The strict environment helped my grades, but I continued my life of drugs and sex. Once I attempted suicide by taking all the aspirins in a huge bottle. They pumped my stomach and I was very sick. I thought I would just as soon die.

While at the farm, my father died suddenly. I was allowed to go to the funeral, but at my mother's request I was not allowed to return home.

I did go home from the farm at the end of the school year. I returned to my old ways, and by the beginning of December, I was kicked out of school again. I attended an "alternative school" that had minimal requirements for attendance and curriculum. I was living from day to day, trying to stay as high and loaded at all times as possible, but I finally graduated from high school.

When I turned seventeen, I moved to another state for a year. I worked odd jobs, and got into booze and heavy drugs. Finally, a friend phoned my mother and new stepfather and told them if they wanted to see me alive again they had better send me a ticket home. They did, and tried to have me dried out—with little success. Six months later they moved. When my mother left, she gave money to my sister for me, "for either a doctor, lawyer, or mortuary," because they were sure I'd need at least one of them.

At that point, I started living in my car. A cult called "The Children of God" took me in. I straightened out for a year or two, but left them because of their sexual practices.

Then I went to live with my parents for a while. It was the happiest six months of my youth. I turned twenty-one during this time.

I met the young man whom I later married, had a good job, and have kept pretty steady employment since then. But though we wanted to have children, I was unable to become pregnant. Tests have shown large amounts of scar tissue in my uterus. Frustrated, I started drinking heavily again. Six years later, during a drinking binge, I attempted suicide with a gun. I had it loaded and set up when a friend discovered me.

I went to the hospital for two weeks, and finally came to terms with why I was trying to destroy myself: I had killed my own child, so I felt I didn't deserve anything. I know now that my Father in heaven has the same love for me as He has for my child.

Though I still have no baby of my own, my husband and I have adopted two wonderful older children. Best of all, I know that God has truly forgiven me. I want others to know about the pain and anguish a woman can go through from abortion, and I'd like them to know the forgiveness that Jesus has for us.

THREE

The Evidence from the Pro-choice Side

The women who contributed their stories to this book have all had one thing in common: they have all reconciled themselves to their abortion experiences by (1) openly coming to grips with the realization that they made a wrong choice; (2) claiming spiritual and/or personal forgiveness for themselves; and (3) working to save other women from making the same mistake. All of these women suffered emotionally and psychologically from abortion, and all of them complain that they were not adequately warned about the psychological impact of abortion. But were such warnings really necessary? Or are WEBA-like experiences uncommon? Are these women just the unfortunate few? Or are they, instead, typical examples of the twenty-five million, or more, American women who have had abortions since 1973?

In this chapter we will see that WEBA women are not simply the "unfortunate few." Instead, we will find that even the pro-choice literature helps to prove our thesis that abortion is almost always a negative experience. Whenever women who have had abortions are interviewed, even by pro-choice authors, they always report the same ambivalence and pain. Thus, the research of the pro-choice authors confirms that the WEBA-like experience is far closer to being the rule than the exception.

PASSAGE THROUGH ABORTION

In 1973, sociologist Mary K. Zimmerman began a comprehensive study of how women experienced abortion. Published in 1977, her book *Passage Through Abortion: The Personal and Social Reality of Women's Experiences* summarizes the results of her surveys, includes excerpts of her interviews, and dwells on her own analysis of the abortion experience. Though she occasionally lapses into pro-choice rhetoric and seems to rely exclusively on pro-abortion literature for her supplemental material, the core of Zimmerman's own work is an impartial and systematic study of the short-term abortion experience.

Zimmerman's study was based on a Midwest city with two abortion clinics serving a metropolitan population of approximately 165,000 people. With cooperation from both clinics, letters from Zimmerman were distributed to women seeking abortions. The letter explained the nature and purpose of her study and asked for their participation. Attached to the letter was a short survey. Six to ten weeks after each woman's abortion, Zimmerman interviewed each patient. During these interviews, Zimmerman followed a systematic outline of questions in order to elicit responses on a variety of topics. Forty such interviews were done, and these make up the body of her study. This number was selected as being sufficiently large to be significant, yet small enough to be manageable.

It should be noted, however, that certain restrictions surrounding the selection of these forty women biased the sample in several respects, a fact noted by Zimmerman herself.

First, women who had undergone previous abortions were excluded from the study sample. This exclusion was deemed necessary since repeat aborters are likely to report greater negative reactions than women who are "naive" about abortion and experiencing it for the first time. Zimmerman felt that this variation in reactions could not be "adequately handled and so it was eliminated."[1]

Second, women undergoing second or third trimester abortions were excluded in order to confine the study to those women undergoing suction abortions. This limitation was made in order to study reactions to similar abortion experiences. This limitation, however, eliminated some of the most negative abortion experiences from the sample, since late-term abortion procedures are more traumatic, both physically and emotionally, than vacuum curettage.[2]

A third bias was placed on this study's sample not by Zimmerman, but by the abortion clinic director, who told staff members "not to give the client [Zimmerman's] letter, consent form, and questionnaire if, in their judgement, it would be inadvisable clinically." In other words, if the patient was already displaying signs of being upset, guilty, or extremely ambivalent, she was screened out of the sample. This staff "screening" of clients not only prevented the study from including the "worse case" examples of the abortion experience, but also allowed the clinics to put their "best" clients forward. Thirteen percent of the women aborted during the timeframe of this study were eliminated from the sample at the option of the clinics. Most were under twenty-two years old and unmarried, and were often accompanied by a parent with whom there were arguments and hostility, an indication that parental pressure was being exerted to secure the abortion.[3]

While these limitations may have been necessary for the purpose of standardizing the study in relation to first-trimester, first-abortion experiences, the fact that the results are thus biased cannot be overlooked. Over one third of all abortions in the United States are repeat abortions, and nearly one tenth are performed in the second trimester or later. In addition, the screening out of 13 percent of the "most sensitive" cases at "clinic discretion" must clearly have affected the study's final results.

Lastly, of all the women asked to participate in the study, 36 percent refused. How the characteristics of the women who refused to be studied would have affected the study is not known. However, it can be speculated that the women who were unwilling to participate in the study refused primarily because they wanted to "get it over with" and did not want to face the prospect of a later interview. This implies strong negative feelings prior to the abortion and suggests that strong negative reactions would have occurred afterwards as well. Thus, the women who "screened" themselves out of the study were probably at a high risk of suffering post-abortion sequelae, and knew it. (*Sequelae* is a medical term meaning physical or psychological aftereffects.) Most of these women probably refused to participate in order to insulate themselves from any prolonged association with a negative experience.

All of the "screening" mechanisms mentioned above suggest that compared to the truly "average" sample of aborted women, Zimmerman's study disproportionately represents the "best" patients under the most "ideal" circumstances. But with this strongly "positive" bias, Zimmerman's findings are disturbingly bleak and mirror the result of the survey described in Chapter One.

Contraceptive Use Of the study group, Zimmerman found that 7 percent of the women had been consistent users of a "reliable" method of birth control (defined as either the Pill, the IUD, or the diaphragm). These women became pregnant by contraceptive failure. On the other hand, 80 percent were sporadic users of various contraceptives or had suddenly discontinued use of a "reliable" method just prior to becoming pregnant, often due to health reasons or because they were in transition periods between relationships. Finally, 13 percent were not using any method. Confirming numerous other studies, Zimmerman reports that almost all of the women studied were familiar and experienced with birth control methods. Abortion resulted not from ignorance, but from "carelessness" or "indifference."[4]

Reaction to Pregnancy   After first becoming aware of their pregnancies, 63 percent of the women studied initially tended towards abortion, 24 percent tended towards childbirth, and 13 percent were uncertain.[5] Zimmerman notes, however, that although

> ... two-thirds of the women were displeased upon learning that they were pregnant . . . this does not mean that two-thirds of the women did not want the baby. In the final analysis, only a little more than a third explicitly stated that they did not want the child. While all of the women studied eventually made the same decision about abortion, they did *not* all adopt the same stance on wanting the baby.[6]

In fact, 30 percent told the interviewer that there had been a strong desire to have and keep the baby, but they had felt that circumstances did not allow it. Another 33 percent deliberately ignored the question of whether or not they wanted the child. These women instead focused on the life constraints which "forced" them to abort. Whether or not they wanted the baby was a moot and dangerous question for these women. Since outside pressures were "forcing" them to abort whether they wanted to or not, any desires to continue their pregnancies were consciously ignored or denied. Some of the women in this latter group expressed joy and happiness about the pregnancy through indirect means. Thus, for no less than 30 percent of aborters and possibly up to 60 percent or more, the abortion involved the destruction of a "wanted" or at least "acceptable" child, not out of "choice," but because of circumstances.[7]

The Decision   In 95 percent of all cases studied, the male partner played a central role in the abortion decision. A significant majority of the men agreed to, supported, or actively encouraged the abortion option. In 20 percent of the cases where the woman's initial decision was to abort, however, the male opposed the abortion. On the other hand, in another 20 percent of the cases the woman's initial decision was to continue the pregnancy, but the man insisted upon the abortion and eventually the woman submitted. Thus, no fewer than 20 percent felt "forced" to abort by the man.[8]

Overall, Zimmerman records that 35 percent of the aborted women studied remained confused throughout most of the decision-making process. Many were not clear about what they would do until right before the abortion was performed.[9] Of the 65 percent who expressed that the decision to abort was clear, most saw it not as a choice but rather as their only alternative. In general, the choice seemed clear because all the persons with whom they consulted positively encouraged and supported the abortion option.[10] Altogether, over two-thirds of the women made statements suggesting that they had "no choice" or had been "forced" to have the abortion.[11]

Reasons Given for Their Abortions   The two most frequent reasons given for the abortion were financial problems and being unmarried.[12] The expectation of financial hardship after the birth of the child was a major concern for both married and single women. For single women, refusal by parents to help support her and her child was frequently the overriding pressure to abort. In some cases, parents insisted on the abortion.[13] Being unmarried, having a partner unwilling to marry, or being unwilling to marry an undesirable partner is also a major determinant in abortion decisions since the prospect of being a single parent appears overly burdensome, or even impossible.[14] "Almost all of the women studied, regardless of the exact configuration of circumstances, felt that *the time was not right* for a baby. Most wanted to become pregnant again in the future, but only when the circumstances were just right. Rather than deal with the problems that having the baby posed, they chose abortion."[15]

Disruption of Relationships   In 50 percent of the cases, the abortion was quickly followed by disruption and termination of the relationship with the man involved in the pregnancy. In 5 percent of the cases, a major disruption occurred with other family members.[16]

Their Ethical Views of Abortion   Fully 70 percent of the women studied expressed disapproval of abortion, seeing it as deviant and immoral.[17] But seeing themselves as forced by others, by their circumstances, or by society at large, they frequently attempted to deny responsibility for what they believed was an immoral act.[18] In other words, 70 percent of these aborted women felt forced to compromise their own values and ideals.

In order to avoid upsetting the women in this study, Zimmerman asked no specific questions concerning the nature of the fetus. But though unasked, nearly 25 percent of the women interviewed stated that the aborted fetus was a life, a person, or a human being. In many of these cases, they admitted a sense of having killed or murdered another being. Another 25 percent expressed confusion about the nature of the fetus. In these cases, the women generally believed the fetus was human but denied that abortion was killing. Zimmerman suggests that this contradictory stance was taken in order to maintain their self-image as moral persons. Finally, only 15 percent maintained that the fetus was *not* a person or human life, but even these women expressed themselves in terms of denial rather than with arguments to support their beliefs. For example, "I feel that it's something there, but I don't really feel that it's a life yet."[19]

Reaction to the Abortion Experience   Before evaluating the reactions of women to abortion, Zimmerman attempted to measure and define two classes of women receiving abortion: the affiliated and the disaffiliated. She defined affiliated women as those who were "well-integrated or 'tied in' to their social worlds. These women are clear about their obligations, expectations, and futures. They knew who they were and where they were going . . . a pattern characterized by persons who are securely rooted or enmeshed in social life." These women were more likely to be from a higher upper economic level and social class, had strong career goals, and were more likely to abort for self-serving, pragmatic reasons. Disaffiliated women were defined as "less firmly attached to their social worlds. They had fewer and weaker social ties, role relationships, and other forms of systematic social participation. They also appeared to have less a sense of purpose [plans for the future] than the former group." Because these women tended to be less certain about their futures and less assertive, they were more likely to abort in order to please others (i.e., their boyfriends or families).[20]

In her interviews, Zimmerman found that only 26 percent of the "affiliated" women expressed such "troubled thoughts" as guilt, regret, sadness, and loss. In contrast, 74 percent of those classified as "disaffiliated" expressed "troubled thoughts." Altogether, 48 percent of the women studied described themselves as disturbed by the abortion.[21]

Even when taken at face value, these percentages indicate a relatively high level of negative reactions to abortion. But when examined in the full context of the study, these figures clearly represent only the tip of the iceberg. Two factors indicate that these are minimized figures. First, Zimmerman's sampling limitations, plus the clinic's "screening" of sensitive cases, eliminated several classes and situations most prone to post-abortion depression. Second, Zimmerman's interviews took place only six weeks after the abortion. Other studies show that the percentage of women experiencing post-abortion sequelae increases with time. Many of those who reported few problems early after the abortion may face long-term distress from repressed feelings. Indeed, even Zimmerman notes that many of the affiliated women who seem to be coping best with the abortion are able to do so primarily because they are the most proficient at blocking it out of their minds, or at making it seem like an "unreal" memory.[22]

Whether such blocking out of the abortion feelings at six weeks is sufficient for a lifetime is questionable. Indeed, the WEBA experience strongly suggests otherwise. At six weeks, the women in Zimmerman's survey had not even faced the common triggering experiences for abortion trauma, such as the date when the child should have been born, the anniversary date of the abortion, the birth of a later child, the death or miscarriage of a later child, and so on.

Despite its limitations, the Zimmerman study provides valuable insight into the abortion experience and helps to confirm that the thrust of the WEBA experiences are by no means "rare" or "unusual."

THE AMBIVALENCE OF ABORTION

One of the most haunting tales about the experience of abortion was published in May 1976 on the Op-Ed page of the *New York Times* under the title "There Just Wasn't Room in Our Lives Now for Another Baby." The author, Linda Bird Francke, was a professional journalist, feminist, and pro-choice activist. When faced with an unplanned pregnancy which would have interfered with her and her husband's rising careers, the couple decided to have an abortion. But as the time for the abortion approached, Francke became increasingly ambivalent about their choice, and as she and her husband sat in the waiting room, she began to panic: "Suddenly the rhetoric, the abortion marches I'd walked in, the telegrams sent to Albany to counteract the Friends of the Fetus, the Zero Population Growth buttons I'd worn, peeled away, and I was all alone with my microscopic baby." Intellectually, she tried to concentrate on how small the fetus was, and therefore how impossible it was for it to be human, but she had borne children before and the feel of her own body kept telling her that there was real life growing within her. "Though I would march myself into blisters for a woman's right to exercise the option of motherhood," she writes, "I discovered there in the waiting room that I was not the modern woman I thought I was."[23]

By the time she entered the operating room, Francke was desperately hoping for some release from her predetermined course. She longed for her husband to valiantly "burst" through the door and stop it from happening. When he failed to do so, and the doctor began to dilate her for the surgery, she herself begged him to stop. But the doctor told her it was too late and completed the surgery anyway. At that point she gave in: "What good sports we women are. And how obedient. Physically the pain passed even before the hum of the machine signaled that the vacuuming of my uterus was completed, my baby sucked up like ashes after a cocktail party."[24]

In the months following the abortion, her ambivalence continued. During times of relaxation when she had time to reflect on the beauty of the world, she experienced the common reaction of "visitations" from her aborted child. Her benign "little ghost" would come to her and wave. And she would tearfully wave back to reassure her lost baby that if only it returned, they would now make room for him or her in their busy lives.[25]

The *New York Times* account was published three years after Francke's abortion, only when the "guilt and sadness" associated with the experience had waned. Two years later, drawn once more to reinvestigate her own mixed feelings about abortion, Francke published a book entitled *The Ambivalence of Abortion*, in which she transcribed the reactions to the abortion experience of almost seventy women, couples, parents, and men.

Though Francke takes great pains to align herself with the pro-choice position, her book is not primarily intended to be a defense for the pro-choice ideology. In fact, when Francke's ideology comes into conflict with her own negative abortion experience, the result is often a confusing, contradictory series of rationalizations. For example, Francke candidly acknowledges that she feels she destroyed a life saying, "When I became pregnant five years ago, there was no doubt that life was right there, in my womb." Yet she still supports abortion, and would have one again herself, because there are "no neat answers," just a lot of bad options.[26]

Thus, despite Francke's passion for pro-choice rhetoric, her book is not intended to defend abortion per se. Instead, she seems to have two other goals in mind. First, by painting such intimate portraits of the women forced to seek abortion, she is attempting to convince anti-abortionists to leave these poor, troubled women alone. She is attempting to show that women do not take the decision to abort lightly. Their reasons are well thought out; the problems and obstacles they face are severe. Abortion is difficult enough as it is; women should be simply left alone.

Second, and perhaps more important, Francke's book is intended as a form of group therapy for her fellow aborters ("See, others have gone through the same thing") and a cautious warning for future aborters. Indeed, if there is any single theme that Francke returns to time and time again, it is to the warning that while abortion is an "undeniable right," it is an experience never "easy" to undergo or "easy" to forget. Instead, it is a choice which carries with it many unresolved and ambivalent feelings. She warns that every one should know that abortion always involves a "period of great stress for every person involved"—women, men, relatives, and even the doctors and nurses. To ignore the emotional risks of abortion, she writes, is blind foolishness.[27]

Filled with so many varied interviews, *The Ambivalence of Abortion* is *must* reading for anyone wanting to understand the abortion experience, but it is not without faults and limitations. The weakest portions of the book are the introductory and concluding chapters in which Francke attempts to describe the history of abortion and argues the pro-choice line. To the well-informed, these chapters are obviously filled with a large number of factual errors. It is probable that these errors occurred because Francke was overly dependent on the biased materials supplied to her by pro-abortion foundations.[28]

The second major limitation of Francke's work is that she gathered her interviews primarily in abortion clinics just prior to or immediately after her subjects' abortions, thus limiting the range of reactions. This is a severe problem since studies show that the number of women who experience negative feelings about their abortions increases with time. On the other hand, this limitation is also one of the book's strengths. The immediacy of these interviews provides an intense view not seen in the settled, matured WEBA stories. These are women in the midst of their crises. They have not yet reconciled themselves to what they have done; they have not yet settled on whether it was right or wrong, only that it was necessary. As Francke herself points out, these women are frequently incoherent and inconsistent, struggling to understand and rationalize their actions.[29] Almost every testimony reflects deep-rooted ambivalence and unresolved doubts. In their stories, one sees WEBA women who have not yet come to see how they have been exploited, who have not yet been able to admit their mistakes.

Besides the limitations of whom and when she interviewed, Francke's interviewing style does not encourage stories which are easily analyzed. Unlike Zimmerman, a sociologist who carefully guides each woman through a routine of relevant questions, Francke is a journalist who allows each woman to tell her story in her own way. This approach provides for much more varied and interesting reading than Zimmerman's clinical study, but it is less patterned and consistent. Some women reveal themselves in intimate detail; others are brusque and short. Some go into great lengths describing their feelings and emotions; others limit themselves to factual descriptions as to when, where, how and why the abortion was obtained, but give no glimpse of their innermost feelings. Because the interview process was not patterned and consistent, each woman tells only what seems most significant to her at that moment, only what she is willing to reveal to this sympathetic and understanding reporter. But even for those who are most comfortable with Francke and her tape recorder, significant feelings, too sensitive to be revealed to oneself much less a stranger, are obviously being held back. The interviews gathered by Francke, therefore, reflect only what the women were *willing* to share and what was currently at the "top of their minds." They are less circumspect than they are spontaneous.

Despite these limitations, *The Ambivalence of Abortion* offers a wealth of information. Though it can in no sense be considered unbiased or fully representative, the data which can be culled from these interviews substantially confirms this researcher's own findings which show that abortion almost always has a negative impact on women's lives. Examining the forty-nine interviews with women and couples which Francke includes in her book, the following facts emerge:

Sexual Coldness   Eleven women (22 percent) volunteered information which described how the abortion resulted in sexual coldness towards their mates, or men in general.[30] A few mentioned that having to abort their pregnancies made them "angry at men," or even resulted in feelings of "hatred" towards all men. For others, sexual coldness was directed more inwardly. One women said she felt "my body get cold and dry up" whenever her boyfriend approached her. Another felt guilt over the abortion whenever she and her husband made love. One woman slept with her boyfriend for three years after her abortion but never made love with him again. Others simply lost all pleasure in sexual intercourse, or became fearful of sex believing they would be forced to go through a second abortion.

Desire for Pregnancy and Child   Twenty-two of those interviewed (47 percent) mentioned an initial happiness over the pregnancy or said that they had a desire to keep the baby.[31] It is this tension between wanting the baby (or at least feeling a sense of duty to accept it) versus the practical necessities not to have a child which is central to the emotional ambivalence towards abortion. In order to do the "practical" thing, women are forced to compromise their own values, deny their own "impractical" desires, and submit to the humiliating but "necessary evil" of abortion.

Because of this conflict between wanting the child and rejecting the responsibilities of motherhood, many of the women interviewed told stories filled with confusion and contradictions. For example, one woman insisted that "I never thought about the fetus. I had a pre-political feeling of what was inside me and my rights. It was something that didn't belong there and had no place in my life at that time." But she also told Francke: "The whole time [before the abortion] I had a fantasy of keeping the baby. I wrote a few poems with earthy words in them like 'seed,' and 'bloom,' and 'blossom,' but it was cynical. This seed? Let this seed grow? No way."[32]

Frequently those who expressed a desire to keep the baby said they were aborting only out of a sense of duty to their boyfriends.[33] Others only aborted under extreme pressure from parents.[34]

Abortion as a Violation of the Body   Several of the women interviewed by Francke described the abortion procedure itself as horrible and degrading. One woman equated the humiliation of having her body invaded by the abortionist with brutal rape.[35] For some, the pain of abortion helped to divert their attention away from their moral dilemma. Their pain was seen as "payment" for what has happened. For others, the worst part of the abortion was the unnaturalness of the act, the emptiness felt afterwards, the feeling that the body was in a state of "limbo," lost and waiting to complete what it had begun.[36]

One woman interviewed by Francke, though basically pro-choice in attitude, described abortion as a violent disruption of the female body's natural balance. This disturbance of the body's natural "ecology" has far-ranging effects. In short, this woman says, abortion is "just nuts, it's bad karma, it's negative anti-life force. It's a no. It's not allowing things to flow their natural way."[37]

Negative Feelings Thirty-five of the women interviewed by Francke (71 percent) clearly expressed some type of negative feeling about their abortion experiences.[38] Some described their experience and its aftermath in extremely negative terms; others avoided details of their feelings but admitted to a general feeling of ambivalence, confusion, or doubt.

The most frequent complaint was from women who described themselves as feeling "guilty" or "dirty." Many said they felt that they had killed or murdered their babies: "I hated myself. I felt abandoned and lost. There was no one's shoulder to cry on, and I wanted to cry like hell. And I felt guilty about killing something. I couldn't get it out of my head that I'd just killed a baby."[39] Others reported looking at other children and imagining possible similarities to their own aborted children.[40] Guilt led one woman to attempt suicide with an overdose of tranquilizers.[41]

For some, feelings of guilt were not immediate. Instead, remorse came tumbling in during later periods of crisis. One woman, for example, reported a sudden onslaught of post-abortion guilt only when she faced problems with a later wanted pregnancy: "For five weeks I was flat on my back and the abortion just wouldn't go out of my mind." Not only did she then miscarry, but she also found out that she was suffering from blocked fallopian tubes. From this period onward, her guilt and fears increased, ultimately requiring psychiatric therapy to deal with her repressed feelings.[42]

The desire to forget the abortion experience, "put it out of my mind," or the firm announcement that she "just won't think about it" is common to almost every story. But Francke found that, just as many WEBA members report, even the most determined efforts to push the abortion memory out of the mind often fail:

> I just wanted to forget it, but after a year I started having anxiety attacks. I didn't think the abortion was causing them though. I thought

that was all past. On the anniversary of the abortion it got really bad. I started to shake and cry. I huddled on the floor and felt like I was screaming, and my breathing became heavy and uncontrolled. I started having two or three attacks a week, and it was scary. I went to a counselor at the university and finally talked about the abortion.[43]

For many, rationalizations were maintained only by a conscious effort: "I didn't think of it as a baby. I just didn't want to think of it that way."[44] For others, their rationalizations only added to their confusion. A woman back for her third abortion insisted to Francke that she was well-adjusted to the first two, but then she went on to describe the symptoms of post-abortion syndrome, such as compulsive fascination with other people's children, anger, denial, and rationalization. No longer knowing what to believe, she finally concluded: "Maybe I should go to a psychiatrist, but I really don't have the money or the interest. Truth is hard to take, and I just don't know if I'm ready for it."[45]

Denial. Thinly veiled self-deceptions. Again and again the women interviewed by Francke reveal how difficult it is to balance reality against rationalizations, feelings against ideology. For many, peace of mind is gained only at the great cost of closing out all feelings and emotions. One woman, for example, described herself after her abortion by saying, "Mostly I felt dead a lot of the time." Still another found relief only when she "just stopped feeling altogether."[46]

For others there can be no rationalizations. These are women who were originally against abortion but felt forced by circumstances to compromise their values: "We were convinced that the abortion was the best thing rather than the right thing. If you asked me how I felt about abortion I would say I was against it. I feel very hypocritical."[47]

Despite the limitations and biases mentioned earlier, Francke's interviews support our findings that for the vast majority of women, 71 percent in her sample, abortion is a negative experience which women try desperately to forget, but rarely with success.

Positive Experiences? But what of the other 29 percent of the women interviewed by Francke? Is abortion an easy or even a positive experience for this minority? Probably not. Most of the fourteen interviews which do not contain negative comments about the abortion say little or nothing about the woman's feelings. Many of these interviews are uninformative because they were taken just prior to the abortion, minutes afterwards, or only two weeks later. Most of these women had nothing negative to say because they had not yet had time enough to reflect on the experience or to face later situations which would call their abortion back to mind. In these interviews, the women's minds were focused on the anticipation of the abortion to come or on the relief that it was finally over.

Despite these obvious time limitations, Francke tries to use a few of these interviews to "prove" that for some women, at least, abortion is not emotionally damaging and thus is a "good choice." For example, only two weeks after her abortion, one woman told Francke that she had not had any regrets or emotional problems. She and her husband chose abortion because they were simply "not willing to make the sacrifices necessary to raise a child." But, she admitted, during the two weeks between her abortion and the interview she had been so busy dealing with the physical complications which occurred that she had not yet had time to notice any emotional reactions.[48]

Another interview which Francke numbers among the "positive" cases is much too short to sustain her conclusion. Indeed, this interview is less than a hundred words long and was taken when the woman was on the recovery table, only minutes after the abortion was completed, where she told Francke, "I don't feel any guilt. I don't feel no nothing except tired [sic]. It was simple and the only thing to do."[49]

This is hardly one of Francke's more open and revealing interviews, and yet she lists it as one which proves that for some women there is "little difficulty reaching their decision and no appreciable trouble afterwards."[50] But obviously this unfortunate woman felt forced into her abortion by her financial circumstances, felt no "freedom of choice" in reaching her decision, and had not yet had time to reflect on what had really happened. In these first few minutes after her abortion, this woman was holding to the relief she felt at having it over and done with. Her statements are hardly fitting proof that abortion can be an easy or positive experience.

Yet another story selected by Francke to show that abortion is sometimes "a positive experience and a period of personal growth" seems anything but positive. Indeed, the most amazing thing is that Francke can interpret it in that way. Interviewed two weeks after her second abortion, this woman described her first abortion, saying: "I just couldn't stop crying the whole time. All I could think was that I was going to be a mother and that this child would love me and I was hurting it. I lay on the table and kept cradling my arms as if there was a baby in them. I could swear I heard it crying. . . . I thought I was going crazy."[51]

Afterwards she described herself as becoming promiscuous for a time, and then suddenly stopped when she realized she was "turning into a whore." A year later she deliberately became pregnant a second time. Then, to punish herself and her boyfriend, she had her second abortion: "I really wanted to punish myself, and I guess I was setting the guy up to be a victim too. . . ."[52]

Her interview was conducted two weeks after this second abortion, one she described as equally painful—both physically and emotionally—as the first. But this woman concluded her story by saying that during the last week she and her boyfriend had been trying to talk, trying to let their angers and frustrations out, without rushing into a reunion. ". . . So that's the way I feel right now, this abortion's really been a positive one. And maybe it's going to be okay now."[53]

From this *hope* to change her life, this resolution to try again, Francke concludes that this young woman's second abortion experience was a "positive experience and a period of personal growth." Though everyone would hope that this woman's bad experiences have motivated her to make constructive changes, her qualified hope that "maybe it's going to be okay now" clearly indicates that she was trying to talk herself into a positive attitude, not that it had been achieved through her second abortion.

Several of the women interviewed by Francke insisted that they were emotionally unaffected by the abortion, but were nonetheless extremely bitter towards the man, or men in general, and often displaced this anger towards the child. Though these women did not admit to any negative feelings stemming from their abortions, the intensity with which they denied doubts and regrets reminds one of fireworks being used to disguise tears.[54]

Even the few women who insisted that the abortion had a positive effect on their lives expressed discomfort, insisting that they don't ever want to go through it again.[55] Strangely enough, Francke frequently interprets a woman's comment that she is taking greater precautions to prevent ever needing another abortion to mean that her first abortion was a "positive experience."[56] Ironically, it seems, any woman who resolves never to have another abortion is said to have "grown" from her experience. Only repeaters, she implies, have failed to grow. But this discrimination against repeaters implies that there is something wrong about abortion, that abortion is something to be avoided. For if abortion is to be avoided a second time, why shouldn't it be avoided the first time? If it is dangerous or irresponsible to undergo many abortions, why is it not also dangerous or irresponsible to undergo one?

In sum, if one reads the stories recorded by Francke looking for signs of pain, one will find them in every story—though occasionally buried under tough and bitter words. On the other hand, if one reads her collection looking to find women trying to cope with their pains, trying to reconcile themselves to what has happened, trying to avoid future mistakes, future abortions, one will find this common search for hope too. But pro-abortionists are too willing to ignore the former fact and emphasize the latter as proof that abortion can be a "positive, growing experience." Though no one doubts that women who undergo abortions learn something from that experience, that does not mean abortion is a desirable lesson. Indeed, it might very well be a lesson which should be avoided at any cost.

The testimony of WEBA women confirms this latter point of view. These women have learned from their abortion experiences; they have experienced growth, but it is growth which has been achieved by recognizing their errors and the evil of abortion, not by defending it. For many, abortion led them to the pit of despair where they found and accepted the forgiveness of God. Growth came not in defending the pit of abortion as their "right," their home, but in seeing the pit for what it is and crawling out of it. Growth came not because abortion is a positive experience, but because they were able to finally recognize and condemn it as a negative experience.

IN NECESSITY AND SORROW

A third powerful book which examines the abortion experience from a pro-choice perspective is *In Necessity and Sorrow: Life and Death in an Abortion Hospital* by Magda Denes.

As with Francke, Denes' book was an outgrowth of her own ambivalent abortion experience. Three times she entered a private hospital with an appointment to abort her pregnancy. Twice she changed her mind and left in tears; the third time she stayed and was aborted. Two weeks after her abortion, Denes returned to the hospital and asked the director if she could conduct in-depth interviews with consenting patients, relatives, and staff. When informed that Dr. Denes was a university professor and a certified psychologist, the director gave his blessings to the project, feeling that it would help shed light on an important topic.

During the "many months" that followed, Denes became a fixture at the hospital, quietly observing, befriending and interviewing. Her book is a narrative of her experiences, a diary of her reflections, and a summary of her interviews. It is often slow, frequently cynical, often morbid, but always revealing.

What was the motivating force behind Denes' book? Twice she walked out of the hospital before finally returning for her own abortion. In this ability to waiver and feel uncertain, she felt that she was among the lucky few. She had a secure home, secure finances, and a husband who would have supported her even if she had chosen not to abort. But she was forced to wonder about other women: "I wanted to know most urgently what lies behind the abortion myths," she writes. "What happens to women who are not as privileged as I and who can not freely choose but are rather compelled by circumstance to renounce their child? Do they grieve less, or more?"[57] This is the question that prompted her study, but after returning to the hospital to begin her study, it was the "now" of abortion, not it's aftermath, which caught her eye.

The time and place to which Denes confined her research was very limiting. Her study began slightly before the 1973 Supreme Court decision legalizing abortion in all fifty states, and ended a short time later. The place was New York City, the abortion capital of the nation, where abortions were easily and legally obtainable since 1970. The place was a private hospital which specialized in providing second trimester abortions.

In addition to the limitations imposed by this timeframe and setting, Denes' perspective of the abortion experience in this hospital was constrained by the position and rank with which the patients she met perceived her. By way of comparison, Zimmerman's approach to this topic was as that of a sociologist. She carefully and consistently interviewed aborted women under formal conditions, following a uniform outline. Francke, on the other hand, was less clinical, less formal. Hers was a reporter's style. She interviewed women in clinics around the country. She was out in the trenches, out among the people, "one of them," so to speak, and this position allowed for some startlingly candid interviews. But Denes had none of the trust and advantages accorded to a "normal" woman. She was a "doctor," no mere pedestrian. At times, as she herself points out, this rank became a barrier between her and the patients she interviewed. Cautious and circumspect, already filled with doubts and ambivalence, many were afraid of confiding in a "shrink."

Like most of those with whom she worked at the hospital, Denes had an honest compassion for the patients. Furthermore, having been aborted herself, she clearly identified with them. Still, the patients soon became passing figures, one sad face after another, one sad story after another, and Denes' senses became dulled by the recurring dramas. Instead, the hospital and staff—always the same day after day—took on a greater reality and permanence both in her mind and in her book. It is this reality, the abortion hospital, which is the true focus of her book. The patients Denes talked with are seen only from the hospital point of view, what the counselors heard, what the doctors saw. There were still tears, doubts, terror, and most of all determination to have it over with as soon as possible. But all these interviews were from the "before" point of view. She never follows up to see how the patients were reacting after abortion had sucked the life from their wombs.

Denes' book includes interviews with seventeen abortion patients: ten saline, seven D&C (dilation and curettage. See Chapter Five for further information). The interviews are all relatively short, and most are conducted *before* the abortion actually took place. But the stories follow what is, by now, a very familiar pattern. Many of the women interviewed were being pressured to abort by boyfriends, husbands, or parents. Since they all were second trimester aborters who had delayed in their decisions, almost all had strong feelings of ambivalence. Some openly desired to keep the child; others were already plagued with guilt.

Some of the women Denes talked with openly discussed their feelings of guilt. For example, one woman who was being pressured to abort by her husband told Denes: "Like when you have an abortion you just destroying [sic] a part of yourself, that's the way I feel anyhow. I just feel bad inside, that's all. I didn't really want to do it. It's a sin."[58]

But more typically the women were simply trying to block out their negative feelings. As one woman told her: "I made up my mind to do it and like I could let it drive me crazy, any woman could, but you can't, because you've got to live with it and there's really no sense in letting it drive you right off the edge."[59]

As a trained psychiatrist, Denes knows to look beyond the words of those she interviews. She sees that words of bravery are used to disguise fears, words of calm to hide doubts. For example, when introducing the interview of one patient, she writes: "All that she says sounds honest and straightforward. It is only when she refers to the abortion that she lies, not so much to me as to herself."[60] But seeing through these self-deceptions does not mean that Denes criticizes them. Instead, she justifies denial as a necessary defense mechanism by which all people protect themselves from their worst sides. "Oh yes," she writes, "these people lie, they kid themselves, testify falsely, confess in bad faith, shirk responsibility, only pretend to honor, bracket the past, and invent their lives. And who among us does differently? Especially in times of crisis. Especially in times of irreversible choice."[61]

Self-preservation is the name of the game, and Denes clearly sees that sanity in the abortion clinic can be achieved only by a strict adherence to the rules of the game. Both patients and staff collaborate in this conspiracy of self-deceptions. Describing her interviews with both staff and patients, she writes: "Above all, this is a document on the evasions, multifaceted, clever, and shameful, by which we all live and die."[62] In the abortion hospital, she adds, "Reality is a matter of courtesy. A matter of agreement not to rock the tempest-torn boat."[63]

It is a primary task of abortion personnel, then, to assist patients in constructing and maintaining this tunnel-visioned view of reality. It is their task to keep the patients from becoming afraid, doubtful. Thus

Denes perceives the abortion routine as being designed to carry the patients along, to numb them against reality. This is done in often contradictory ways: busy them, push them, coddle them, ignore them. The routine minimizes questions, stifles doubts, and fans the hope that soon it will all be over with:

> As I sit watching these two women, I am overwhelmed by the bureaucratic banality of suffering. Obscure chatter, legal forms, repeated signatures, waiting, these are the structured anesthetic that oil the machinery of institutions. At this hospital, downstairs they wait, in this unit they bear witness, further up they are delivered. In between they endure the purgatory of routine and fear, of lab-tests and regrets and reaffirmations of purpose. Until it is over. Until the crisis recedes, and the dull comfort of monotony asserts itself once more.[64]

In Necessity and Sorrow is filled with such commentaries. Denes' style is like that of a funeral dirge: solemn, sad, respectful of both the living and the deceased. Although she recognized the need for patients and staff to hide from the reality of abortion, she herself feels compelled to confront this reality in its most grisly forms. In this sense, her book is less an examination of others than an examination of herself. It is her own ambivalence towards her own abortion which she returned to the hospital to confront, and it is this confrontation which is most illuminating.

Some of the most disturbing portions of the book are those in which Denes cautiously and fearfully investigated the inner sanctum of the abortion hospital: the operating rooms. There she watched frightened, often sobbing women undergoing saline abortions. There she saw surgeons who were compassionate and cruel, efficient and mercenary. She heard tales of severe complications, near deaths, and even of aborted babies born alive. She saw contradictions, paradoxes, and pain:

> I am drawn to the [saline] unit, irresistibly, by my reactions of disbelief, sorrow, horror, compassion, guilt. The place depresses me, yet I hang around after working hours. When I leave, I behave outside with the expansiveness of one who has just escaped a disaster. I have bad dreams. My sense of complicity in something nameless grows and festers. I consider giving up the research, but it is unthinkable to not return to the saline floor without knowing more.[65]

After returning day after day, Denes finally began the process of interviewing doctors, nurses, and patients. But she still felt drawn to know the full truth. She needed to see it all for herself.

Half-heartedly, Denes makes several attempts to see a saline abortion through to completion, to see the laboring birth of the dead fetus. But she never quite succeeds in this task. Other duties call her, and somehow she seems to always miss seeing that unpredictable event. Finally, she writes:

> I decide to put an end to my stalling and spend an uninterrupted afternoon on the floor. Nothing happens, not even screaming. Toward evening I turn in desperation to one of the nurses. "Isn't anybody going to give birth today?" Before she can open her mouth, her face tells me that I have spat in the soup. "Doctor, that is not what happens here." "I am sorry, I mean deliver the baby, I mean fetus. To hell with it, nurse, I am going home. Good night." The next afternoon I return determined, regardless of where I am at the time of delivery, to look inside the buckets. . . . Planting myself in front of the table . . . I remove with one hand the lid of a bucket. . . . I look inside the bucket in front of me. There is a small naked person in there floating in a bloody liquid—plainly the tragic victim of a drowning accident. But then perhaps this was no accident, because the body is purple with bruises and the face has the agonized tautness of one forced to die too soon. Death overtakes me in a rush of madness. . . . I take the lid off all the buckets. All of them. I reach up to the shelf above this bucket graveyard tabletop and take down a pair of forceps. With them I pull aside in each bucket the placenta, which looks like a cancerous mushroom shrouding the fetus. With the forceps I lift the fetuses, one by one. I lift them by an arm or a leg, leaving, as I return them again, an additional bruise on their purple, wrinkled, acid-soaked flesh. I have evidently gone mad. I carry on the examination, whose sole purpose by now is to increase the unbearable anguish in my heart. I lift a very large fetus. . . . I look at the label. . . . This is Master Atkins—to be burned tomorrow [in a hospital incinerator]—who died like a hero to save his mother's life. Might he have become someday the only one to truly love her? The only one to mourn her death? "Nurse, nurse," I shout, taking off my fancy gloves. "Cover them up."[66]

Like the woman who aborts again and again, determined to prove to herself that it doesn't really hurt, Denes forced herself to look at all the horrors of abortion again and again, hoping despite the tremors to find the reasons why, the justifications, the apologies for this "evil necessity." Eventually, her purgation in this chamber of death achieved its desired effect:

> In a month's time I acquire a sort of wooden torpor to the screams that periodically shatter the humdrum noises of the floor. Tears cease to unsettle me. I am unmoved by wailing. I take it for granted that we are in the business of death here, and the tenor of each day will

be heartache. . . . I am shell-shocked, as it were, stunned by being spoken to. Staggered by these readily revealed dramas, whose plots are loneliness, whose resolutions are defeat.[67]

Numbed by the saline floor, Denes pressed on, forcing herself to face even greater shocks. By superficial appearances the D&C floor was more controlled and "civilized" because the abortions were quick, finished in minutes rather than days, and the patients were anesthetized. But the D&C procedure itself was more graphic and gruesome. Still, Denes was determined to witness it in full.

At the first D&C abortion she attended, the disorienting noises and smells drove her from the room, nauseated and shaken. She had yet to see anything. The second time was only slightly better. She remained at the patient's head for the whole time but again saw none of the procedure itself. By the third time Denes was determined to witness everything. And she did.

Watching an abortion at the surgeon's end of the table, Denes' first reaction is one of shock at how the patient is put to sleep, spread-eagled, and violated with cold impunity. It is coarse, degrading, and even defiling. But it is not until the fetal parts are removed that all her feelings are deadened by the enormity of what she sees:

He pulls out something, which he slaps on the instrument table. "There," he says. "A leg." . . . I turn to Mr. Smith. "What did he say?" "He pulled a leg off," Mr. Smith says. "Right here." He points to the instrument table, where there is a perfectly formed, slightly bent leg, about three inches long. It consists of a ripped thigh, a knee, a lower leg, a foot, and five toes. I start to shake very badly, but otherwise, I feel nothing. Total shock is passionless. "I have the rib cage now," Holtzman says, as he slams down another piece of the fetus. . . . "There, I've got the head out now. Also a piece of the placenta." I look at the instrument table where next to the leg, and next to a mess he calls the rib cage but that I cannot recognize, there lies a head. It is the smallest human head I have ever seen, but it is unmistakably part of a person. My vision and my hearing though disengaged, continue, I note, to function with exceptional clarity. The rest of me is mercifully gone.[68]

After this, Denes left the hospital completely "exhausted," but she returned again and again. Forcing herself to witness these terrors again and again, Denes soon discovered the deadening comfort of repetition. Her dearly bought callousness was tested one day when she watched the most morbid of spectacles without a quiver of distaste. On this day, one of the nurses lost her wedding ring in the operating room, so she and another staff member pawed through a bag of blood and fetal parts hoping to recover it. At first, the scene did not arouse Denes' normally keen sensibilities. She writes:

> I am all for them. It is frightful to lose one's wedding ring. The event is completely divested of its larger context. Hours later when the scene reasserts itself in my mind, I do not recognize myself. Is inhumanity a habit? Is indifference the result of the attrition of meaning? If so, one must watch the self like an enemy.[69]

If numbness to abortion was what Denes had been seeking, then that is what she found. By the end of her stay at the hospital, Denes is so benumbed by the months she has spent in this abortion hospital that she is indistinguishable from the rest of the shell-shocked staff. Together, she and other members of the abortuary sit in the hospital's cafeteria and find hysterical laughter in jokes about a menu of "fetus-stew" and "mince meat pie."[70]

Ironically, one of the few incidents which Denes describes with joy is when a young girl fled the clinic, running from her pressuring parents:

> There are exceptions. One is a young girl barely sixteen. She is scrawny, Puerto Rican, uneducated, poor, and headstrong. Some say she is crazy. I love her as she takes off down the corridor, screaming, her white gown flying in a blaze of glory. "Let me outta here. I won't do it. It's my baby." Six weeks pregnant—afflicted with an abstraction, one might say—she leaves triumphant, with two sulky parents who have been hastily summoned by Dora. Will this madness cost her her life? . . . I have no opinion except to observe once again that the question of which life, whose life, is a frequent and unanswerable dilemma in this hospital. To note also that after her departure, all the women—patients and nurses—set their faces a little tighter.[71]

All these others, it would seem, are struggling against the same "crazy" impulse to flee. But they are all too strong, or too weak, to take that other route.

The glue that holds it all together—the hospital, the staff and the patients—is weak and precarious. It is always on the verge of collapse and always maintained by sheer willpower, by the collective agreement that what must be done, must be done. There is no room for questions:

> The most threatening pitfall in this hospital is a creeping conviction of absurdity. Daily, terror and desolation dictate decisions, the meaning of which are obscure to everyone. This life against that. Why? That life against this. Why again? Because patients can speak, and fetuses are mute? Things happen. Situations arise. We do what we

can, which is not much. Will, God's or otherwise, appears an obsolete notion. The most frequent gesture is a shrug. The most prevalent phrase is "I don't know."[72]

But this game of denial and the tunnel-vision it breeds, Denes sees, has a high cost. There is insensitivity. There is forced isolation, because to come too close is to shatter the illusion. For example, she records an incident in which a frightened patient asks a nurse for the time when a clock is in plain sight. When the nurse answered, "Quarter past four, dear" and ignored this subtle plea for attention and reassurance, Denes wants to shout and expose these pained masks, these silent absurdities, but instead she remains silent, thinking, "To uncover reality here would mean to turn this place into a madhouse. Therefore I am silent, and clutch my stomach, and go for a walk down the corridor."[73]

What does Denes think of all these games of denial? "Sometimes acquaintanceship with reality makes people sane, at other times it drives them mad," she writes. "Who is to say what is the right path? Certainly not anyone with a heart."[74] Oddly, this rhetorical question seems to argue that isolationism can be substituted for compassion. She could just as well say: "Who are we to interfere? Let them make their own mistakes. Whether the path they choose leads to sanity or madness, it is the path they choose *alone.*"

Though Dr. Magda Denes is personally committed to the pro-choice philosophy, her book, like Francke's, is never embraced by the pro-choice movement. It is too dark, too questioning, too disturbing. Despite the author's pro-choice perspective, *In Necessity and Sorrow* is a powerful indictment *of* abortion. It is an indictment which Denes did not want to make, but an indictment which cannot be avoided by one who would report the facts she observes. Denes herself is unsettled by the tone of her writing. Despite her intellectual belief in abortion, her writings had taken on a dark nature of their own:

> On reading it, my book appears to me boobytrapped. It seems a mined object ready to explode in utter destructiveness at the slightest corrupt or careless touch. For in fact I am for abortions. My rage throughout these pages is at the human predicament. At the finitude of our lives, at our nakedness, at the absurdity of our perpetual ambivalence toward the terror of life and toward the horror of death.[75]

The reason both Denes' and Francke's books are so anti-abortion—despite the opposite leanings of their authors—is simple. When one studies the effect of abortion on women in an intimate and personal way, it is never an encouraging story. What emerges is always much more sorrow than joy, much more guilt than relief.

The pro-abortion/pro-choice philosophy is admirable only when stripped of its reality, only when worshiped as an ideal, believed in the abstract. When examined from the viewpoint of women filled with despair, dread, guilt, and denial, pro-choice rhetoric is cold and uncomforting. When examined from the viewpoint of torn limbs, saline-burnt bodies, scarred uteruses, and infertility, it is a mockery.

Denes herself finds little reason to cling to her pro-abortion stance other than for the abstract ideal of "choice." With a candor unusual for a pro-choice advocate, Denes readily admits that abortion is "a type of murder," that its victim is "alive and human." But she sees abortion on demand as justifiable murder because it "saves the life" of the woman, or at least "saves" her from an unwanted burden.[76]

In sum, speaking as one who has been there, Denes favors abortion on demand purely on the grounds that women should be given a choice. Yet, she is discomforted with that choice, for even under the most ideal circumstances, even if abortion on demand were "provided free by the state, [and] supported with mercy by the church," she believes that such a pure freedom to abort would only accentuate the horrors, doubts, guilts, and other problems which are *inherent* to abortion. "For if we remove abortions from the realm of defiance of authority," she writes,

> . . . if we permit them to be acts of freedom as they should be, their meaning, private and collective, will inescapably emerge in the consciousness of every person. . . . I think it is a far, far lighter task to regard oneself as a martyr and to battle the world than to know the private sorrows of unique commitments and the heartache of self-chosen destiny. I wish, therefore, to be taken for what I am. A proabortionist with a bad secular conscience.[77]

OTHER TESTIMONIES

The three books discussed above provide perhaps the widest collection of interviews by pro-choice authors. They are not, however, the only sources wherein aborted women provide testimony about their experiences. Bits and pieces are scattered wide and far. Small batches and single stories can be found throughout the general media, in pro-life publications, and in pro-choice publications. To gather all such stories together would be impossible task, but a brief review of some of these other sources supports our finding that abortion is never an easy experience for the women involved.

Looking first to pro-choice literature, one can hardly miss *Our*

Bodies, Ourselves, compiled in 1973 by the Boston Women's Health Book Collective. Written from a radical feminist perspective, this book covers a wide range of women's health topics and includes sections on female sexuality, lesbianism, reproduction, and abortion. The abortion chapter is devoutly pro-choice, but there is a reluctant admission that although abortion brings a relief from immediate problems, "Even the most positive feelings afterward tend to be mixed with negative ones."[78]

As examples, the Boston Women's Collective prints a few quotations from aborted women, such as: "I began my mourning during my short pregnancy. I feel there has to be a mourning in some form for the life that was never allowed to continue." Another reports: "I was so relieved not to be pregnant any more that I didn't think I had any sad feelings at all. Then a few days later, on my way to a friend's house, I saw a young couple walking a new baby and I burst out crying right there on the street."[79]

Besides the few brief testimonies such as these, *Our Bodies, Ourselves* contains the complete abortion testimonies of two anonymous feminists. Both resemble the "typical" stories of ambivalence encountered so far. The only difference is that each ends her story with an appeal to feminist ideology and the glories of self-determination.

The first of these stories recounts an illegal abortion in 1967. At first the woman was pleased to learn she was pregnant, but then she went through a process of trying to talk herself out of having the child. This impulse seemed to stem from a feminist belief that reproduction is a crude, secondary function of the female body, and a binding and enslaving one at that. From this viewpoint, then, every pregnancy should be regarded with suspicion. One's "biological" yearnings to keep the pregnancy should be weighed against the more important needs of the woman's "rational" being. Thus, this woman chose to suppress her strong desires to keep the pregnancy and instead chose to prove her "rational control" over her own life. To her, her pregnancy was the test case which would determine whether she was a feminist, free and independent, or a weak-willed victim bound by her biology and the conventions of a "male-dominated society."[80]

In order to fight her "biological" impulses and proceed with the abortion, she writes, "I shut myself down emotionally," and even years later "my total emotional reaction to it escapes me." But she ends her tale with pro-choice bravado, telling women that there is no reason to feel guilt over abortion despite "societal taboos" because "it is my nature and my right to determine my destiny as a woman."[81]

The second story, also intended to reinforce the pro-choice philosophy, is even more ambivalent than the first. This time it is the story of a legal abortion by a married woman, a mother, who was in the process of returning to college. Her plans were upset, so:

> I kept hoping for a miscarriage. The idea of abortion—the word— came in and out of my head but was quickly dismissed. I felt strongly that abortion was not a choice for me. I, as a person I thought I had begun to know, did not have the freedom to make that choice. I had believed abortion was every woman's right, but those were hollow, liberal thoughts for me. It's so easy to be liberal when you're comfortable. For me abortion was a whole life-death question that I could not bear to settle. . . . It's important to say that my husband was adamantly opposed to a third child, which didn't help me at all in making a decision. We argued bitterly—I defending anything he was against. . . . I kept getting very entangled in the sanctity of life: this fetus was growing within me whether I was awake or asleep, all the time. When does one have the right to destroy a life, potential or real? When is life real? . . . [I was] confused by the realization that I could consider aborting a fetus. Fetus—to me a child. I was completely muddled—and I had nowhere to go. But friends kept helping and supporting—women supporting no decision, just me as I was.[82]

At this point her friends convinced her that she had to take responsibility for making her own decision. She learned, as all aborting women do, to shift away from the moral question, "Is it a life?" to the practical question, "Do I want a child?" For this would-be feminist, facing this practical question was a challenge to be a "mature woman" and "make your own decision" independent of past "conditioning" or social norms.

> I had to take on the responsibility of saying "I want to have this child, and I will accept that" or "I do not want another child and I must accept the responsibility for aborting this fetus." I had to say that I was real, that my life was real and mine and important. Those feelings were very hard to come to. I don't think I believe in them fully even now. . . . [But] there was a certain strength in knowing that I could make a choice that was mine alone and be entirely responsible to myself. On the strength that I had begun to feel as a woman I made the decision to have an abortion. There was no decision of right or wrong or morality—it simply seemed the most responsible choice to make. It is still upsetting to me—the logic of it all—but somewhere within me it is still very clear, and I'm still very sure of that decision. . . . I was very sure of my decision that day [of my abortion], much more than at any other time, but my emotions were somewhat shut down. Perhaps it was in self-defense. I had questioned my decision so many times that I just had to stop. . . . What in reality hap-

pened was that I had become a person I control— someone who is able to say "This is the way my life must go." In retrospect, my feelings are very contrary and complex—some high, some low. I do not feel guilt—almost rather guilty over my astonishing (to me) lack of guilt. I have felt at many times very strong and sure in my identity as a woman—a very real person.[83]

Like the first story, this testimony is intended to teach aspiring feminists, modern and independent, that abortion is bearable if one fixes one's eyes on the ideal of self-determination—no matter who must suffer to achieve it. Abortion, then, is seen as the "badge of honor" by which women reclaim control over their own lives.

Despite the bravado of these testimonies, however, the doubts and ambivalence which these women feel is clear. Their closing remarks about the virtues of the "freedom to choose" may have been necessitated by the editorial slant of the volume to which they contributed their testimonies. But it is more likely, as Denes put it, that they are "evasions, multifaceted and clever," intended to convince themselves more than their readers.

Quite honestly, these two stories from *Our Bodies, Ourselves* are the most "positive" abortion testimonies one can find. Clearly, abortion is *never* free of sour doubts and pains. Those who are "completely satisfied" are few and far between. But even when such "satisfied" aborters are encountered, their claims of being untroubled by their abortions must be taken with a grain of salt, since such women have far more reason, if only to reinforce their own self-images, to hide negative feelings and insist that the decision to abort was good and right. To admit otherwise is to open the door to reevaluation, doubt, self-reproach, despair.

Periodically, letters from aborted women will appear on the editorial pages of the popular press. The pain they describe almost always follows the same pattern. For example, a letter which appeared in the *Tampa Tribune* said in part:

> I am 34, married seven years. I had an abortion not quite four years ago. The pain of the knowledge of what I did is permanent, deep and fresh again when I least expect it. A word about a child, Mother's Day, a song—can literally rip me apart. There is never any warning. In the middle of the happiest moments, something will trigger a sadness for my action. I can't make you feel how I feel or how I felt. I would be writing for hours. Even if I talked to you, you could not know the pain I've set myself up for. It's not just babies that abortion kills. It's mothers, too.[84]

This observation is substantiated by the testimony of Dr. Julius Fogel, a seventy-five-year-old psychiatrist and obstetrician who has been a long-time advocate of abortion. Dr. Fogel estimates he has personally performed about 20,000 abortions. Although he clearly approaches abortion from a "pro-choice" perspective, Dr. Fogel is deeply concerned about the "psychological effects of abortion on the mother's mind." According to Dr. Fogel:

> Abortion is an impassioned subject. . . . Every woman—whatever her age, background or sexuality—has a trauma at destroying a pregnancy. A level of humanness is touched. This is a part of her own life. She destroys a pregnancy, she is destroying herself. There is no way it can be innocuous. One is dealing with the life force. It is totally beside the point whether or not you think a life is there. You cannot deny that something is being created and that this creation is physically happening. . . . Often the trauma may sink into the unconscious and never surface in the woman's lifetime. But it is not as harmless and casual an event as many in the pro-abortion crowd insist. A psychological price is paid. It may be alienation; it may be a pushing away from human warmth, perhaps a hardening of the maternal instinct. Something happens on the deeper levels of a woman's consciousness when she destroys a pregnancy. I know that as a psychiatrist.[85]

Occasionally stories of grief over a past abortion turn up in the most unexpected places and at the most unexpected times. For example, during an interview on the "Donahue" show actress Shelly Winters was discussing the love affairs in her life when suddenly she blurted out: "You know, I find myself agreeing with the Catholic Church on some issues. You all will probably not like me for this . . ." and she proceeded to tell the audience that despite her reliance on contraceptives she had had two abortions in her life. "I am a very lonely woman," she confessed. "I would give up everything—my money, my academy awards, my career—if only I could have those children now." With that, she broke into uncontrollable sobs. As the audience roared with sympathetic applause, Donahue switched to a commercial.[86]

Another great star who lived in the shadow of an abortion was Gloria Swanson, America's sweetheart in the 1920s and 1930s. Remorse over her abortion experience was so central to her life that her autobiography, *Swanson on Swanson*, begins and ends with lamentations over her aborted child. After having aborted to preserve her reputation and career, Swanson writes: "I could never view my life or my career in the same way again." Even fifty-four years later, she was still crying "fresh tears out of guilt." Near the end of her life, at eighty-four years of age, she writes that "the greatest regret of my life has always been that I didn't have my baby, Henri's child, in 1925. Nothing in the whole world is worth a baby, I realized as soon as it was too late, and I never stopped blaming myself."[87]

The trend is clear to anyone who looks. The negative WEBA-like abortion experience is the rule rather than the exception. Many aborted women will deny it by hiding their emotions and tell little or nothing of their experience. Others may hide it behind the anger and bitterness they feel toward others who were involved, especially against the male. But most will admit they are troubled; they simply don't know what else to do other than to try to forget it and move on.

Most of all, the stories of aborting women are stories of isolation and despair. What they are saying is that they did not really need a "solution" to *avoid* their problems, but instead, wanted love and support to *face* their problems.[88] As one WEBA woman has said: "The responsibility of carrying a child for nine months—and even of raising that child, if one chooses, for twenty years—is far less than the responsibility of having taken another's life."

The Granberg Study   The purpose of this chapter has been to illustrate that the negative reaction of WEBA women is typical of nearly every aborted woman's experience. Even the evidence gathered by pro-choice authors confirms this view. The titles alone, *In Necessity and Sorrow* and *The Ambivalence of Abortion*, are evidence that the consensus of women who have been aborted is indeed very negative.

But if this case against abortion is still in doubt, we offer one last bit of evidence supporting our contention that the vast majority of aborted women regret their decisions. Ironically, this evidence is again supplied by a pro-choice source.

In 1981, Planned Parenthood's *Family Planning Perspectives* published an article by Donald Granberg entitled "The Abortion Activists." In this article, Granberg unearthed figures which, if properly interpreted, indicated that the "outbreak" of WEBA women banning together to denounce abortion was not unpredictable. What these figures really reveal, though carefully disguised behind a pro-choice bias, is that aborted women are much more likely to become anti-abortion activists than pro-choice activists.

In this study, sociologist Donald Granberg compared the membership characteristics of the nation's two largest organizations supporting and opposing abortion—the National Abortion Rights Action League (NARAL) and the National Right to Life Committee (NRLC). Surveying approximately 450 members of each group on a broad number of questions, Granberg was able to contrast many of the broad opinions and characteristics of each group.

Most of Granberg's results were unsurprising. He found, for

example, that NRLC members were more likely to have larger family sizes, were much more likely to think religion was important in their lives, and were much more likely to reject sexual activity outside of marriage. NARAL members, by contrast, preferred smaller family sizes, held religion to be moderately or minimally important, if at all (40 percent listed themselves as being atheist or agnostic), were much more permissive about all forms of sexual activity, and were more likely to belong to higher social and economic classes.[89]

In terms of favoring abortion for any given circumstances, of course, the two groups held diametrically opposing positions. Notably, however, 73 percent of anti-abortionists approved abortion when necessary to save a woman's life. Pro-choice advocates, on the other hand, showed less than absolute support for freedom of choice than their rhetoric would suggest, with only 58 percent approving of abortion as a means of sex selection, though 85 percent also claimed a woman should be able to obtain an abortion "for whatever reason." This hostility towards the use of abortion for sex selection suggests that many NARAL members place at least a minimal value on the unborn life when compared to "trivial" reasons for abortion.[90]

But the most unexpected, and least analyzed, result of the Granberg survey was the response of women members from each group to the question of whether or not she had ever had an abortion. In response, 32 percent of NARAL's female members reported having had an abortion compared to 3 percent of NRLC's female members. Granberg carefully twists these figures to reach the pro-abortion conclusion that "women who have abortions tend to strongly support the availability of legal abortion for others." He admits, however, that "it is recognized that the bulk of women who have had abortions do not join any organization on either side of the abortion controversy. Many of these women, no doubt, feel a real and sometimes abiding ambivalence about the abortion."[91]

Granberg's focusing upon the *percentage* of aborters in each group is, in fact, a ploy for hiding an uncomfortable truth which his statistics would otherwise expose. Percentages are useful only in relationship to a whole, and when the percentage of aborters Granberg discovers in each group are applied to the whole groups from which they were drawn, an entirely different picture emerges.

According to the *Encyclopedia of Associations*, at the time of the study NARAL had a total membership of 156,000, whereas NRLC has a total of twelve million members.[92] It is in this fundamental difference in the size of the organizations from which he draws his survey sample that his deception is revealed.

Granberg himself finds that 78 percent of NARAL's members are female, compared to a 63 percent female membership in NRLC. Therefore, based on Granberg's own figures, 32 percent of NARAL's female members have had abortions, yielding a total of 39,000 aborters. On the other hand, 3 percent of NRLC's female members yields approximately 245,000 aborters.[93]

In other words, women who have had abortions are six times more likely to work *against* abortion than for it.

A few more points should be made about this comparison of the number of aborters working for and against abortion. Those who have joined NRLC were probably motivated by remorse and guilt over a previous abortion. It can be assumed that few, if any, had their abortions after joining the pro-life group. The NARAL women, on the other hand, were not asked whether they had joined the pro-choice group before or after their abortion, a missing factor which would be important to understanding the motivation behind their pro-choice activism. It is possible that many of these women had their abortions *after* becoming involved with NARAL. In these cases, the abortion decision reflected on prior political feelings, and perhaps the abortion was even seen as a "badge of honor" reflecting one's commitment to the cause, proof of one's liberation and freedom. For others who aborted *prior* to joining NARAL, it is possible that for some the vocal defense of abortion was a way of denying underlying feelings of guilt and psychological distress. By joining an organization which loudly proclaims that abortion is moral and good, they surround themselves with the comforting presence of people who will confirm their choice and reassure them of their integrity.[94]

SUMMARY

Even studies done by pro-choice researchers show that the abortion experience is almost always negative and is often harshly disruptive of one's life. It is never a trivial act; it will always continue to be a major part of a woman's life.

The WEBA-like experience recorded in this author's survey and in the chapters included in this book is a close match to the "typical" abortion experience. The only "atypical" aspect of this sample of aborting women is that the vast majority of this group has come, or is coming, to terms with their abortion experience through a radical renunciation of abortion. They are freeing themselves from ambivalence and guilt by openly admitting their ambivalence and guilt. In a society which urges women to hide and suppress their post-abortion feelings, this is a radical approach.

FOUR

Feminists Who Abort

As seen in the previous chapter, abortion is almost always an unsettling experience, even for the staunchest of feminists. As Linda Bird Francke writes: "Though I would march myself into blisters for a woman's right to exercise the option of motherhood, I discovered there in the waiting room that I was not the modern woman I thought I was."[1]

Despite the claims of some abortion clinics, abortion is *never* "as simple as having a tooth pulled." No matter how much a woman believes in women's rights, or the rhetoric that her unborn human fetus is only a "potential life," she cannot deny or ignore the fact that during an abortion her body becomes a battleground where a life force within her is destroyed. Furthermore, this destruction is an irreversible event which alters the future of her life forever.

For some feminists, a negative abortion experience will draw them deeper into the feminism where they hope to find answers to the uneasiness they feel. They may even hope to become abortion reformers by drawing on their abortion experience to bring more compassion and caring to family planning and abortion clinics. Some may find this satisfying, at least for a time, but many others eventually become disillusioned with the pro-choice rhetoric and seek peace through renunciation of their abortions and even turn to pro-life activism.

Approximately 30 percent of the WEBA members surveyed were pro-choice advocates prior to their own abortions. Many were active feminists, and many are still pro-life feminists. Their changes of view are a result of their abortion experiences.

KAREN SULLIVAN

Karen became pregnant when she was twenty-two. Unmarried, career-oriented, and a proponent of "free choice," she chose abortion as the

best way to preserve her lifestyle. Afterwards she worked as a coun-
selor for a feminist health collective in California until she became
pregnant a second time. The birth of her son compelled Karen to
reevaluate her abortion experience and eventually led her to become
a pro-life activist.

At the time of my abortion, I was living in California. I had recently
moved there to be near my boyfriend, who was attending the
University of California at Berkeley. I didn't know anyone there, so
when I found out I was pregnant, I went straight to Planned
Parenthood. It was from that organization that I had received my contraceptives a year earlier.

The counselor, a man, painted a bleak picture of parenting alone,
and never told me that I would be eligible for WIC, food stamps, welfare, and medical aid should I carry my baby to term. Instead, the counselor told me that I had to explore my career goals before having a child.

I gave my decision much thought; in fact, I was obsessed with it.
I was very pro-choice in my philosophy. Although I wasn't active in
any feminist organizations, I felt the feminists had it all together, and
I was very sympathetic to their pro-choice reasoning. Within one
week, I decided to go ahead and have the abortion.

On the day of the abortion, my boyfriend took me to the Choice
Clinic in Los Gatos, California. At the time, our relationship was very
shaky and tense. While we were there, we were situated with four
other women, and were "counseled." Actually, we all just sat there,
nervous and tense, looking at each other, and trying to convince ourselves that we did really want to have an abortion. A few minutes
before we were to be ushered in to have the abortion, we were offered
five or ten milligrams of Valium. I didn't take any, because I wanted
to be wide awake and conscious of what was happening to me.

I was twelve weeks pregnant, so they performed a suction abortion.
They inserted dilators into my cervix, one after the other, until the largest
one was as big around as my little finger. It was really, really painful. I
wasn't told that it would hurt that bad. They turned on the suction
machine. I could feel the baby being torn from my insides. It was really
painful. Not having had any pain killers, I felt all of it, completely and
totally. Three-quarters of the way through the operation, I sat up. To my
right, and down, I saw the tube that led out of me, from the vacuum
aspirator, and it led into a glass cylinder. In the cylinder I saw the bits
and pieces of my little child floating in a pool of blood. I screamed and
jumped up off the table. They took me into another room and I started
vomiting. They responded by offering me Seven-Up and cookies. It all
was just repulsive to me, and I just couldn't stop throwing up.

I stayed there for a couple of hours, and then Mark, my boyfriend, took me home. While we were saying our feelings about all this to each other, I begged him to stay with me: "Please don't leave me, I don't want to be alone tonight." He said he had homework and that he had to leave, but that he would check back with me the next day or the next week, but sometime soon. I haven't seen him since. It's been four years, and there's been no word or sight of him since.

A few days afterwards, I began to feel relief. There was no tummy, no shame, and I wasn't pregnant anymore. I felt pretty good. But I did not escape the aftermath of abortion. I had nightmares and reoccurring dreams about my baby. I couldn't work my job. I just laid in my bed and cried. Once I wept so hard I sprained my ribs. Another time while crying, I was unable to breathe and I passed out. I was unable to walk on the beach because the playing children would make me cry. Even Pampers commercials would set me into fits of uncontrollable crying.

I tried to establish a post-abortion counseling group for women, and hung a notice of a meeting on a bulletin board at a women's health collective. But nobody showed up at the meeting, so I just dropped it.

After that, I joined the women's health collective and began working as a women's health counselor. It was a feminist clinic, and they were really anti-men. There were a lot of lesbians working there. And because of my grief, I submitted myself to counseling with a therapist who was homosexual and living with another woman. And I couldn't figure out why her counseling didn't help me—now I know, but at that time I didn't.

Her counseling tried to get me to the point where I could deny my grief, where I would be "healthy" enough to not ever admit that abortion was wrong, but to say, "Hey, I had an abortion. No big deal." To get to the point where I could counsel other women to have abortions would be to have "arrived," that I could cope. But I never got there. By her standards, I guess, I was a total failure. She never ever dealt with my guilt. I was a walking talking pile of guilt, but she never ever dealt with that. Her response was like, "Guilt is just something imposed on us by our religious, male-dominated society, and we women have to fight against it." I was just supposed to "take control of my life" and deny my guilt. I was in counseling with her for about six or seven months.

But counseling which tells you to have the abortion and then forget about it just doesn't work. Even at an early stage of pregnancy a bond is formed between the mother and the child, a physical bond, of course, and a psychological bond. It is natural for mothers to bond with their children. Abortion puts an unnatural halt to the natural bonding. Eventually, nature will strike back.

All this time, I continued to work at this pro-abortion facility dedicated to presenting an alternative to regular health care. There's safety in numbers. I didn't feel really awful about my abortion as long as everyone where I worked was patting me on the back. But I never really came to believe in their philosophy; I never really "arrived." I just never could bring myself to talk anyone into an abortion.

I got pregnant again while I was working there. I conceived my son the very week that my aborted baby should have been born. It was no accident; I set out to get pregnant. My son is an "atonement baby" for the child I lost. I had felt that by my abortion I had taken something precious out of the world and so I wanted to put something back into it. At first, though, I had a strong impulse to terminate this second pregnancy. But luckily, a friend made me aware of what I was doing: "You're going to have abortion after abortion. Your life will be hell." My friend convinced me that I was running scared, and that I didn't hate my baby. Now I love my son for who he is, though he was definitely conceived out of my grief for my first baby.

At the counseling center, though, my becoming pregnant by a man was like a "sin" to them. You see, they were very hostile towards men, very anti-male. So for anyone who was working there to become pregnant was like a betrayal since it was proof that you had "known" a man. Abortion, to them, was the way you killed the "thing" the man had made in you; it was a reaction against men. For this reason, when counseling women they definitely pressed for abortion as the "best solution." (My lesbian therapist had had a child by artificial insemination, but that was OK with them.)

I was already on the outs with them then, just by being pregnant, but halfway during my second pregnancy when I felt the baby move inside me, I really began to feel funny about all this abortion advocacy. I certainly wasn't what you'd call a pro-life person, but when I got "caught" praising a woman for choosing not to abort, that was the last straw. I was fired.

I had my baby and moved to Arizona. By this time the full impact of what I had done hit me. I felt like a criminal, like I was the worst person on this entire earth. But I still wasn't pro-life or anything. Then one Sunday, about a year ago, I had the impulse to go to the Grace Lutheran Church, though I had never been there before. But I went, and there I heard a woman speaking about abortion and pro-life, etc., and something just clicked in my mind: "Yes." At this time I was still really struggling with my own abortion, but with all the love and support of the pro-life people, I began to get over it. Then I heard about WEBA and decided, "I want to get involved with that." And ever since I became involved with the right to life movement, my whole life has changed. Now I'm able to use my own experience to help other women avoid abortion. There's a lot of hope in that.

CAROL ST. AMOUR

Carol has had two abortions. She has little or no memory of her first, but her second abortion experience eventually drove her to severe depression, alcoholism, heroin, and violence against her husband.

My story begins almost a year before the abortion, because of the circumstances and people who touched my life and led to the decision. I was divorced and struggling to raise two children—my daughter born out of wedlock when I was eighteen, and a son from my first marriage.

I was working as a bartender at a local pub when I met Jim. He managed a local band and was a very handsome, intelligent and determined man. He showed up at my apartment one night, claiming that he and his wife were through. Our love affair began.

As the months passed, it turned into a family-type relationship. He was helping to raise my children, and loved them the best he knew how. We talked of marriage but made no definite plans. I felt insecure, because his ex-wife kept interrupting our happy home. I felt bitterness toward his former family, but I tried to remain supportive.

Several months after this, I started having difficulty with birth control. I had an IUD, but had trouble with it, and had to have it removed. I tried the Pill, but after one week my breasts swelled and had lumps everywhere. So I discontinued use, and became pregnant. I was very satisfied, nearly ecstatic about our baby. I saw it as a bond between our children, and it gave me a sense of belonging and purpose in our relationship besides being the sympathetic ear to Jim's previous marital problems.

After I left my doctor's office, when I found out I was pregnant, I stopped and talked to the wife of one of the members of the band that Jim managed. News spread quickly, and the band members were all very excited for us.

Jim, however, didn't feel that way. At first he was very quiet about it, and didn't speak to me for over a week. When I pressed him about it, he stated he did not want me to have the baby, and that if I did, he'd leave me. I was crushed. I was a very open-minded, pro-choice feminist . . . but this was HIS child, too. So I talked to a friend about abortion alternatives, and she said, "Well, you can always have more children, but there's only one Jim. So if you love him . . ."

So I weighed the costs, and wanting very much to please him, plus being fearful of his leaving me, I made an appointment to "discuss" this with my doctor. Upon my arrival at the doctor's office, and sharing Jim's reaction with him, the doctor made arrangements to have the pregnancy terminated the following week. The place was "Women's Medical Services"; I found out later that the doctor operated this place outside his ob/gyn practice.

This was to be my second abortion. The first time had been a D&C in 1975. I was asleep during it. I guess that's what kept me a pro-choice person after my first abortion: I didn't really know what an abortion was until I experienced the horrors of it while wide awake.

Now it was 1979. I went in on a Thursday for the insertion of a laminaria, and returned the next day for the "procedure". Jim took the day off work (big of him, huh?) to go with me. He was the only guy in the lobby of about fifteen girls. There was a HEAVY silence there. I had an inward battle going on inside me that only God and perhaps other women who have had abortions could possibly understand. It was like the cartoon of the person who has the devil on one shoulder and the angel on the other: one is whispering, "You're doing the right thing, life will be better, he'll love you more for it," while the angel is saying, "Leave this place, you'll be OK, he's not worth it, it's your baby, a part of the man you say you love."

Finally I was ushered into a room, given a gown to put on, and given 5 milligrams of Valium—big deal. I remember the assistant's very cold, businesslike manner, not too talkative. I wasn't impressed by any of the people working there—there was no compassion or counseling, just an attitude of "let's get it over with, there are many patients to deal with." I was instructed to get up on a table, put my legs in the stirrups, and relax (easy for them to say).

My "doctor" came in, dressed in a surgical gown. The doctor began inserting this and that, and then the machine started. The noise was unforgettable—I can still hear it, even now. I grabbed at my chest and closed my eyes and started praying. Then I felt this gripping pain—it hurt so bad that I cried out. The doctor told me to "shut up" because there were "other girls" and the "walls were thin."

The ride home was short. Jim asked if I was alright, and I lied and said I was. We got home at 1:00 P.M., and I went right to bed and cried all day and night. This depression worsened as several weeks went by. Jim's compassion and concern began turning into anger, as I started lashing out at him—"I want my baby back!"

One night Jim's band was playing at a local club and he insisted that I go with him. Up until that point I hadn't left the house. I reluctantly went. I was beginning to enjoy myself as we slow-danced, and I laughed for what seemed the first time in months.

Then something happened that I should have expected, but had forgotten about: these people still thought I was pregnant. One of the wives came up and said, "You must be thrilled! When's the due date?" I about died, and had to think fast. My emotions about it all were rushing again, and as I looked at Jim, I could honestly say that I hated him. First the abortion and now this! I knew I'd have to lie to protect his rapport with our peers. I sadly told her that I had miscarried. We left shortly thereafter because I couldn't handle the sympathy these people were giving me—ME, a murderer!

Our relationship was like a roller coaster ride, but we were married in December, eight months after the abortion. Now I believe that on his part, he married me out of pity and guilt. The eight months leading up to our marriage were filled with knockdown, drag-out fights. During this time I began drinking heavily and doing drugs, mostly amphetamines.

I hated myself and Jim so much that I could no longer keep it inside. I was very pathetic, instigating fights between us, saying things like he loved his ex-wife and children more than me and our dead baby. We went for secular counseling during this time. Our therapist said that I was experiencing a mourning period and overwhelming grief. To me it was a baby, my baby. To Jim it was a product-of-conception blob, a problem. He understood my feelings, but he couldn't handle it.

In November, during a bitter fight, I grabbed a twelve-inch butcher knife and cut up his good brown suit, stabbing at it and crying. He began hauling things out of the house, leaving and taking his possessions with him. I was furious. We began throwing things at each other, spitting, name-calling. As I watched him load OUR car with his things, something clicked in me that I wanted to kill him. I lunged at him with the butcher knife, and he hit me as a full-grown man would hit when fighting with another man. He picked up an oxen yoke from the porch (I collected antiques) and used it as a baseball bat on me. It knocked me off my feet and drove me six feet into the house. There I lay, I couldn't move. My kids were running around screaming, crying, and attacking him, hitting him for hurting me.

That was the end of our marriage—I went downhill from there. I neglected my children because I was too busy at bars with other men, looking for love or free drugs. I finally began using the destructive drug heroin. I enjoyed the drug, and that scared me enough to stop. I closed down the day-care center I operated in my home because I couldn't cope with looking at babies anymore. I packed up my kids and moved to Virginia Beach where my dad lived.

There I read my daughter's Bible and asked God to save me and help me. After three months in Virginia and reading the Word of God, it was impressed on me to go back to Michigan and make amends. I asked Jim to forgive me, which he did. But he was happy now and wanted nothing to do with me.

I became involved in a pro-life, Christian fellowship and formed a chapter of WEBA in December of 1983.

Soon after, in March of 1984, following months of symptoms of physical illness, a friend forced me to see a doctor. After the abortion I had vowed never to see a doctor again. My friend sought out a pro-life doctor, put me in a car, and drove me to my appointment. I was informed that I had cervical cancer. It was a new mountain to conquer, as it was a severe case of invasive cancer that was inoperable. I underwent a series of radiation treatments and radium implants.

It was a traumatic experience, but I survived it. There is now a study being done by a medical/psychological team at an Ohio medical school to investigate the increase of cervical/uterine cancer in aborted women. Their suspicions are that the psychological aftereffects such as I have suffered from abortion have triggered this cancer growth. Only time and research will tell, but I believe in my heart that the two are definitely related.

Anyway, the radiation treatments left me hopelessly sterile for life. Not only that, but I must take progesterone ten days each month and estrogen daily. I am thirty-one years old and experiencing mid-life crisis. My strong desire to have another baby is heartbreaking, but I'm learning to cope and compensate by saving others.

As a feminist—and former "pro-choicer"—I believe that the feminists have gone too far in supporting legal abortion. I know that my body is not my own when I am pregnant. That baby is its own person.

Where was the feminists' protection of my rights at the doctor's office and the abortion clinic? No feminist was encouraging my male chauvinist pig boyfriend to take a walk. None of my feminist friends offered to *really* help me. No, they rallied to *his* side. Nobody was there for me but the Lifegiver, and for that I am thankful.

P.S. July 23, 1984: Today I had to go see my oncologist (cancer specialist) because the radiologist found another "spot" on my cervix. I was led into an examination room and told to undress from the waist down. After the nurse left the room I started looking around, checking things out. To my shock and complete loss of control I saw, two feet from my left foot, a suction aspirator machine! I freaked out. I had a total flashback of the abortion experience. I began crying uncontrollably, got up, dressed, and ran out into the hall, hyperventilating. I found the nurse, and was near hysteria as I explained why I couldn't go back in there. She understood, and tried comforting me, reassuring me their office did not do abortions but that the machine was used for other purposes. She took the machine out of the room. I returned shaken and surprised at my lack of self-control. I wonder . . . will it ever end?

(*Author's note: Carol did die of cervical cancer. She was only a little over thirty years of age. Recent medical research is corroborating a statistical link between abortion and cervical cancer, as well as breast cancer.*[2])

DEBORAH HULEBAK

Deborah underwent four abortions. With each abortion she became more hardened and more angrily pro-choice. Of the four, only the decision to have her first abortion was very difficult. In that case she wanted to keep the baby but was pressured by her doctor into accepting an abortion for eugenic reasons.

My story begins in January of 1972. I was eighteen years old. I had been married for only a few months when I found that I was pregnant; it was my first pregnancy. My husband was in the military, so I was receiving medical care from the military doctors in Palo Alto, California.

When I found out I was pregnant, I was really excited. The thought of being pregnant had always appealed to me, and I was really anxious to start a family. I'd always just loved children, so my initial feeling was overwhelming joy. But when the doctor told me I was pregnant, he immediately asked me, "What are you planning on doing?" I guess I misunderstood the question, because my initial reaction was, "Well, I was going to go home and call my husband and tell him."

But then it occurred to me that the doctor was not thinking in those terms. The look on his face was very sober, and he said, "Had you considered abortion?" And my heart fell to the floor. It was as if he had come into my hospital room after I had delivered the baby and said, "Your baby is dead." I felt as if he had just signed my baby's death certificate. I told him, "No, I'd never thought about it."

The look on my face prompted the doctor to explain about the medication I'd been taking for thrombophlebitis (blood clots in my legs), coumadin, an anti-coagulant. He said in a very matter of fact way, "This drug causes birth defects." In this whole conversation, I don't remember saying anything. I had so many thoughts; it seemed like he did all the talking. But I remember very clearly what he said: "I would be running a risk if I even gave you a fifty-fifty chance of having a normal child."

My immediate answer was "NO. I will not even consider an abortion." He wanted to know why not, and I'm sure I said something like, "I just don't want to do that. This just can't be the only answer—there has to be another answer."

He said, "Why don't you go home and think about it, and let me know what you decide in a few days." I remember feeling greatly eased by that, and I went home.

I don't remember a lot of emotions; you know, I find that I seem to have blocked a lot of this out. I do recall calling the doctor and telling him that my husband had just received notice that he was to be stationed in Vietnam and at that point I would not consider an abortion. My reason to the doctor was that I did not expect my husband to return from Vietnam alive, and I wanted to have this baby, regardless of how it would turn out. I felt very confident in my decision that I did not want that abortion.

The doctor was very concerned about my decision not to have an abortion and literally pleaded with me not to go ahead and have it. He begged, "Please reconsider this. I don't know why you would want to do this to yourself and your husband. The baby would be a burden to you." He had no respect for my decision, and kept saying things like, "You have GOT to be kidding. There is NO WAY you can carry this baby to term. There are so many dangers involved. You're a fool to think of not aborting." Before I hung up, he said, "I want you to consider it again carefully, and call me if you change your mind." In the years since, I've suspected that the doctor was so adamant with me about the abortion because he was afraid that if the baby did have birth defects, I'd hit him with a malpractice suit.

I did change my mind, and made the decision to go ahead with the abortion. I'm not sure what prompted it, other than that my husband called me a couple of weeks later and informed me that he would not be going to Vietnam. Instead, we were going to be stationed in Germany. I also gave some thought to the fact that though my husband wanted children he didn't want them right away. This compounded my fear. I remember thinking, "If I have a deformed child, he's going to blame me. He's going to say that it was my fault, because I could've gotten rid of the kid but didn't."

Looking back now as a thirty-one-year-old adult and mother of three children, assuming these things made me more mature, I would say that the primary reason for my decision came from a seed that the doctor had planted in me. It was his mannerism, his firm belief that I should have that abortion. He was so serious that it frightened me: I felt fear at NOT having the abortion. I felt justified because the doctor was so determined for me to have the abortion. That really played the biggest part in my decision.

After informing the doctor of my decision, the first thing they did was another examination, to verify that I was pregnant. Then I had to receive some "supposed" counseling from two psychiatrists. (This was 1972, and abortion on demand was not yet legal.) I remember that the psychiatrist asked me why I was having the abortion, and I told him it was because my baby would be deformed. That was about it. He never dealt with my thinking or my emotions. For example, he never asked, "Do you think you're going to be really upset when you find out that your baby is dead?" or "Do you realize that you're killing a child? How do you feel about killing this child?" They never referred to this baby as a baby, they never referred to my maternal instincts, to missing my child . . .

They did ask me how my husband felt about this, and I said I didn't know, that I didn't think he cared. And the truth of the matter was that he didn't care. He and I never really discussed the abortion that much, except when we were in Germany together six months later. A couple of nights I would wake up with nightmares about the abortion, and he would comfort me. Other than that, we never really talked about it.

Anyway, they put me in the hospital, and I had to be on anti-coagulants because of my blood clots, and I had to stay three days. After the abortion, I remember waking up as I was being wheeled to my room. I heard my mother's voice saying, "That's my baby." And I could hear crying in her voice. I looked up and saw my mother and her best friend standing over me. I felt something soft next to my cheek, and looked over and saw that they had brought me a stuffed animal. Bless her heart, I'm sure she was thinking that I would need something to replace that baby. But you know, I never thought of that. At that point, there was no baby, there had never been a baby; it was never referred to as a baby to me. But I remember the pain in my mother's voice and the tears in both women's eyes as they stood over me.

And then it occurred to me, for a split moment; I felt cheated, deprived, angry, hurt, and alone. At that moment, no one could comfort me. I didn't cry then, but I did later. I'm not sure if they were tears for me or for the baby, but I think they were for me, because I felt like such a rotten person.

When I left that hospital, I put up a wall within myself, with a big sign on it that said, "Don't ever think about this experience again. What you did was the right thing to do. Don't ever think about it again." I used to think that wall was put there by God to protect me, it was Him comforting me saying, "It's OK." But now I know that that wall was put there not only by the Enemy, but also by those doctors and nurses, the medical staff. They put it there to protect themselves, they instill those thoughts in you: "Don't think about it, don't dwell on it."

After that, I joined my husband in Germany. My life went to alcohol and hard drugs all the time. I was so distraught and terribly depressed, and I had to be hospitalized for depression. When he was scheduled to return to the U.S., I came back ahead of him. I was so unhappy. He was abusing me quite severely, and I wanted to get away for a while, to try to start a singing career.

Looking for love, I had an affair with a married man. His wife and I got pregnant at the same time. SHE got her baby; he gave ME $300 for an abortion. This abortion triggered me into coldness about abortion, for it was done in anger. At the time, the first one was justified because of the possible birth defects. But this one was a lot easier—I was saying to myself, "You're real tough. You can do this and it won't hurt a bit."

After this second abortion, I developed an extremely serious uterine infection and had to be hospitalized. The doctor couldn't even examine me the first day. He said, "There is so much blood and pus in there that I can't even get in." I was on antibiotics for a week.

In addition to drugs and alcohol, I now found myself being very promiscuous. I had always been insecure and needed a lot of attention. I needed to be popular and needed to be accepted. I hated school, so the only way, in my mind to get attention was through sex and drugs and partying. I had never had a "solid" father in my life. I realized that by sleeping around, I got attention and affection. I soon found myself in need of a third abortion. By now, though, I was "tough" enough that I could laugh about having it.

I talked real openly about abortion. I was pro-choice, and I talked to other women about the value of having an abortion. During my first abortion, I would have said, "No, I don't think abortion is right. But in my case, since this baby might be deformed, it's OK." But with each successive abortion, my attitude got worse and worse. I became increasingly pro-choice, to the point where I would say to other girls, "Big deal if you get pregnant—you can have an abortion. I've had three and it hasn't hurt me a bit!"

I found that in talking to other women about abortion, their decisions to abort satisfied something in me. It made me feel better about what I had done. It was almost like I was gloating in their misery. If I'd had an opportunity to work at a counseling center to counsel women before their abortions, I would have done it. It would have strengthened my own decisions to abort.

I did have an opportunity to get close to this situation. In between my second and third abortions, I worked in a hospital lab, doing blood work. You knew when these patients were having abortions, because it would say right on the labels "AB," which stood for "abortion."

Sometimes I'd be tempted to ask them why they were having their abortions. I remember thinking that if I asked them, part of my heart would be saying, "Wait! Think about it!" But then another part of me would be thinking, "Yes, that's the best thing."

Working there also gave me the chance to see the effects of an abortion. I walked into the lab one day and saw these big plastic bowls with lids on a table. As I walked toward them, the lab technician said, "I don't think you want to look in there." So I picked it up and looked in underneath, and I saw a baby floating in there. It had little legs, fingers, toes, eyes. It shocked me, but I set it back down. I was so hardened at that point that I just didn't let it get to me. But I know it did something to me; I've never been able to get that picture out of my mind.

There was one girl who came in for abortion blood work, and just started crying. I asked her what was wrong, and then asked, "Are you pregnant?" She just started crying harder and said, "I don't know what to do." I don't remember counseling her one way or the other, but I do remember saying, "Maybe you better think about this some more." She left, then came back a couple weeks later. She said, "I decided to keep the baby, and my boyfriend and I are getting married." I remember feeling happy for her, but there was something in me that felt a little defeated, too. It was like, "SHE got to do it, but I didn't." I was envious, because she'd been braver than me.

I think I acted that way out of bitterness. I was trying to cover up my true feelings. When I think back now, in between abortions, I can recall actually talking to my aborted babies. I'd comfort them and tell them that I loved them. I'd tell them that it just wasn't the right time in my life to have them. I cried sometimes, thinking about it. But you know, until I received my healing and was forced to bring all this sadness back to the surface, I never remembered these sad times. I only remembered making myself think, "It's easy to have an abortion. I'm tough enough to do it."

Anyway, my lifestyle didn't change. In between my abortions, I did give birth to one child, a daughter. But when I became pregnant a fifth time, I went ahead and had my fourth and last abortion.

I've thought about why I kept doing that to myself, getting pregnant and having abortions in an endless cycle. I feel like I did it because I had to prove to myself that I was right. I had to prove to myself that it didn't hurt, that I could go through it over and over again and it wouldn't hurt. The more I did it, the less it hurt, physically and emotionally. I deadened myself to pain—and to right and wrong. Until finally, with the last one, it didn't hurt at all. It was one of the "quickies" at the clinic. You go in, pop a Valium, take a shower, hop up on the table, they suck it out, and it's "*adios*, hope we never see you again." On the way out the door, they hand you a brown paper sack full of birth control: foam and prophy-lactics and things. The father of that baby, I even swindled out of him an extra three hundred dollars to keep my mouth shut. I went out and bought myself some new clothes after the abortion, that same afternoon. And then I got drunk that night.

I started to think about my life then—and something clicked in me. I began to realize that everything I had done—the abortions, drugs, affairs, depressions—had all been a result of the circumstances of my first abortion. After that, I couldn't make any decisions at all. I knew that all the sex and drugs were wrong, but my mind was so clouded with negatives that I wasn't in any position to get my life straightened out. I just went with the flow of everything around me. I don't want to totally blame the doctor and other people involved with my first abortion, because I know that in the end I made that decision. But my decision to abort distorted my ability to make other decisions.

It's amazing how you can think that you know all the answers and that what you're doing is right and good. And then ten years down the road, you look back at your actions, and you realize that you were just living a bunch of lies, and that each lie just seems to compound the other ones and force them deeper and deeper into your subconscious. It has taken me so long to admit and discuss this. God has healed me, and God is using my stories to heal others, and maybe, prayerfully so, He's using my stories to prevent others from doing what I did.

Thinking along those lines, I started to recover. I married my high school sweetheart, the only man I ever really loved, and the man I knew the Lord wanted me to marry. We tried to conceive a child. I had a miscarriage, then I had an ectopic pregnancy, which resulted in the loss of twins. At that time, I asked my doctor if this was all related to my abortions, and he very hesitantly suggested that it was. But he was reluctant to talk about it. What he did tell me was, "Your right fal-lopian tube is nearly destroyed. I can't tell what the left one looks like, but I can tell you that there is no guarantee that you'll ever success-fully conceive a child." They then had to remove the right tube, and didn't leave me much hope about the left one.

Fortunately for me, I had just received the Lord. Jesus made it pos-sible for me to conceive my second and third children. But before I conceived the second child, I had yet another miscarriage. Then again before my third child, I miscarried.

Please go public with my story. I have nothing to hide. In fact, I have everything to share. If my stories, no matter how badly they hurt or embarrass me, will prevent one baby from being destroyed, it's worth that to me; it's worth a lot.

FIVE

The Physical Risks of Abortion

A bortion is a surgical procedure in which a woman's body is forcibly entered, and her pregnancy is forcibly "terminated." Because it is intrusive and because it disrupts a natural process (pregnancy), abortion poses both short-term and long-term risks to the health and well-being of the aborted woman. Abortion is never without risks.

A few abortion advocates continue to insist that abortion is so safe as to be virtually "risk free," but such claims are exaggerations resulting from some blind belief in the slogans and clichés fostered by the early abortion reformers.[1] In contrast to these few abortion zealots, most defenders of abortion, particularly those in the health fields, admit that there are inherent risks to abortion. Within the medical profession the intense debate is not over whether there are risks or not, but over how often complications will occur. Some claim the risks are "acceptable," while others insist they are not.

Answering the question "How safe is abortion?" is crucial to any public policy on abortion, but it is even more crucial to the women facing the abortion decision. Unfortunately for hundreds of thousands of women, their "safe and easy" abortions proved to be neither safe nor easy. Even more outrageous is the fact that almost none of these women were given a realistic assessment of the risks of abortion.

A SYSTEMATIC COVER-UP

Maintaining abortion's image of "safety" is important to groups supporting abortion for a variety of reasons. Obviously, for abortion referral agencies, abortion counselors, and the abortionists themselves, financial success depends upon their ability to assure clients that abortion is "safe." For population control groups that encourage abortion, achieving their long-range goals for population control depends on their ability to promote abortion as a "safe" and even "preferable" alternative to childbirth. And finally, the ideological success of the pro-choice philosophy in feminism depends on the "desirability" of abortion. After all, if abortion is found to be dangerous to women, its legalization can hardly be claimed as a triumph for "women's rights." For these reasons and others, abortion providers, population controllers, and pro-choice feminists are all anxious to believe that abortion is safe, and they are even more anxious to spread this belief to the general public. They support the contention that abortion is "relatively" safe by citing national statistics which report a "low" incidence of abortion-related deaths. But are these statistics accurate? Probably not.

In the first place, accurate statistics are scarce because the reporting of complications is almost entirely at the option of abortion providers. In other words, abortionists are in the privileged position of being able to hide any information that might damage their reputations or trade.

How can this be so?

Federal court rulings have sheltered the practice of abortion in a "zone of privacy." This prohibits any meaningful form of state or federal regulation other than broad "general requirements as to the maintaining of sanitary facilities and . . . minimal building code standards. . . . "[2] As a result, any laws which require that deaths and complications resulting from abortion be recorded, much less reported, are unconstitutional.[3] Thus the only information available on abortion complications is the result of data voluntarily reported. Since abortionists want to hide their failures, underreporting of complications is the rule rather than the exception.[4]

The deliberate underreporting of abortion complications occurs primarily for three reasons: 1) Abortionists are seeking to protect their personal and professional reputations; 2) By minimizing the existence of unfavorable records, abortionists can minimize the availability of damaging evidence in the event of malpractice suits; and 3) Abortionists want to maintain the general myth that abortion is safe.

But even assuming that abortionists were totally willing to report complications, underreporting would still occur for other reasons:

1) Most outpatient abortion clinics do not provide follow-up examinations. Without these, the clinics simply assume there are no complications unless they receive a complaint. Other clinics do provide post-abortion exams, but these are usually brief and superficial.

2) Even if a post-abortion exam is insisted upon, conditions which

may develop into long-range complications, such as sterility or an incompetent uterus, are not easily detectable without prolonged surveillance.

3) Many women hide their identities when seeking an abortion and may fail to return for a post-abortion exam even when one is available.

4) Over 60 percent of the women who need emergency treatment following an outpatient abortion go to a nearby hospital instead of going back to the abortionist. In these cases, an abortionist may never know that a complication occurred.[5]

5) When women are treated for long-term complications such as infertility, they may hide their past abortion experience or simply not realize that it is relevant.[6]

What all these factors add up to is simply this: complication records from outpatient clinics are virtually inaccessible or nonexistent, even though these clinics provide the vast majority of all abortions. Even in Britain where reporting requirements are much better than in the United States, medical experts believe that less than 10 percent of abortion complications are actually reported to government health agencies.[7]

When treatment for a complication takes place in a hospital, however, the records are much more likely to be contributed to the health agencies which compile national health statistics; but this still does not mean that the records will be completely accurate. Instead, complications due to abortion are often listed under other categories. Sometimes this is done to disguise the cause of death. In one case, for example, a twenty-one-year-old woman died only a few hours after a saline abortion, and her death was creatively listed as due to "spontaneous gangrene of the ovary."[8] The reason for the cover-up is relatively obvious—abortionists don't want to be held legally and financially responsible for the complications and deaths that are a natural result of "routine" abortions.

In many cases, even physicians who are not involved with performing abortions contribute to the cover-up. There are primarily two reasons for this: loyalty to one's patient and loyalty to one's profession. Examples of the first category occur when young women who have been aborted want to hide the cause of their hospitalization from their families and friends, even when they are in danger of dying.[9] Thus, what begins as an attempt to avoid embarrassing a woman and her family ends up as an omission of facts in the hospital's official records and, subsequently, as a distortion of national abortion statistics.

Secondly, there exists in the medical profession, as in most professions, an unstated code of "brotherhood" which discourages pointing fingers at the mistakes of other physicians. Therefore, in keeping with the general rule of the fraternity, "see no evil; speak no evil," the physician attending an abortion complication at a local hospital is quite likely to simply treat the condition and avoid recording that it was the result of an incomplete abortion performed by his colleague down the street.

All of the above factors have been mentioned to explain the lack of complete records on abortion complications in America. Political and financial motives, as well as respect for personal privacy, all hinder the reporting of these statistics. With these factors in mind, it should be remembered that the figures which will be cited in the following sections are minimum complication rates based on partial studies. They reflect only what is voluntarily reported, not what is actually happening.

ABORTION MORBIDITY

The rate of complications following a medical procedure is known as the morbidity rate. For the reasons cited above, the morbidity rate due to abortion in America is unknown, though a few hospital studies have been done. But while the rate of complications is uncertain, the variety of complications which occur is well documented.

Over one hundred potential complications have been associated with abortion. Some of these can be immediately spotted, such as a puncture of the uterus or other organs, convulsions, or cardiac arrest. Other complications appear within a few days, such as a slow hemorrhage, pulmonary embolisms, infection and fever. Still other complications are long-term in nature, usually the result of damage to the reproductive system, and may result in chronic infection, an inability to carry a subsequent pregnancy to term, or sterility. These latent complications may not be apparent until a later pregnancy is attempted or until the uterus is so infected as to require removal. Thus, an abortion recorded as complication-free in a short-term study might in fact have caused long-term damage. Thus, as many investigators have discovered, short-term studies of abortion complications reveal only the tip of the iceberg. Indeed, the longer women are kept under surveillance after an abortion, the higher are the reported rates of latent morbidity.[10] Women who may appear physically unaffected by an abortion after a one-year follow-up may be found to be severely affected by the abortion as many as ten to fifteen years later.

Because of the large number of possible complications, it is difficult for any medical study to check for them all, especially the more elusive ones. Furthermore, because of the great time variation between short-term complications and long-term complications, no major scientific studies have been done to tabulate both.

After noting all of these qualifications, a few general observations can be made. First, every type of abortion procedure carries significant risks. Second, the earlier the abortion is done, the lower is the rate of immediate and short-term "major" complications. Third, every type of abortion procedure poses a significant long-term threat to a woman's reproductive health. Fourth, the younger the patient, the greater the long-term risks to her reproductive system.

Overall, the rate of immediate and short-term complications is no less than 10 percent. This figure is based on a reported 100,000 abortion complications in 1977, when the total number of legal abortions in that year was approximately one million.[11] This 10 percent morbidity rate, it should be remembered, is an undisputed minimum rate for immediate and short-term complications. It does not include unreported complications or long-range complications such as infertility. As we will see, the evidence indicates that the actual morbidity rate is probably much higher.

IMMEDIATE AND SHORT-TERM RISKS

Suction Curettage

Almost 90 percent of all abortions are performed by suction curettage, commonly known as vacuum abortions. In this procedure, the vagina and cervix are forcibly dilated with progressively larger tapered cylinders called dilators. Dilation provides the abortionist with the necessary "working room" through which he inserts the abortion instruments, in this case a cutting instrument attached to a high-powered vacuum (twenty-nine times more powerful than a home vacuum). With this device, the abortionist dismembers the "products of conception" (i.e., the unborn child and its placenta) and simultaneously vacuums out the pieces. Abortionists insist that in skilled hands suction curettage is the safest form of abortion. Many physicians disagree.[12]

According to two independent studies, the immediate or short-term complication rate for vacuum abortions is approximately 12 percent.[13] The reported "major" complication rate (strictly defined to include only life-threatening complications) is 4000 per million. Obviously, defining "major" complications in restrictive terms would make abortion appear safer than it really is.[14] Considering both immediate and long-term complications, a major German study found that the total morbidity rate for vacuum aspiration abortions exceeded 31 percent.[15]

Because the abortionist operates blindly, by sense of feel only, the cutting/suction device is potentially deadly. Perforation of the uterus is one of the most common complications (this can occur during dilation or evacuation) which leads to severe hemorrhage and can occasionally result in damage to other internal organs. In a few recorded cases, abortionists have inadvertently sucked out several feet of intestines in a matter of only a few seconds.[16]

Another common complication results from failure to extract all the "products of conception." If a limb or skull is left in the uterus or if a portion of the placenta remains intact, severe infection may result, causing severe cramping and bleeding. Treatment may require another dilation followed by mechanical curettage and antibiotics. If the infection becomes too advanced or is persistent, a hysterectomy will be necessary to remove the diseased uterus.[17]

Third, as with all forms of abortion, suction curettage results in a high incidence of embolisms. An embolism is an obstruction of a blood vessel by a foreign substance such as air, fat, tissue, or a blood clot. Usually, such a blockage is minor and goes unnoticed and eventually dissolves. But if the block occurs in the brain or heart, it may result in a stroke or heart attack. If it occurs in the lungs, it may result in a pulmonary thromboembolism. This condition may occur anywhere from two to fifty days after an abortion and is a relatively frequent major complication. In one group of abortion-related deaths, pulmonary embolisms were the second most common cause of death. Because of the nature of embolisms, these abortion fatalities are unpredictable and often unavoidable. This risk, like most others, is seldom revealed to women during counseling at abortion clinics, even though it is widely known in medical circles. Pulmonary emboli are reported to afflict about 200 aborted women each year.[18]

Fourth, due to the rich blood supply around the uterus during pregnancy, local and general anesthesia during abortions are particularly risky. Anesthesia complications during first trimester abortions are fairly common and unpredictable. When an adverse reaction to anesthetics occurs in an outpatient abortion clinic, there is generally little equipment and expertise available on the site to deal with the emergency. Convulsions, heart arrest, and death are not an uncommon result of these circumstances. In one study of seventy-four women killed by legal abortions, anesthesia complications ranked as the third leading cause of death. The officially reported rate of anesthesia complications is twenty per 100,000 first trimester abortions.[19]

The nine most common "major" complications resulting from

vacuum abortions are infection, excessive bleeding, embolism, ripping or perforation of the uterus, anesthesia complications, convulsions, hemorrhage, cervical injury, and endotoxic shock.[20] "Minor" complications include minor infections, bleeding, fevers and chills, second-degree burns, chronic abdominal pain, vomiting, gastrointestinal disturbances, weight loss, painful or disrupted menstrual cycles, and Rh sensitization.[21]

A word about the last item—only 42 percent of aborted women receive Rh screening prior to their abortions; and even for the minority that are tested, the analysis of the blood samples is often rushed and inaccurate.[22] Unless a woman with Rh negative blood receives a RhoGam injection immediately after the abortion, sensitization may result. In a later "wanted pregnancy" this sensitization may endanger both the life of the mother and her child, a complication which could no longer be considered "minor."

Dilation and Curettage (D&C)

Dilation and curettage is very similar to suction curettage but is used primarily in late first trimester and early second trimester abortions. It differs from suction abortions in that instead of vacuuming out the "products of conception," the abortionist manually dismembers the fetus and scrapes the organs out of the uterus and into a basin. Because it uses sharper instruments and involves more scraping, D&C abortions typically result in much greater blood loss and a higher rate of overall complications.

The types of complications associated with D&C abortions are virtually the same as with vacuum abortions, but are approximately 20 percent more frequent.[23]

Saline Abortions

Each year there are between 100,000 and 150,000 second and third trimester abortions. Most of these are saline abortions. The rate of "major" complications associated with saline abortion is reported to be about five times greater than for first trimester suction abortions.[24]

In a saline abortion, also known as a "salting out," a concentrated salt solution is injected into the amniotic sack surrounding the baby. This solution burns the skin of the fetus and slowly poisons his system, resulting in vasodilation, edema, congestion, hemorrhage, shock, and death.[25] This process takes from one to three hours, during which the distressed unborn kicks, thrusts, and writhes in its attempts to escape. Twelve to forty-eight hours after the child dies, the mother's hormonal system shifts in recognition of this fact, and she goes into natural labor. Normally, within seventy-two hours after the injection, she will deliver a dead fetus.

The technique of saline abortion was originally developed in the concentration camps of Nazi Germany.[26] In Japan, where abortion has been legalized since the 1940s, the saline abortion technique has been outlawed because it is "extraordinarily dangerous."[27] Indeed, in the United States saline abortion is second only to heart transplants as the elective surgery with the highest fatality rate.[28] Despite this fact, state laws attempting to prohibit saline abortions because of their great risk to aborting women have been declared unconstitutional by the courts.[29]

Severe infections and hemorrhages are extremely common following saline abortions. In addition, seepage of the salt solution into the woman's blood system may result in life-threatening coagulation problems. Incomplete abortions and retained placentas occur in from 40 to 55 percent of all cases, the correction of which requires additional surgery. Furthermore, infections or uterine damage incurred during saline abortions frequently requires removal of the uterus.[30]

Prostaglandin Abortions

In a technique similar to saline abortions, the chemical prostaglandin is injected into the amniotic fluid. But instead of killing the unborn outright, this method induces intense contractions of the uterus and causes forced labor. Usually the child dies during the trauma of premature labor, but frequently it does not. This results in one of the most disturbing "complications" of prostaglandin abortions, a live birth.

When prostaglandins were first introduced, there was great hope among abortionists that this new technique would be safer than saline injections. But when six women died and a large number of "aborted" babies were delivered alive, the enthusiasm for prostaglandins dwindled rapidly.[31]

Frequent complications associated with prostaglandin abortions include spontaneous ruptures in the uterine wall, convulsions, hemorrhage, coagulation defects, and cervical injury. Incomplete abortions are also very common. In these cases the decay of retained tissue may result in severe infections, prolonged hospitalization, additional surgery, and in many cases the need for an emergency hysterectomy.[32]

In sum, rather than replacing saline abortions, prostaglandins have simply caused a debate within the aborting community as to which method is the most dangerous. Oddly enough, however, although the evidence seems to indicate that prostaglandins are slightly less dangerous, most abortionists continue to prefer saline abortions. The reason for this is simple. Live births following prostaglandin abortions are extremely disturbing to both the medical staff and the mothers. In other words, a higher priority is being placed on killing the fetus than on providing the safest way for a woman to be rid of her pregnancy.[33]

THE LIVING COMPLICATION

Except when dilation and curettage is used, second and third trimester abortions always run the risk of producing a live-born aborted baby. These premature infants generally die within a few minutes or hours. Some, however, live for days, and a few live to adulthood.[34]

Besides the extraordinary trauma which a live birth abortion poses for a woman, live births constitute the most difficult ethical and legal dilemma faced by abortionists. Is a physician who is being paid to kill an unwanted fetus one moment, required to attempt to save an unexpected baby the next? According to Dr. Robert Grist, a Kansas City abortionist, "the abortion patient has a right not only to be rid of the growth, called a fetus in her body, but also has a right to a dead fetus."[35] But when witnesses reported that they saw Dr. William B. Waddill choke and kill a live-born baby which resulted from a non-lethal saline abortion, the physician was subjected to trial for murder.[36]

Though most doctors do not actively attempt to kill live-born babies following an abortion, most do attempt to ensure death through neglect. Following most second and third trimester abortions, abortion staffs make a conscious effort not to discover whether the child is alive or dead. Any signs of movement or breathing which might be noticed are dismissed as "reflex," unless movement and crying reach a level which cannot be ignored. One abortionist describes his policy this way:

> At the time of delivery, it has been our policy to wrap the fetus in a towel. The fetus is then moved to another room while our attention is turned to the care of [the woman]. She is examined to determine whether complete placental expulsion has occurred and the extent of vaginal bleeding. Once we are sure her condition is stable, the fetus is evaluated. Almost invariably all signs of life have ceased.[37]

Wrapping the fetus in a towel accomplishes two things. First, it conceals all "signs of life" which may be disturbing to the patient and staff. Second, if the premature baby is not already dead, the towel will prevent the baby from getting the oxygen it needs to survive.

Most abortionists will do anything to avoid treating a live-born aborted baby.[38] One of the most shocking examples occurred in Pine

Bluff, Arkansas, where an abortion resulted in a kicking and screaming baby:

> In the examining room after the abortion, the doctor wrapped the
> baby in a towel and laid it aside while he finished caring for Marie.
> The infant continued to squirm and cry.
>
> Soon afterward, Marie left the doctor's office for a friend's house
> nearby. The physician then placed the child in a sack and gave it to
> one of the two friends who had accompanied Marie. . . .
>
> In a few minutes, the woman with the sack arrived at the house
> where Marie was waiting. She said the doctor had told her to "take
> it along with you, and pretty soon it will stop moving."
>
> After Marie fell asleep, the friends kept their death watch over
> the aborted infant until they decided to seek help.[39]

In this case, even after prolonged neglect, the baby survived.
Marie, filled with guilt, is glad that her child lives.

Live-birth abortions occur in the United States at a rate of 400 to
500 times per year, literally an everyday experience.[40] The number may
be higher since: 1) there is no effort to determine if a child is live-born,
and 2) most abortionists avoid reporting live-birth abortions. Dr.
Williard Gates, chief of abortion surveillance at the Center for Disease
Control in Atlanta, describes the cover-up this way: "It's like turning
yourself in to the IRS for an audit. What is there to gain? The tendency
is not to report because there are only negative incentives."[41]

In order to avoid the "complication" of live births, abortionists
are experimenting with more deadly techniques for second and third
trimester abortions. One new technique involves the injection of a poi-
sonous dose of digitoxin directly into the unborn child's heart. As with
most experimental abortion procedures, women are generally not
informed that the procedure is untested.[42] These new techniques may
solve the "abortionists' dilemma," but they may also pose unforeseen
dangers to the health of women.

LONG-RANGE RISKS

A high risk of infection is common to all forms of abortion. Infection
may result from bacteria and viruses introduced into the womb during the abortion or from the decay of damaged uterine tissue or unre-
moved "products of conception." In one series of 1,182 abortions
which occurred under closely regulated hospital conditions,
researchers found that 27 percent of the patients acquired post-abortion infections resulting in fevers lasting three days or longer.[43] The

infection rate from outpatient "abortion mills" is probably much higher.

Many infections are dangerous and life-threatening, and severe pain will typically prompt the patient to seek emergency treatment. But the majority of infections are of a milder order. These lesser infections will cause only minor discomfort, if any. Eventually a woman's body will overcome these milder infections, but long-term damage may still result.

Mild or severe infections may extend from the uterine lining to the fallopian tubes or to organs adjacent to the uterus. Scar tissue left by the infection may block the fallopian tubes, resulting in total or partial infertility and an increased probability of ectopic pregnancies. If a chronic infection results, a total hysterectomy may be required several months or even years after the abortion.[44]

Studies have shown that a woman's risk of an ectopic pregnancy dramatically increases following an abortion. One study suggests that the risk increases 100 to 150 percent, another study suggests a 400 percent increased risk, and a third indicates an 800 percent increased risk.[45] Since the legalization of abortion in 1973, there has been a 300 percent increase in the occurrence of ectopic pregnancies in the United States.[46] Other countries with legalized abortion have witnessed the same effect.

Treatment of an ectopic pregnancy requires major surgery to remove the impregnated fallopian tube before it bursts. For every 100,000 cases of ectopic pregnancy, 300 women die due to rupture and hemorrhage.[47] These deaths are always listed under the "maternal mortality" category rather than as "abortion deaths," even though abortion may be the root cause of most ectopic pregnancies today.

If the scar tissue caused by post-abortion infection is severe enough to completely block the fallopian tubes, total sterility will result. Women who undergo just one induced abortion are three to four times more likely to suffer from secondary infertility than non-aborted women.[48] Numerous studies have found that 3 to 5 percent of all aborted women are inadvertently left sterile by the operation.[49] If a woman is infected by a venereal disease at the time of her abortion, the risk of being rendered sterile is even greater.[50]

After infection, cervical damage is the next leading cause of post-abortion reproductive problems. Damage to the cervix may occur during the "scraping out" in a vacuum or D&C abortion, or during the "expulsion" in a saline or prostaglandin abortion. But undoubtedly, it is during the forced dilation of the uterus in vacuum and D&C abortions that most cervical damage is incurred.

Normally the cervix is rigid and tightly closed throughout the pregnancy. Only at the time of birth does it begin to naturally soften and open. But in an artificially induced abortion, no such natural change occurs; the cervix is hard and "green," designed by nature to resist intrusion and to protect its charge. In this context, it is clear that abortion is an attack not only on the unborn, but also on the woman's reproductive organs, which are designed to protect the child. Thus, during the forcible dilation which occurs in all early abortions, a tremendous stress is placed upon the woman's "green" cervical muscles. This stress virtually always causes microscopic tearing of the muscles and occasionally results in severe ripping of the uterine wall (a "major" complication). According to one hospital study, one in eight suction curettage abortions required stitches for cervical laceration.[51] Another study indicated that laceration of the cervix occurred in 22 percent of aborted women. Again it should be remembered that in outpatient abortion clinics, such lacerations are frequently not noticed, much less treated.

In any case, whether the dilation damage to the uterine muscles is microscopic or macroscopic, this damage frequently results in a permanent weakening of the uterus. This weakening may result in an "incompetent cervix" which, unable to carry the weight of a later "wanted" pregnancy, opens prematurely, resulting in miscarriage or premature birth.[52] For this reason, the chance that a later "wanted" child will die during pregnancy or labor is at least twice as high for previously aborted women.[53]

Cervical damage is extremely frequent in young women pregnant for the first time because the cervix is much more rigid in women who have not previously given birth.[54] This fact is particularly unnerving since nearly 60 percent of all abortions are for first pregnancies. Most of these women will later seek a "wanted" pregnancy, but because of cervical damage they may instead face the traumas of repeated miscarriages and premature births.

According to one study, the risk of a second trimester miscarriage increases tenfold following a vaginal abortion. Similarly, the risk of premature delivery also increases eight to ten times. Though normally only 5 percent of all babies are born prematurely, this rate jumps to 40 percent among women who have had abortions.[55] In another study of first pregnancy abortions, a researcher found that 48 percent of the women studied suffered from abortion-related complications in later "wanted" pregnancies. Women in this group experienced 2.3 miscarriages for every one live birth.[56]

These figures reflect the increased risks for the average woman undergoing an abortion. But when the woman is only a teenager, the frequency and severity of the damage is even worse since a teenager's "green" cervix is still growing and changing. This fact is best illustrated in a comparative study done by Dr. J. K. Russell. In this study, Dr. Russell tracked the reproductive lives of sixty-two pregnant teenagers. When first pregnant, fifty of the girls had abortions, eleven gave birth, and one miscarried. Of the eleven teenagers who gave birth, nine later became pregnant with "wanted" children and delivered with no complications and a 100 percent success rate. Among the fifty girls who had undergone abortions, there were forty-seven subsequent "wanted" pregnancies. Of these forty-seven "wanted" pregnancies, 66 percent ended in defective births (including nineteen miscarriages and seven premature births). Only 34 percent of the pregnancies among the previously aborted group ended with a full-term delivery of a healthy child.[57]

Induced abortion may cause not only cervical incompetence, but also cervical rigidity. Permanent damage to the uterine wall may result in the faulty placement and development of the placenta during later pregnancies. A 1981 study at Vanderbilt University found that after a single abortion the risk of placenta previa in later pregnancies increases seven to fifteen times.[58] Abnormal development of the placenta due to uterine damage increases the risk of fetal malformation, perinatal death, and excessive bleeding.[59]

Due to uterine damage, previously aborted women also face much more difficult and dangerous deliveries in later pregnancies. Aborted women face at least three times more labor complications than nonaborted women.[60] Previously aborted women require longer periods of labor during all three stages of labor; they are more likely to require manual or instrumental assistance to complete their labor; they are more likely to suffer from retained and adherent placenta following delivery; they are more likely to experience rupture of their uterus during labor; and they are more likely to suffer from severe hemorrhage at parturition and experience substantially greater blood losses than their nonaborted sisters.[61] In short, abortion places women and their future children at much greater risk during both their pregnancies and their deliveries.

Finally, there is a large class of long-term complications which is only now being investigated. For example, a recent study performed by California researchers found that the risk of breast cancer doubled among women who aborted their first pregnancies.[62] Two known studies are now underway to determine if there is a link between abortion and the high incidence of cervical cancer among aborted women.

The explanation for increased breast cancers and cervical cancers among aborted women lies in the unnatural disruption of their changing bodies. Early in pregnancy, the breasts and uterus undergo a rapid growth and change. Suddenly disrupting these changes before their completion may render these cells susceptible to "neoplastic stimuli" (tumor initiation) or might hasten the growth of cells which are already malignant.

Only the future will reveal how many other side effects result from abortion. But already it is clear that because of its many immediate and long-term complications, legal abortion is perhaps the leading cause of gynecological and obstetric emergencies in the United States.[63] This is reflected in the trend in medical malpractice insurance toward creating a new "ultra-risk" category for surgeons who perform abortions.[64]

THE UNDERREPORTING OF ABORTION DEATHS

On June 14, 1977, Barbaralee Davis underwent a routine suction abortion at the Hope Clinic for Women in Granite City, Illinois. After the customary period of observation in the clinic's recovery room, she complained of weakness and was sent home with instructions to rest. Alone in her bedroom, she slept and quietly bled to death. Her body was found less than twelve hours after the abortion. After the incident was reported in the local press, Michael Grobsmith, chief of the Illinois Department of Public Health's Division of Hospitals and Clinics, commented on the death: "It's unfortunate, but it's happening every day in Chicago, and you're just not hearing about it."[65]

One year later, during an investigation of only four Chicago-based clinics (in a state with over twenty abortion clinics), the *Chicago-Sun Times* uncovered twelve abortion deaths that had never been reported.[66] Even when abortion-related deaths such as these are uncovered, they are generally not included in the "official" total since they were not reported as such on the original death certificates.[67] If there are this many unreported abortion deaths in one city from only a few clinics, in a state with regulations as strict as any allowed by the courts, how many more are there across the country?

As with other abortion complications, there is no accurate mechanism for gathering statistics about abortion-related deaths. The Supreme Court's abortion cases have struck down all requirements for reporting abortion-related complications and deaths on the grounds that such reporting might discourage women from seeking abortions.[68] This new freedom allows abortionists and others to disguise abortion deaths under other categories when filling out death certificates.[69] Even the Centers for Disease Control, a data bank for U.S. health statistics which is strongly pro-abortion in its editorial opinions, admits that the reported rate of deaths due to legal abortion is being deliberately kept low through selective underreporting.[70]

But though there are no precise figures for the number of deaths from legal abortions, there is no doubt that the figure is much higher than the officially reported totals. On one occasion, for example, Dr. Lester Hibbard, chairman of the Los Angeles County Medical Society Committee, which is charged with keeping track of maternal deaths, told a newspaper reporter that there had been only four abortion-related deaths officially reported as such. But, Dr. Hibbard added, he *personally* knew of at least four other deaths that had followed legal abortions but had not been reported as such on the death certificates. Furthermore, he said he was certain that these unreported abortion deaths were only the tip of the iceberg.[71] According to one estimate, less than 10 percent of deaths from legal abortion are reported as such.[72]

The degree to which abortion deaths are underreported is hinted at in the results of a 1974 survey which asked 486 obstetricians about their experience with complications resulting from legal abortions. Of the doctors surveyed, 91 percent had treated patients for complications, 87 percent had hospitalized one or more patients, and 6 percent (twenty-nine doctors) reported one or more patients having died from a legal abortion.[73] It can be assumed that these doctors witnessed these deaths between the years 1968 and 1974, since 1968 was the first year in which abortion became legal in some states. Therefore, extrapolation of this 6 percent sample rate to all 21,700 obstetricians in the United States in 1974 would indicate a probability of 1,300 patient deaths due to abortion-related complications during the six-year period between 1968 and 1974. But the actual number of deaths from legal abortions reported for that period was fifty-two, only *5 percent* of the projected figure.[74] In order for the reported figure of only fifty-two deaths during this period to be accurate, the 486 doctors surveyed in this study must have coincidentally seen *over half* of all the nation's deaths from legal abortion—a very unlikely coincidence. Finally, this projection of 1,300 deaths between 1968 and 1974 is based on a survey of obstetricians only. Aborted women who died under the care of general practitioners or other health professionals would not be included in this survey, so the actual mortality rate and cover-up could be even worse.

What should be clear is that there is a major flaw in the mortality statistics for legal abortion. It is quite possible that only 5 to 10 percent of all deaths resulting from legal abortion are being reported as abortion-related. Even if 50 percent were being accurately reported, that extra margin of risk is far greater than women are being led to believe. Indeed, based on the *reported* abortion deaths alone, abortion is already the fifth leading cause of maternal death in the United States.[75]

The most common causes of death from legal abortion include hemorrhage, infection, blood clots in the lungs, heart failure, and anesthetic complications.[76] These can occur after any type of abortion procedure and are generally unpredictable. Some of these deaths result because outpatient clinics are seldom equipped to handle an emergency. But more frequently the death occurs *after* the patient leaves the clinic. According to one study: "43% of abortion deaths occurred on the day of the abortion, 4% on the second postabortion day, 22% on the third day, and 30% thereafter."[77] Obviously, fifteen minutes or an hour in a clinic recovery room (usually under the supervision of a staff person without medical training) is not sufficient to ensure that an abortion is "complication-free." Without daily follow-ups, infections, blood clots, and slow hemorrhages will continue to take their toll.

Furthermore, it should be noted that abortion actually increases the chance of maternal death in later pregnancies. Medical researchers Margaret and Arthur Wynn, who favor abortion on request, state in their comprehensive study of the effects of abortion on later pregnancies that: "Any patient who has had a previous history of an abortion should be regarded as a high risk patient."[78] This is because abortion dramatically increases the risks of ectopic pregnancies, cervical incompetence, miscarriage, and other complications of pregnancy. These conditions increase the risk of death for both mother and child in later pregnancies. But despite the fact that abortion is indirectly responsible for these deaths, deaths resulting from these conditions will be included only under the maternal mortality column; they will *not* be proportionately attributed to abortion.[79]

Finally, the present claims for a low abortion mortality rate in the United States should be compared to experience prior to *Roe v. Wade* when states with permissive abortion laws were allowed to require reporting of abortion-related deaths. Of course, this did not guarantee that all deaths would be reported, but failure to report might result in legal problems and even the revoking of a physician's license. Under these conditions, Oregon reported 13.9 abortion deaths per 100,000 legal abortions compared to only 8.4 maternal deaths per 100,000 live births. Maryland reported 40.5 deaths per 100,000 legal abortions as compared to 23.1 maternal deaths per 100,000 live births.[80] According to these pre-*Roe* state statistics, the mortality rate for legal abortion is nearly twice as high as the overall maternal mortality rate.

The only state which claimed an abortion mortality rate lower than the maternal mortality rate was New York. There, a public health official, citing the official records, claimed only 5.3 deaths per 100,000 abortions. But these New York figures are widely recognized as invalid because only 32 percent of all the abortions performed were included in the follow-up. Any deaths among the other 68 percent would not have been recorded. Indeed, even among the abortion-related deaths that were reported, at least seven known deaths were arbitrarily excluded from the "official" total for strained, technical reasons. In addition, a large number of other known deaths which had occurred after the patients had flown back to their homes out of state were also excluded from the "official records."[81]

In contrast to New York's "official" safety record for abortion, a 1971 study done by Dr. Joseph J. Rovinsky concluded that the actual abortion mortality rate in New York was no less than 38 per 100,000.[82] Indeed, by 1972, the year prior to *Roe v. Wade*, the *reported* number of women who had died from legal abortions exceeded the number dying from illegal abortions by almost two to one.[83] Only after all requirements for reporting were struck down did the number of reported deaths from legal abortion even begin to level off.[84]

The experience in other countries also confirms that abortion mortality rates, even during the first trimester, are invariably larger than their respective maternal mortality rates. For example, in Sweden the death rate for legal abortion is 39 per 100,000, and in Denmark the reported death rate is approximately 30 per 100,000. These rates are more than double the maternal mortality rates of these countries.[85] Canadian figures list 36 deaths per 100,000 abortions.[86] And in one British study at Glasgow University, fifteen deaths were found in a series of 20,000 legal abortions yielding an unexpected fatality rate of 75 per 100,000.[87]

In sum, what can we say about abortion mortality rates? First, not all abortion-related deaths are reported as such. Indeed, circumstantial evidence indicates that only a minority of abortion deaths are reported as abortion-related. Second, for the average, healthy woman, *abortion is far more risky than childbirth.*[88]

But it should be remembered that in terms of practical decision-making for the individual, mortality rates for both abortion and childbirth are virtually meaningless. As Dr. Thomas Hilgers points out:

> If a woman achieves pregnancy and carries it through to term with the delivery of the infant, her chances of surviving that pregnancy are 99.99 percent. In fact, her chances of surviving that pregnancy are higher, at all age levels, than her chances of simply surviving the next one year of life.[89]

Likewise, the chances of surviving an abortion are only slightly worse or slightly better, depending on whom you believe. The vast majority of pregnant women will survive either childbirth or abortion.

In terms of a pregnant woman's decision-making, comparing the *complication* rates of abortion and childbirth is far more important than the mortality rates. When judging the comparative health risks of abortion versus childbirth on the basis of morbidity rates, it is an indisputable fact that the risk of long-term complications following an abortion is ten to twenty times greater than the risk of *any* complications following childbirth.[90]

The question women considering abortion must face is not so much one of survival but the question of how well they will survive. Since abortion is frequently damaging to a woman's reproductive system, women who may wish to have children at a later date are especially at risk.[91]

Decisions to Be Weak

For some women, the choice to have an abortion is never truly made. Instead, buffeted about by the pressures they face and the advice of well-meaning friends, they feel themselves carried by some outside momentum toward the unwanted but seemingly inevitable solution of abortion. One survey respondent writes:

> I didn't want to kill my child; I just made the decision to be weak and not care about any of it. . . . I made a decision not to make a conscious choice at all. In fact, Planned Parenthood and all the abortion mills tell you that you have NO CHOICE but to get an abortion. This is the irony of the "pro-choice" rhetoric.

Similarly, when Kathleen Trueland Smith became pregnant as a junior in high school, she too found it easy to abdicate responsibility for her decision to her parents.

> I reasoned that I had already disappointed my parents once by getting pregnant, so I didn't want to disappoint them again by having the baby. By this time I was in such an emotional state that I turned off all logical thinking processes. I let my parents take over; it was so easy to have them make the decisions for me.

Often women faced with unplanned pregnancies find that they lack the courage which is necessary to assert their desire to keep the baby. They desperately pray that someone else will step into their lives and give them the encouragement they need to "do the right thing." For example, even as she was sitting in the abortion clinic, Renate Penney was looking for even a small word of hope: "I waited for someone to talk to me. I wanted someone to tell me not to do this. Anyone. But no one did. And it was done."

Thus, just as a despondent person will threaten suicide in the hope that someone will reach out and care, so too do many women threaten abortion hoping to be talked out of it. But instead, they all too often discover that others are only going to encourage the dark option of death. One WEBA member writes:

> I called a priest who was counseling me and said, "I want to get an abortion." I couldn't believe I would ever say such a thing. He put me in touch with a woman who had had an abortion and she escorted me to the clinic. No one *ever* counseled me about financial and emotional help—nothing. If that is pro-choice—where is the *choice!* I could have been counseled and led to find a "joy in living and procreation"—instead I was allowed to run from life. Those two people had a chance to intervene in my life. Instead they were passive wimps.

By not choosing, or by letting others choose for them, some women hope to avoid responsibility for their abortions. But while this strategy may help to divert blame for negative feelings which occur after the abortion, it does not prevent those bitter feelings from occurring. Indeed, these women experience even a greater sense of exploitation, and they suffer even a greater loss of self-esteem.

What most women faced with problem pregnancies want is nothing more than encouragement and love. Instead they are given abortion—an act of despair and lovelessness.

CAROLYN WALTON

When Carolyn became pregnant under difficult circumstances, she went into a state of "shock." She didn't know what to do. But her well-meaning relatives did. They took over her decision-making for her and had her undergo an abortion at a Cleveland clinic. The trauma of her abortion made her lose complete control of her life. She found herself abusing drugs and alcohol, sterile from abortion complications, and dangerously suicidal.

Ten years ago I found myself pregnant, divorced, and virtually alone. The first emotion was that of sheer panic. I only had a small income and was working two jobs. I had a four-year-old daughter to support. The baby's father immediately retracted his marriage proposal as soon as he found out I was pregnant. I had no money, no medical insurance, and didn't realize that there were places to turn to for help.

As I turned to friends and relatives for advice the whole matter became more confusing. Advice poured in from all sides. I felt like I was being put through the third degree. "What is a divorced woman going to do with such a small income? You already have one child to feed. How will you pay the hospital bills?" As I think back, not once did anyone just put their arms around me and ask my feelings or allow me to even have time to have any. Just some positive love and support would have been a relief. A relative who had had an illegal abortion twenty-five years before talked to me about abortion. After all, it was now legal and "safe." She had never been able to have children because of her abortion, but strangely enough, advised me to have one anyway! I felt like I was in a tailspin. There was no time to think.

My relatives went about their business of making all the arrangements while I remained in a total state of oblivion. I felt like someone on the outside looking in. It was as if it was happening to someone else. I don't blame anyone, they only did what they thought was right; that is why educating people about what's really right is so important.

Anyway, I was soon whisked off to Cleveland and dropped off at some friends' house. The next day I was again dropped off at the abortion clinic. My heart told me I was wrong, but my mind, like a robot, did what it was told. After I got inside (alone) I paid my $200 and was given a pregnancy test and a locker (just like in a gym). I was given a paper gown and told to put it on. The place was cold and the people formal. No compassion, no understanding. It was like a busy assembly line.

I then waited in a small room until my name was called. I was taken to another room and told to get up on the table, put my feet in the stirrups, and scoot down. It was so cold—I shivered and have never been so scared or felt so alone. I was soon to find out that the "painless" procedure I was promised was anything but painless. As my baby was ripped from my body the pain became unbearable, and tears streamed down my face. I was told to be still, it would soon be over. After the abortion, I walked to another room and was allowed to lie down for thirty minutes, after which I was told I could leave. I went to my locker, got dressed, and was told to see my family doctor in six weeks. I asked if I could use a phone to call my ride and was told they had no phones for public use but there was a pay phone down the street I could use.

I walked down the street. It was November, and very cold. As I walked back to wait for my ride outside the clinic, I felt cold, nauseous, dizzy, alone and empty. When my ride picked me up she had a friend with her. They were going to a steak house for lunch and I had to go along. You would have thought I had just gone to get my eyes checked for all anyone cared.

Later that day, another relative took me home and dropped me off in front of my apartment. It's amazing how everyone was there to give advice before the abortion, but afterwards I was on my own.

What was to follow was more like a nightmare than reality. I began having nightmares about my murdered baby. I began drinking more and more until I was up to five bottles of alcohol a week. I sometimes went so long without eating that when I would try to eat, I would vomit. I finally went to the doctor and found out that I had an infection from the abortion. He started treatment but it didn't help. I told him about the nightmares and my nerves and he gave me tranquilizers—no comfort, no counseling—just pills.

So I started taking tranquilizers to help me sleep, and pep pills to keep me going during the day. Four times I deliberately overdosed, trying to commit suicide. I don't think I really wanted to die, I only wanted someone to care, to help, to listen. I wanted the pain to go away. The doctor continued to try treatment after treatment on the physical problem. But to no avail. I finally changed doctors and had to have surgery because the infection caused by the abortion had destroyed the cervix and the uterus. This helped for a short time.

I finally met the man I am now married to; with his love and support, I started to put my life back together. We started to attend church, and I came to find Christ as my Savior. I then knew I was forgiven, but it took time before I was able to forgive myself. I was finally alive after being dead and living in hell.

But the physical problems caused by the abortion started cropping back up. More infections and more damage. I changed doctors again. I had a D&C. I was filled with tumors by this time and had endometriosis. A hysterectomy was inevitable, but we put it off as long as possible. But March 15, 1984 it finally came to pass. *Everything* had to be removed, for it was totally destroyed. It took ten years of constant problems, but the abortion finally took its final toll.

As I look back, if I had had love and support, and above all, the true facts, I would have never even considered an abortion. The pain never goes away, it's always there.

I really believe WEBA needs to be heard; we have a right to be heard. The thought of anyone going through what I went through (although I know that there are literally millions who have) is heartbreaking to me.

ALICE GILMORE

Sometimes women are pushed into abortion by circumstances, and find themselves in and out of the abortion clinic without really under-

standing what has happened to them. Such was the case for Alice Gilmore. Though naive about abortion before she walked in the door of the Kansas City abortion clinic, Alice spent the next six years experiencing the traumatic physical and psychological problems caused by that abortion.

I was eighteen years old when I first became pregnant. A few weeks later, I went to the doctor so I could be sure, but I was very naive about what to expect. My boyfriend was not encouraging; he said he was too young to be a father. So I went to a girlfriend, who suggested that maybe I could have an abortion. She gave me the name of a place that did abortions.

So I called them, and they told me what to do to prepare myself. I didn't even know what abortion really was. So I went up there the next day—it all happened really fast—and the woman at the reception desk asked me the reason for terminating the baby. I said that "I would like to keep it, but I can't." She said, "Well then, you don't want it, do you?" I said, "No, I want it, but I can't keep it." I had no support from anybody at that time. She wrote down anyway that I didn't want the fetus. That hurt me really bad at that time, because I did want my baby.

She didn't mention any alternatives whatsoever. In fact, everybody that I talked to was very rude to me. It seemed like they were all angry. I went to this other room for counseling, or what they called counseling, but it wasn't really. They didn't give any alternatives, either. Their counseling was to tell us about what they were going to do. Then they showed us pictures of ways to prevent birth next time. They wanted us to get an IUD—they said that was the best thing to get. So they sold me an IUD, and they put it in me after the abortion.

The doctor told me I was almost four months along. I asked the doctor, "Is the baby alive?" He said, "No." I never had prior instruction in school as to the development of a baby, so I didn't know any better. All I had to go on was what he told me, and that's all he said.

From there, I had to get ready. There were two or three of us sitting in this room, right next to where we would go in and lay down. Although we couldn't see what was going on, we certainly could hear. There was a girl in the next room crying very loud. Then it was my turn. I went in and lay down on the table. They gave me my choice of a local or gas. They made a big point of telling me that the gas cost $50 more. "If you don't want to pay it, you get a local." But I didn't have the extra money.

So they gave me the local and it made me feel sick. I told them, "I'm going to be sick." And the doctor said, "Oh, she's going to be sick. Get her something." The nurse said, "Alright, alright." They were very, very rude about it. They were not nice at all. They acted like I was an inconvenience to them. So the nurse got a bowl and laid it next to me.

So the doctor started, and said, "You'll feel a little pinch; it will be very, very minor." But it hurt an awful lot! It felt like they were pulling my insides out. I don't think I've ever felt that much pain.

Afterwards, I just felt badly, and I had a lot of pain. I felt no relief at all. I didn't realize why I felt bad. My boyfriend took me home. It wasn't long after I got home that I knew—it just hit me—that I had killed my baby. That's what I said to myself: "I killed my baby."

After the abortion, I started to bleed a lot. They had told me that I would bleed for about six weeks, and that unless I had clots bigger than an inch across, not to worry about it. I went way past the six weeks; I bled for over a year. I bled a whole lot for the first nine months. I didn't go to the doctor, because I was ashamed, especially at first. And secondly because the clots weren't very big—half an inch across, but never an inch. I was bleeding so bad that I couldn't get away from the bathroom for more than fifteen minutes. I had to have double protection to keep the blood from going through my pants.

I also began to feel a great deal of pain during intercourse. This lasted for many years. From what I've been able to learn since, I probably had a torn cervix. And I still have pain now.

I also became very, very depressed. I had a lot of trouble concentrating, I couldn't keep my mind off the abortion. I cried a lot. I don't think I ever got out of the depression. I used to laugh a lot; I used to be known in school as the class clown. But afterwards I could never laugh. People tried very hard to make me laugh; but I just couldn't laugh, even at something very funny. I went through a complete personality change.

A lot of times I wanted to die—I was very, very lonely. There was no reason to live, not really.

I had six years of depression after my abortion. I developed into a really weird person. I hated myself, I had no self-confidence. My boyfriend started to feel really guilty, too. Right after making love I'd say, "I killed my baby." And he started feeling really bad. Things started going downhill. He started lying to me and going out behind my back.

Two years after my abortion, we broke up. I met my husband-to-be the next day. We started to live together, and I got pregnant right away. I guess I was a very lenient-type girl; I grew up with no love. I told my boyfriend, "I won't have another abortion; I already went through that once; I won't go through it again." He said, "I wouldn't ask you to." He was very good about it, he wanted to marry me right away when he knew I was pregnant. I kept saying, "No, I don't know you. I don't love you."

We lived together while I was pregnant. He wanted to marry me, but I kept saying no. Finally I told him to quit asking me and I would let him know when I was ready to get married. Two months after my son was born, I decided that he wanted me and the baby, so we were married.

Several years later, I started reading the Bible, especially the New Testament. For a long time my husband ridiculed me because he hadn't been born again yet. But later we both became active in a Christian church. It was only then that I could start to forgive myself, but that was the hardest part. I knew the Lord had forgiven me, but I couldn't forgive myself. Within myself, it took about a year and a half to completely heal.

I really feel sorry for women who have had abortions. It's never a good thing, not even in the case of incest. I've been through incest with my natural father—though I never became pregnant—but even in the case of incest, abortion is wrong. It would only hurt the girl more, physically and emotionally.

SEVEN

Decisions to Take Control

While many women abandon their decision-making power to others and are pressured into abortion, others make a clear and independent choice on their own. For these strong-willed women, the choice for abortion is a choice to control their own destinies. These are modern, liberated women. They are assertive and they know what they want. And one thing they do not want is an unplanned pregnancy which will disrupt their plans for their future. Unfortunately, they seldom realize that the short-term solution of abortion will eventually be just as disruptive—if not more so.

DONNA MERRICK

Donna was just finishing nursing school and was looking forward to her career when she discovered she was pregnant. Despite the desperate pleas of her boyfriend, Donna aborted their child. Today her sense of guilt includes her mistreatment of both her baby and her boyfriend.

I found out I was pregnant on my twenty-first birthday. For a fleeting moment I let myself kind of giggle inside. I had always had my sights set towards being a mother, and I figured that's where I would eventually end up. I had just graduated from nursing school, and I enjoyed nursing. Yet I wanted to get married; I wasn't too crazy about myself, and I wanted somebody to love me, hug me, and tell me I was OK. I'm sure I'm not the only one who's ever been through anything like that.

When I found out I was pregnant, then, it was almost like everything that "little girl Donna" had been looking forward to and playing house about had finally arrived: I was PREGNANT. But I didn't let myself consciously think that I was going to be a mommy, because that would have led me to think that I was also going to kill this child that was going to make me a mommy. Still, I did give a squeal of delight, subconsciously thinking, "Oooh I'm pregnant—how neat! I can do it!" I mostly remember experiencing a shudder of joy—what a contradiction in terms.

So when the nurse on the phone said, "Yes, Donna, your test was positive—you are pregnant," all I said was "Oh." Then she said, "Do you want to terminate?," and I said "Yes." She set up an appointment for the following week. I was in New Hampshire, as a summer nurse, at a camp. I had to drive to Springfield, Massachusetts, to the doctor's, where I also got my abortion.

One reason I chose to abort was simply because I didn't want to tell my parents that I had made a mistake. I knew they would have loved me through the entire thing, should I have decided to bring the baby to life, and I knew they would have supported me if I had still decided to abort after I told them. My parents were like that—unquestioningly supportive. We just didn't have a communicative relationship. But in my mind I felt that I needed to attain certain goals to keep them pleased with me. That was something I needed—to have them pleased with me. Becoming pregnant definitely did not fit into the scheme of things.

I remember thinking about this friend I had in nursing school, who had problems with her ovaries. She wasn't sure if she could conceive, so she allowed herself to get pregnant on purpose to see if she could get pregnant. Then she went and had an abortion. I remember thinking at the time that was a really stupid thing to do. The way she used her boyfriend, that's what I thought about too. I looked up to her—I was trying to learn from her. The blind leading the blind, I suppose . . .

Anyway, it was July of 1974 when I found out I was pregnant. I drove into town and told my boyfriend about it. It shocked me, but he looked at me and asked if he was the father. That took me back for a minute—I was almost insulted. But I said, "Of course you're the father." He asked me what I was going to do, and I told him I was going to have an abortion. Then he asked me not to do it. He wasn't very forceful about it at first; I think he saw in my face that I was more or less resigned to having the abortion. But then he did try to talk me out of it, saying he was ready to get married, even though we'd been seeing each other for a month maybe, at the most. In fact, he begged me to marry him. I remember that night, when we were in bed, he put his hand on my tummy and he cried, because he didn't want me to have the abortion.

But I wasn't ready to get married, or I didn't think I was. I'd just graduated from nursing school, I had a (supposedly) "glorious" future ahead of me, and I was determined not to be so old-fashioned or inhibited as to get married right away. I wanted to fit in with the intelligent, free-thinking people. I respected those people and looked up to them, because I felt I had never been one of them and I was trying very hard to be like that. So at the time, abortion seemed the best option.

My boyfriend didn't want me to have the abortion, but he didn't know what else to do. We talked about homes for unwed mothers, but they left such a lousy taste in my mouth. Just saying "homes for unwed mothers" made me think of girls with long, stringy hair sitting in dark, dingy rooms just waiting for their babies to be born, so they could go back home and walk around with their eyes to the ground for the rest of their lives, knowing what they had just done. I certainly didn't want to face that prospect. I was a chicken; abortion is not a courageous decision—it is a cowardly decision. It is a decision to sweep your mistakes under the rug and not face up to them. It needs to be realized that for an unwed mother to give life to her unborn child is a courageous and noble decision.

Anyway, by the time I got around to telling my boyfriend about my planned abortion, I really hadn't thought much about his feelings. I didn't think that he had much to say about it. I didn't really think about whether I should involve him in the decision or not. So, I was the only one to make the decision. My boyfriend was brought up a good Catholic, desperately wanted to have children, and knew that abortion was wrong. He tried to convey that to me.

But I can't remember any kind of reason that I would have accepted. I think that's a characteristic of women who have made a decision to abort, especially in the circumstances that I was in.

Anyway, my boyfriend agreed to take care of me after I had the abortion. But he would not go with me, though I don't remember asking him. I guess I thought it was something I had to do on my own. I think it had something to do with my "coming of age," that I could do this all by myself, and be stalwart, and not be affected by it. In my heart of hearts, though, I was dying to have him with me through the whole thing. I was so scared; I had no idea what was going to happen to me. We hadn't touched on abortion in nursing school.

When I went to the clinic, then, I was by myself. In the waiting room were three or four other scared-looking women, like myself. There wasn't a smile on any of their faces. It was very quiet. Some of the girls had their boyfriends there. I kind of envied them; they were all hugging up to each other like scared little kids.

While we were all sitting in the waiting room, a counselor called us in one by one. When it was my turn, I wasn't sure what to expect. I remember that it was very traumatic for me to go through that "counseling" session. The woman wasn't what I would call one of the most compassionate people in the world. One of the things I remember most vividly was that the counseling was very demeaning. She asked me if I was using birth control when I got pregnant and I said no. She asked me if I had ever used birth control and I said yes. Then she burst out with, "Well, how in the world did you get pregnant?" She made me feel like a jerk all over again; I felt stupid enough as it was, without her hammering on me.

I was sitting there trying desperately not to cry; I remember just wanting to scream. I felt so stupid and I felt so ashamed throughout that whole session. I felt so much guilt and shame that I was just trying to sit on it, instead of allowing myself to cry. I never cried through the whole thing. I was very calm and cool and in control; I wanted to be in control.

I think that's a characteristic of women who have set their minds to having an abortion. Once they've made the decision, it's almost tunnel-vision: making a decision feels so good. That's because being pregnant at this time is an uncontrollable aspect of your life. To make the decision to abort is taking control of this situation that is horrifying to you at this time in your life. That's how the repression of feelings begins. If you let yourself cry, you may become hysterical and uncontrolled; that is NOT the name of the game.

Anyway, the only other thing the woman asked me was, "Have you considered adoption?" I said, "No, I don't think I could do it." "Oh," she said, and that was the end of that.

Of course she asked me what kinds of plans I had for my life, and why I didn't want to get married, and how my boyfriend felt about it. I told her that he didn't want me to have the abortion. She asked me how I felt about that. I answered that I wasn't happy that he didn't want me to have the abortion, and that I wished he would support me. Nothing was said about the baby.

So after we all got counseled (and verbally whipped—that's how I felt), we walked into the hospital into the day surgery rooms, which were next to the delivery rooms. I laid down on the table and put my hands behind my head, determined to be "cool" until the end. That's how I needed to cope with it. The doctor and nurse walked in and saw me like that. The doctor made some comment that made me feel very ashamed for lying there with that nonchalant attitude. They gave me some Demerol IV. I was conscious, but I didn't feel very much pain. I felt cramps and pinches, and the doctor told me how each step would feel, and what he was doing. Then he turned on the suction machine, and it was all over.

I went back to my boyfriend's apartment. I felt so relieved, and so pampered. He had a pitcher of ice water next to the bed, and he had the blankets turned back. But he wasn't there; he didn't want to be there. I went to sleep, but only for a while. I had to be back to camp that night. My boyfriend came back, and was concerned about me being able to drive during the hour and a half trip. But I had to be back, so I waved good-bye.

That was the last time I ever saw him. I came back to his apartment three weeks later, to pick up some things I had left there, and he wasn't there. When I asked his roommate where he was, he said my boyfriend wasn't going to come, that he didn't want to see me. That was the end of the relationship; he couldn't face me.

That's where I remember feeling guilty. At that time I was angry, and very, very hurt. I knew this man loved me; he did. I had told him I loved him, though not enough to get married. I expected him to come crawling after me and keep pursuing me; that's what I wanted. But it never occurred to me then that he just couldn't look me in the eyes, knowing what I had done to his child.

That's been one of the hardest things for me to deal with, following the abortion. I began to realize it about two or three months later, when I returned to his town to see some other friends. It happened to be the day he was getting married. The things that had transpired during those three short months were that he broke a leg, dropped out of nursing school, got engaged, and rejoined the Army. It blew me away to find that out; his many years in the Army had not been a happy time in his life—I knew that something must be wrong, and that he was in a bad state of mind. I felt completely responsible for all of these things.

I tried to get on with my life, and moved in with my sister in Philadelphia. I began to work in a nursing unit there, and ironically enough, I got a job in a nursery, working with premature babies.

But I became very promiscuous after that. I got introduced to the periphery of the feminist movement. I would read *Cosmopolitan* magazine from cover to cover every month, because it told me that the lifestyle I had chosen was the right one, a noble one, a fulfilling one. I needed a fix of that, somebody to tell me that what I was doing was OK. I didn't feel very fulfilled, though. I'd go to clubs at night, and I'd be with a different man every night. Every morning I'd wake up, and they'd be gone, and I'd feel dirty, physically and emotionally. It was just a vicious cycle. But I hung on to my *Cosmopolitan* magazine like my Bible.

About a year after my abortion, I found myself thinking that I was pregnant again. I was panic-stricken. I confided in my sister, whom I had told that I had had an abortion, that I thought I was pregnant. She asked me what I would do, and I said I didn't know, but that I knew I couldn't have another abortion. She didn't ask me why, and I didn't know why either. I just knew that it had made me feel bad, and I didn't want to do it again. But I have a feeling that if I really had been pregnant at that time, which I wasn't, that without other options, I would have had another abortion. I wasn't ready to deal with myself responsibly yet.

Though I didn't want another abortion, I didn't see anything wrong with other women having abortions. I went along with the thinking that a woman should have a right to choose, a right to her own body, and on and on. I felt that way quite strongly.

When I met the Lord, it was about two or three years after my abortion. I hadn't really connected my promiscuity or increased drug use with my abortion, but now I know it was all hooked together. When I met the Lord, I knew right away that what I had done was wrong. It was the first time I'd ever consciously admitted it to myself: my having the abortion was a bad thing to have done. It was a great relief to admit it. I knew that the Lord had forgiven me for it, and that He still loved me. I realized that there isn't anything in our lives that the Lord will allow to go to waste. God is big enough to even use abortion to bring people to Him.

About three years later, living in New Mexico, I saw Nancyjo Mann on television and I really started to think about my abortion. I wrote to her, and she called back and told me I was the first one she had ever heard from in New Mexico, and would I consider directing a chapter here. After much thought, I accepted. It has been a tremendous healing process for me, because I've been able—I've been forced, actually—to look at what abortion does to women, at what causes women to have abortions, and at what they go through afterwards.

I feel that women are being deceived when they go in to have an abortion because they aren't being shown pictures of what their child looks like. Women are being deceived before they get to that place in that they're being sheltered from this truth. Women are being deceived about the procedure they will undergo. I wasn't told that it would be a blind procedure, that the physician cannot see inside my uterus. Women should see pictures representing the child inside of them, and they should know beforehand the side-effects of abortion. They should know that there may be as much as a 25 percent chance of never having another child. Can they live with that? That should be included in the counseling. Without it, that's deception; women aren't being allowed to make a truly informed decision about their abortion.

MONICA HARSHBARGER

Monica had a legal abortion in Colorado in 1971. Though she was afraid that a baby would spoil her teenage fun, she soon found that the complications she suffered from the abortion weren't worth all the "fun" in the world.

In 1971, at the age of seventeen, I became pregnant. I had been a pretty rebellious teenager, and I went through a lot of emotional turmoil at that time. I now know that most of that was due to the fact that my parents divorced in my early teens. I lived with my mother, but loved and missed my father more than I knew, or at least was willing to admit at the time.

I guess I fell in with the wrong group of kids when I was in junior high school. We were experimenting with drugs and casual sex. Oh, we knew about birth control, thanks to our local Planned Parenthood. But it is my belief that teenagers are not responsible enough to handle any form of birth control. I now know that abstinence is the only sure form of birth control.

When I discovered I was pregnant, I was devastated, and could think of no one but me and my life. No one else mattered, because I was having fun, and I knew it all. A baby would have spoiled that. I didn't think I could give birth to a child and give it to someone else. I knew at seventeen that I was not capable of raising a child.

I had heard that abortions were safe and easy. My best friend had had one, and she was fine. She has since had four more; how sad. Needless to say, she is not my best friend now, but we are friends, and I feel terribly sorry for her. She tries so hard to bury her guilt and justify the abortions.

Anyway, I truly believed that what I was carrying at that point, the first trimester, was a blob of tissue. No one ever told me any different, at any time before my abortion. I went to my mother with the news of my pregnancy, and told her that I wanted to have an abortion. She tried to talk me out of it, not because she knew how developed my baby was, but because she believed it was a life, and because of her love and concern for me. But I was determined, and no one was going to change my mind. Then, as now, a parent had no legal influence over their minor child when it came to abortion or birth control.

My father was the one who paid for the abortion; my mother wouldn't.

My friend's sister was a nurse, and she gave me the name of her ob/gyn. Abortion was liberalized in Colorado several years prior to the 1973 Supreme Court decision, for the "health" of the mother. I now know what a generalization that is: it can mean anything. For me, it meant a half an hour in a psychiatrist's office, telling him that I did not want to have a baby. He recommended in favor of the abortion.

I then had a physical examination by the ob/gyn. My mom went with me, I think in hopes of changing my mind. After the exam, we met with the man who called himself "doctor." He never informed us on the development of my baby. He never informed us of the dangers, the possible complications to me.

I returned the day before my abortion, for the insertion of a laminaria tent to start dilation. I returned home, and the next morning checked into a Denver-area hospital. (Before 1973, all abortions were done in a hospital.) Mine was a twelve-week suction abortion.

I remember laying on the stretcher outside the operating room, everything so sterile and so white. Everyone pretended to be so compassionate. You know, I believe I even had a crush on that man who took my baby—he was my savior! What a fool I was then . . .

I believe I had a moment of hesitation: "Am I doing the right thing? I can't turn back now. And it really is for the best." Then they came and rolled me into the operating room.

They put me to sleep. I spent the night, and then left the next morning. I was a bit numb, but relieved. It was over; now I could get on with my life.

The next Friday night, I was out at a party, having a good time, when I went into labor. It was the most horrible pain I would ever experience. My mom picked me up and rushed me to the emergency room. There I underwent a second suction abortion, to remove the parts left behind the first time. When the pain was gone, I was relieved. The doctor told me that either I had had twins, and he had only gotten one the first time, or that my uterus was tipped and he hadn't reached all the fetal tissue. Whatever it was, I didn't care.

I'm sure I justified my abortion to other women after I aborted; I know I did. I was pro-choice, pro-abortion. Justification is where it's at for aborted women, who refuse to admit their mistakes and accept the truth. I guess a lot of women are scared to admit their mistake or talk about it, because they are scared of how it will affect them. Often, after telling my story to a group, I will have a woman come up to me with tears in her eyes, thanking me for having the courage to tell what she has been unable to tell. They are my sisters. And you watch us; pretty soon that fear and doubt will turn into strength and determination, and we will put an end to this degradation.

Anyway, I didn't think about that procedure consciously, until six years later, when my daughter was born. I say "consciously," because when I met my husband-to-be, a couple of years later, at nineteen, I had a strong wish to have a baby. When we were married, I was twenty-two. I went off the Pill immediately, in hopes of conceiving a child soon. After a year or so of trying to conceive, without luck, I went in for some rather uncomfortable fertility tests. We discovered that my fallopian tubes were blocked with scar tissue. My tubes were cleared, and then I became pregnant. How lucky I was!

During my prenatal visits, I can remember crying each time I heard my daughter's heartbeat. But I still did not consciously recall my abortion. Finally, the time for delivery came, and my water broke. I was in labor for twenty hours, but my uterus did not dilate. They had to take her C-section.

When the nurse handed me my baby for the first time, that is when it hit me: what had I done when I was seventeen? Danielle, my daughter, was such a beautiful miracle. From that day on, I started to read and study about the unborn child and abortion. I have been a completely dedicated, pro-life activist ever since.

I will never know if my physical complications—blocked tubes, incompetent uterus, extraordinarily heavy menstrual periods, endometriosis (scar tissue in my uterus), pain in intercourse—were the result of that abortion. When I tried to recover the medical records of my abortion from that office, I was told that they had been destroyed in a fire in 1972—one year after my abortion. But I believe these are all abortion complications.

Emotionally, I have felt a lot of guilt and remorse since finding out that my baby was completely formed at the time of the abortion, and have felt horrible pain. I have trouble telling my story; at times I will break down while telling it.

One other thing: only several years ago did my mother finally unburden herself to me. I wish she'd had the courage when I was seventeen to tell me her story. She had become pregnant when she was seventeen also, and was taken by an uncle to an abortionist. She got up and ran out because she could not go through with it. She stayed in a Catholic convent home until she gave birth to a little boy, John. She kept him there for two years, in hopes that something would work out so that she could keep him. Knowing it was hopeless, she finally gave him up for adoption. We found him a couple of years ago. He's thirty-seven now, and his name is Jerry. This was really a thrill for me.

I really wish that adoption did not hold such a stigma. It is the greatest show of a mother's love, and the best alternative for a lot of young girls today.

EIGHT

Business Before Medicine

Abortion in America is a commodity, bought and sold for the convenience of the buyer and the profit of the seller. Though abortion utilizes medical knowledge, it is not *medical*—that is, abortions are not being prescribed in order to heal the body or cure illnesses. Instead, over 99 percent of all abortions are provided simply at the request of desperate women who hope that by eliminating their pregnancies they can eliminate their problems. Even in the rare cases where extreme medical problems do exist because of the pregnancy, abortion is still not good medicine.[1] Given the physical and psychological risks of this surgical procedure, an informed and truly "conscientious physician" would almost never prescribe abortion.

For the doctors and clinics engaged in the abortion industry, decisions made about providing abortion services are based, not on medical science, but on consumer demand. Rather than being a medical cure prescribed by a trained physician, abortion has become just another service delivered on request, regardless of the patrons' motives and needs. Abortions are handed out like haircuts, to whomever can pay the price—no questions asked—with the hope that it will improve the client's future social life. Thus, today's abortionist-physicians are like the barber-physicians of the Middle Ages who practiced two trades, being both merchants and healers.

This dual role is a far cry from the medical standards that existed less than twenty years ago. At that time, the dignity of physicians lay in their devotion to protecting human life. This high-minded ideal was summed up by their Hippocratic Oath; they pledged to use their knowledge and skills only to save lives and improve health.

But when some physicians began setting aside the Hippocratic Oath—which specifically forbids participation in abortion or any other prostitution of medical knowledge for nonhealing purposes—they also began to set aside their professionalism. Rather than being medical advisors, they became hired hands. Health care became secondary to consumer demand. Whatever patients asked for, they received, regardless of whether or not it was necessary to their medical health.

Having returned to the pursuit of business before medicine, abortionists have shed much of medicine's traditional code of ethics. These discarded professional standards were once seen as necessary to the dignified provision of health-care services, but now these standards are viewed as obstacles to providing efficient and profitable abortion services. The five most obvious differences that separate abortion services from strictly medical services are as follows:

First, abortion is the only medical procedure that may be advertised. Normally, the medical community condemns advertising for business as being undignified and unprofessional. Advertising is forbidden by all codes of medical conduct, and in some states advertising by physicians is illegal. If a physician were to violate this taboo and advertise his or her services, he would be called before a review board and have his license revoked. Abortionists, however, are the exception. The courts have ruled that no restrictions can be placed on the advertising of abortion services. With such judicial support of their trade, abortion clinics routinely advertise in area newspapers and even on radio. Sometimes in order to attract more business, they advertise their clinic under more than one name. These advertisements are seldom coy and are often distasteful. In *The Village Voice*, for example, abortion clinics advertise their services with pictures of smiling women, flowers, or abstract art. To attract customers away from competitors, many clinics advertise loss leaders such as "free pregnancy tests" or "free contraceptive pills." These "medical" services are advertised alongside "adult entertainment" ads for massage parlors and private clubs.[2]

Second, abortion is the only surgery that cannot be regulated by the government. According to Supreme Court rulings, federal, state, and local governments cannot regulate abortion at all during the first trimester (except to require that it be performed by a physician in a reasonably sterile environment) and may exercise only limited regulation during the second and third trimesters.[3] This prohibition is rationalized as being necessary to prevent infringement on the unique "zone of privacy" patients and doctors share when considering the abortion decision. Ironically, minors may be required by law to have parental permission to have their ears pierced, but no law can require parental permission prior to abortion. States may require waiting periods prior to elective surgeries such as sterilization, but not prior to abortion. Abortion alone is immune from government oversight and consumer protections.

Third, abortion is the only surgery for which the surgeon is not obligated to inform the patient of the possible risks of the procedure, or even of the exact nature of the procedure. Indeed, abortion providers are the only medical personnel who have a "constitutional right" to withhold information even when directly questioned by the patient.[4] This right is supposedly granted so that "conscientious physicians" might "protect" women from being frightened by the risks they face or upset by what the abortion procedure will do to their unborn children. Unfortunately, this "right" to totally control and censure the information given to women also allows paternalistic manipulation and deceit. *Abortion is the only medical procedure for which legal and medical codes deny the patient the right to informed consent.*

Fourth, abortion is the only surgery for which physicians routinely demand payment in advance—generally insisting on cash or money orders. For every other medical service cash-at-the-door is considered not only unprofessional, but so unethical as to be punishable by the loss of surgical privileges.[5]

Fifth, abortion is the only medical procedure for which clinics pay cash awards, or "finder's fees," to those who bring them customers. For example, in one year alone, the Los Angeles Planned Parenthood-Clergy Consultation Service received $250,000 in kickbacks from clinics to which they referred women for abortions.[6] In addition, some clinics pay their counselors "bonuses" for each phone inquiry they handle in which they convince the client to abort at their facility.[7] If a physician offered kickbacks for referrals in any other branch of medicine, his license would be revoked.

Since abortion is provided as a commodity, not as a medical necessity, it is only reasonable that abortionists reject medical standards that would encumber their trade. They are free to promote business before health care. While they present abortion under the guise of medicine (since it lends their commodity an air of respectability and quality that cannot be bought with any amount of advertising), they reject all the obligations, codes, and oaths of medicine that through the centuries have given medicine a place of honor. While they label their clinics as a "medical" service, they operate them as businesses. And, as in any business, profit comes first.

MAXIMIZING PROFITS

One point all abortionists agree on is that abortion is a lucrative business. Dr. David Aberman bragged to one reporter that just by moonlighting at an abortion clinic one day a week, he was able to pocket an extra $30,000 dollars per year.[8] Another abortionist, Dr. Kenneth L. Wright, testified at a court hearing that he received $200 per abortion and was able to perform sixty abortions per day, yielding $12,000 worth of business per day.[9] Still another abortionist, Dr. Arnold Bickham, owner and operator of three midwestern clinics, received $792,266 dollars in 1974 for welfare-paid abortions alone.[10] While no precise profit figures are available, it is not unusual for a physician doing abortions to earn more than eight times the average surgeon's income.[11]

Abortion is big business, as abortion clinic owners are the first to admit. And like other businesses, abortion clinics try to cut costs, increase productivity, and maximize profits.

As in any industry, reducing expensive labor costs is the first avenue towards increasing profit margins. Rather than having high-priced engineers assemble the products they design, low-cost laborers are hired to solder the wires and screw the bolts. Similarly, abortion clinics routinely hire low-cost, unskilled staff members to fulfill the quasi-medical tasks normally performed by physicians or nurses.

Though abortion clinic staff bear the major responsibility for counseling the patient and caring for her health needs, there are no educational or certification requirements for abortion clinic personnel. Instead, most of these low-cost workers are simply hired "off the street" and receive on-the-job training. The depth of knowledge abortion staff members have, therefore, is generally far below the usual standards of the medical and nursing professions.

In the typical abortion clinic, these staff members counsel the patients about the procedure, examine the patients, estimate gestation, perform any required tests (e.g., pregnancy tests and blood samples), record vital signs, prepare the patients for surgery, and assist patients in the recovery room. In almost all cases, the physician does not even see the patient until he enters the room to begin the operation. Often the abortionist doesn't even know the patient's name, or vice versa.[12] By delegating responsibility and minimizing patient/doctor interaction, abortionists free themselves to work solely at performing the actual abortions in the least amount of time possible.

This dependency on unskilled workers frequently results in inferior service. For example, at more than one clinic, investigators have found that records of patients' vital signs were "fudged" or blatantly faked both before and after surgery in order to save time or to make questionable cases look routine.[13] Record keeping is held to the minimum, not only to save time and effort, but also to avoid developing too many records which could be used to incriminate the clinic in the event of a future malpractice suit.[14]

Furthermore, in the rush through so many pregnancy and blood tests, abortion clinic lab tests are notoriously unreliable. Nonpregnant women are judged to be pregnant; Rh-negative women are told that they are O-positive; and tests that are paid for are forgotten or mislaid. A lab technician at one abortion clinic shrugged off such mistakes, saying, "We're just too busy to think of everything."[15]

At some clinics, mass-production techniques are used to increase worker efficiency. Workers pre-fill stockpiles of syringes for later use, and unregistered nursing aides even give the shots.[16]

In the busy assembly-line environment of abortion clinics, sanitation standards often deteriorate. Health inspectors at one abortion clinic found:

- Instruments that were "dirty and worn to the point that the stainless-steel finish had deteriorated, and the instruments were beginning to rust."
- Recovery room beds made with dirty linens.
- "Supposedly sterile instruments" encrusted with "dried matter."
- Instruments being "sterilized" with Tide detergent and surgical equipment, including the suction machine, being "cleansed" with plain water.[17]

Besides relying on low-skilled workers to reduce labor costs, many clinics cut back on the medical double-checks normally used to safeguard against accidents. For example, whenever tissue is removed during hospital surgery, it is routinely examined by a licensed pathologist. Tissues extracted during abortion, on the other hand, are often examined only by an on-the-job-trained staff person, *if at all*. A proper pathological examination would determine if there was a failure to extract all the fetal pieces and placental matter. If this common problem is not identified by a pathological exam, the pieces will be left inside the woman's uterus where they may cause lacerations, rotting, and infection. Incomplete abortions such as these are among the most common post-abortion complications.[18]

At many clinics, costs are cut further by avoiding Rh blood tests and expensive Rhogam shots. Most clinics do not provide this service at all, while others offer Rh testing only at an additional cost. A woman who is untested for the Rh factor and is Rh-sensitive is likely to be sensitized during her abortion. If sensitization occurs, the woman's body will become hostile to a later pregnancy with an Rh-positive baby and try to reject it. Thus a woman who is unknowingly

Rh-sensitized during her abortion faces a future health risk to herself and her "wanted" children.[19]

To cut overhead costs even further, many abortion clinics try to minimize such expensive "frills" as "excessive" emergency equipment. As a result of cost-efficient measures, most clinics do not have transfusion supplies and blood type selections available, even though 2 to 12 percent of aborted women bleed enough to warrant a transfusion.[20]

Cost-saving measures such as those described above are intended to reduce overhead and maximize profits. To increase profits even further, abortionists try to work as fast as possible in order to handle as many patients per day as they can.[21] Besides the obvious risks in hurrying a blind operation which involves sharp instruments and vacuum pressures capable of tearing out organs, the rush for efficiency often results in "cutting corners" on normal sanitation standards. As one operating attendant told Dr. Denes:

> Our surgeons have a technique, even though I shouldn't really say this, where they don't really scrub between cases. They'll scrub once and they'll do a case and they'll go next door to the next room and put on a new gown and gloves. Without scrubbing between. The surgery is only three to five minutes long. . . . A person who is eight weeks in term only needs two minutes' worth of surgery from a good doctor. . . . [22]

Similarly, workers at other clinics have reported physicians doing abortions in their street clothes.[23] Despite the health risks posed by such medical shortcuts, these practices do promote quick and cost-effective delivery of abortion services. When everything is flowing smoothly, the assembly-line routine at abortion clinics operates at maximum efficiency. One patient recalls her abortion experience, saying:

> I could swear that there was only one doctor and he just went down the line giving abortions. I started crying because I could hear that little [suction] machine going on and off. He just kept getting closer and closer. I heard his gloves pop off in the next room and then he came to me. He didn't say a word. He came in and did it and walked out in three minutes. Then he started down the hall again. . . . [24]

When clinics employ more than one abortionist, the work goes even faster. As a former nurse at one clinic reports: "The doctors race each other. Especially on Saturdays, they compete to see who can get the most patients done."[25]

Because of the huge profits to be made in supplying abortions, the competition between metropolitan abortion clinics is often fierce. Some offer "lunch hour" prices or special "discount days" to attract customers, and at least one abortion referral service uses a sound truck to hype its "Abortion Hot Line."[26] Operators of big city clinics openly admit their desire to drive their competitors out of business. As the owner of one abortion clinic told his staff:

> We have to sell abortions. We have to use all of the tactics we can because just like my other businesses [a trucking firm, a pollution-control business, and a real estate sales office] we have competition. Now, we have to go by the rules, but rules have to be broken if we are gonna get things done.[27]

But perhaps the most dangerous cost-cutting activity of abortionists is their failure to provide post-abortion follow-up exams. In most clinics, there is little or no post-abortion counseling by the doctor or the staff, and it is extremely unusual for the physician to examine the woman prior to release. Typically, women are told to wait in the recovery room from fifteen minutes to an hour and are then dismissed. By way of comparison, a woman who has a D&C in a hospital is usually hospitalized for observation for two days.[28]

Furthermore, few clinics offer follow-up exams in the days after the abortion. It is rare for any clinic to insist upon the woman's return—except when they have sold her an additional service such as a fitting for an IUD or scheduled her for a sterilization. Instead, most abortion clinics tell women to return only if they experience excessive bleeding or fever. But even this lax standard is not observed by all. Some clinics, not wanting to be bothered further, instruct patients to "go to your own doctor" if problems arise. But since most women simply want to put the abortion experience behind them as fast as possible, very few return for follow-up exams even when one is offered. And others, rather than admit what they have done to their family doctor, prefer to endure any post-abortion discomfort in shameful silence.[29]

Like most big businesses, the abortion industry resists all government regulations that might reduce their profits. For example, it was not women seeking abortion who opposed the Akron city ordinance which established minimum standards of informed consent; it was the abortion providers. In *Akron v. Akron Center for Reproductive Health,* abortionists objected to an ordinance that would have required them to inform women of the health risks of abortion, alternatives to abortion, and what the procedure entailed, including facts about the relative development of their fetus. This information, the abortionists complained, would only discourage women from aborting and have a "chilling" effect on their business. Like any salesmen, abortionists wanted to emphasize only the "good" side of their product.

Similarly, when pro-life sidewalk counselors were sued in California, it was not women seeking abortions who sued complaining that they were being presented with alternatives; it was the owners of the abortion clinic. In this case, the abortionists sued sidewalk counselors for $50,000 worth of "lost customers."[30]

In efforts to prevent any state regulation of abortion, abortion providers have repeatedly gone to court to attack and defeat twenty-four-hour waiting requirements, parental and spousal notification requirements, and state restrictions on welfare-subsidized abortions. They oppose the twenty-four-hour waiting period because it provided too much time for reflection and hindered "impulse sales." In striking down requirements for parental and spousal notification, abortionists have succeeded in separating scared and vulnerable young women from those who might support them and provide them with alternatives to abortion.[31] But their motive for seeking to force state Medicaid programs to pay for abortions is most obvious of all: it is easier to make large profits from the government than from the poor.

CLINICS OF DECEIT: AN INSIDE LOOK AT THE ABORTION INDUSTRY

In the fall of 1978, the *Chicago Sun-Times* ran a series of articles that shocked the state. Entitled "The Abortion Profiteers," the series detailed the results of a five-month undercover investigation of four abortion clinics. The clinics infiltrated by Better Government Association (BGA) investigators and *Sun-Times* reporters were four of the largest in Illinois, all located on Chicago's high-rent "Magnificent Mile." Together, these four clinics performed over one-third of all abortions done in Illinois. By all outward appearances, these were big-time, first-class abortion clinics. But undercover investigators found nothing "first-class" about them. Instead, they found callous treatment of patients, lies, greed, injuries, and death.

In order to cushion the impact of these revelations, *Sun-Times* editorials went to great lengths to insist that the abortion right was a sacred one, which should not be curtailed. The abuses its investigators had uncovered, the paper insisted, could be corrected by better and more vigilant state regulation of abortion clinics. Furthermore, while decrying the profiteering of the four clinics investigated, the *Sun-Times* boldly insisted that most abortion clinics are probably better and safer than the four which they had investigated.

Unfortunately, there is little reason for this optimism. By looking at the list of "abuses" that the *Sun-Times* and BGA investigators uncovered, we will find that most of the practices condemned were perfectly legal, are common throughout the abortion industry, and years later are *still* outside the scope of government regulation.

Abortions for Nonpregnant Women   *Sun-Times* reporters witnessed dozens of cases in which abortions were performed on non-pregnant women. At one clinic, an investigator found that 12 percent of all abortions were performed on women with negative or indeterminate pregnancy test results. As pointed out by the *Sun-Times* reporters, these nonpregnant women were needlessly exposed to the physical and psychological risks of abortion.[32]

Oddly enough, abortions for nonpregnant women is neither illegal nor even uncommon. Such abortions would be illegal only if clinics attempt to profit by *deliberately and knowingly* deceiving nonpregnant women into believing that they are pregnant. But if there is a "reasonable suspicion" that a woman is pregnant—despite negative or inconclusive test results—then doing an abortion is perfectly legal. Indeed, the accepted practice among many professional abortionists is to always abort "suspect" pregnancies. They argue that it is medically safer for the woman to perform an early abortion rather than delay it until tests become conclusive. Furthermore, they insist, performing an early abortion whenever there is a "reasonable suspicion" of pregnancy also saves their patients a great deal of money, time, and worry.

At one national abortion conference, for example, Dr. Ronald Pion, an abortionist from Hawaii, argued that physicians should "protect" women from feeling they killed a fetus by *never* doing a pregnancy test. If a woman could not be sure whether or not an actual abortion had taken place, he argued, she could not feel guilty.[33] At the same conference, New York physician Irwin Kaiser supported Pion's thesis. While admitting that abortion posed inherent risks, Dr. Kaiser questioned the importance of confirming the existence of a pregnancy, saying, "[W]e see no reason at all to be apprehensive about doing a suction evacuation on a patient who isn't pregnant." He added that for the nonpregnant woman, abortion is "probably a very uneventful phenomenon."[34]

Besides "protecting" women from guilt feelings, the most popular defense for doing an abortion when pregnancy is not confirmed is to "be on the safe side." Early abortions are safer abortions and less costly. If a pregnancy is merely suspected, a physician may honestly perform a "menstrual extraction" (a very early abortion which differs from normal suction abortions only in that the pregnancy is not confirmed). Many respected medical authorities even believe that doctors should encourage women to have regular "menstrual extractions" instead of waiting to confirm pregnancy. The problem with this policy of being "on the safe side" is that most of these procedures are unnecessary. Studies have shown that 80 percent of these early abortion procedures are done on nonpregnant women.[35]

Finally, it is not a crime to inaccurately diagnose a pregnancy unless it is done with *intent* to defraud—a very difficult allegation to prove. And since most abortion professionals would testify that abortion of nonpregnant women is a "normal risk" of the procedure, it is doubtful that any federal, state, or local regulation of pregnancy testing would be upheld by the courts, since such regulation would encumber "accepted medical practices" and violate the zone of privacy between "the woman and her physician."[36] Furthermore, even if some sort of regulation were upheld, it would be largely unenforceable unless state inspectors reviewed the results of each and every pregnancy test performed.

In sum, abortion of nonpregnant women is not uncommon. It is not a practice limited only to "shady" abortion profiteers, but occurs in clinics around the country. According to one estimate, as many as 10 percent of all women who receive "abortions" are not actually pregnant.[37]

Exceeding Gestational Limits   According to the Illinois law in force at the time of the *Sun-Times* exposé, second- and third-trimester abortions could only be performed in hospitals. Outpatient clinics were only allowed to do first-trimester abortions. But undercover investigators for the *Sun-Times* reported the "shocking" facts that clinics were doing abortions beyond the twelve-week cutoff date set by state law. But while these "violations" of state abortion laws were a "shocking" revelation when printed on the front page of a major newspaper, the fact that late-term abortions were being performed in clinics was hardly news to any professional abortion observer. Instead, late-term clinic abortions were an accepted reality outside the scope of any practical control.

There are two reasons for this. First, honest mistakes in estimating the gestational period of a pregnancy occur all the time. But once again, it is not a crime for a physician to make an honest mistake in estimating how far a pregnancy has progressed. It is a crime only if his *intent* is to defraud the patient.

Second, the Illinois statute limiting outpatient clinics to first-trimester abortions was of questionable validity, as abortionists well knew. Numerous abortion clinics had successfully challenged similar restrictions in other states. The issue was settled in 1983 when the Supreme Court ruled in favor of the clinics. Today, all outpatient clinics have a "constitutionally protected right" to perform second-trimester abortions.[38]

Abortions Were Not Performed by "Trained" Abortionists
The *Sun-Times* series shocked readers with the warning that many abortions were being performed by "moonlighting residents [and] general practitioners with little or no training in women's medicine." Once again, however, this "revelation" was hardly unique to the four Chicago clinics investigated. Instead, the use of such "untrained" abortionists is perfectly legal and commonplace.

First, the use of medical residents is an accepted practice in all areas of medicine, and abortion is not an exception. Residents are routinely allowed to perform minor surgery in teaching hospitals around the country. How else are they to learn? And since abortion proponents all insist that abortion is a "minor surgery," there is no reason to exclude qualified medical students from doing abortions.

Second, in regard to general practitioners not specially trained in women's medicine, there are no regulations limiting abortion to gynecologists. Indeed, the Supreme Court ruled that the only qualification necessary to perform an abortion is that a person be a medical doctor. Only nonphysicians can be excluded from performing abortions. Attempts to limit abortions to medical specialists (such as obstetricians or gynecologists) have been routinely struck down by the courts as being "unconstitutional."[39]

While it is true that many practicing abortionists have no special training to qualify them to perform abortions, the Constitution as interpreted by the Supreme Court does not allow for any such distinctions in training. Because of this "constitutional law," abortionists are essentially free of oversight by state and local governments or even by state medical boards. Even if an abortionist causes numerous complications or deaths, there is no mechanism to prevent him from continuing to perform abortions—short of imprisonment for criminal neglect.[40]

Callousness Toward Patients   Of all the things that they witnessed, *Sun-Times* investigators seemed most distressed at the discovery that abortionists were "cold, mechanical," and even "sadistic," and often operated with what seemed to be excessive speed.[41] But once more, what these investigators found was not unusual or unique. Instead, as we will see, these traits are common to abortionists at every major abortion clinic.

First, as to the charge of excessive speed, it must be granted that full-time abortionists achieve greater speed with practice. An obstetrician who does only an occasional abortion is unlikely to operate as fast as a full-time professional. In addition, doing abortion after abortion is a monotonous routine, so abortionists tend to develop a pace or rhythm to their surgeries. It is not uncommon for a professional abortionist to do an abortion in less than five minutes, though such speed was seen as shocking by the *Sun-Times* reporters.[42]

Second, the *Sun-Times* investigators reported numerous cases where the attending physician was insensitive and rude to patients about to undergo an abortion. For example, in one case the abortionist walked into the operating room and addressed the patient saying, "What do we have here? Ah, too much weight," and proceeded to do the abortion. Another used foul language and shouted at his patient when she began to scream in pain.[43]

But again, it is not a crime for an abortionist to be "cold and mechanical," or even callous and "sadistic." Instead, from all reports, such attitudes seem to be much more the rule than the exception.[44] Indeed, as we will see later in this chapter, the pressure of doing frequent abortions tends to *make* abortionists callous and "mechanical." Truly compassionate physicians do not have the endurance to keep at the grueling and ugly work of abortion for very long. Only the "tough" (as in "thick-skinned") survive, and it is these abortionists who perform the vast majority of abortions. This inevitable result of the abortion business cannot be corrected by newspaper exposés denouncing "sadism" or by some law requiring "compassion."

Complications and Deaths   *Sun-Times* reporters shocked their readers with reports of aborted women suffering from complications such as excessive bleeding, incomplete abortions, infections, and internal damage, as well as a number of unreported abortion-related deaths. But once again, this shocking "disclosure" was shocking only because it made the headlines of a major newspaper.

Complications and unreported deaths resulting from legal abortions are not unusual. Complications are an inherent and "accepted" risk of the abortion procedure. Whether abortions are performed by incompetent interns or star-studded surgeons, a significant number of complications will always occur. Unless an abortionist intentionally does harm to his patients or is guilty of criminal neglect, the state can do nothing to regulate his practice simply because he has a high complication rate.[45] In fact, in the state of Illinois, as in most states, no physician has ever lost his license because of complications (or even deaths) resulting from his legally induced abortions.[46]

When the above "abuses" were disclosed by *Sun-Times* reporters, loud cries for reform resulted. The Illinois governor called for the establishment of special committees, and there were temporary attempts at change. But in the end, *nothing* changed. In fact, despite all the good intentions of reformers, nothing *could* be changed. All of the "abuses" cited by the *Sun-Times* are within the "zone of privacy" which the Supreme Court established between abortionists and their clients. No reform was possible because any form of state interference would have been an unconstitutional infringement on the super-rights of abortionists.

In 1984 a spokesperson for the Illinois Department of Public Health was unable to identify any lasting reform implemented following the *Sun-Times* exposé six years earlier. The only attempt at change had been a cosmetic redrafting of health and sanitation standards for "licensed ambulatory center treatment facilities" (abortion clinics). With these new sanitation standards, abortion clinics are now inspected four times per year, but these inspections occur *only* after notifying the clinic in advance of the inspection date.[47] Unfortunately, advance-notice inspections are practically useless. With advanced notice, clinic operators take special pains to "clean up their acts" prior to the inspection. Therefore, it is extremely unlikely that these one-day, advance-notice inspections will ever uncover the types of abuses witnessed by reporters who worked undercover *in clinics* for a period of *five months.*

The *Sun-Times* series had even less effect on the careers of the shady abortion providers who were the targets of the articles. Of all the "sadistic" physicians accused of "profiteering" in the series, all but one still practice medicine—and provide abortions—in Illinois.[48] But even that one exception, Dr. Ming Kow Hah, did *not* lose his license because of the incompetent or dangerous abortions he may have performed. Instead, it was learned that Dr. Hah had previously lost his medical license in Michigan due to allegations that he had inappropriately sold 384 prescriptions of a rare addictive drug, which was later sold illegally on the street. Three years later, after numerous delays and appeals during which he continued to perform abortions in Illinois, Dr. Hah's Illinois medical license was revoked on the basis of the Michigan drug-related charges. While the *Sun-Times* accused Dr. Hah of giving the "most painful abortions in the city," his Illinois license was revoked, *not* because of his abortion methods, but because of his past record with fraudulent drug prescriptions.[49]

Of the four clinics targeted by the *Sun-Times* investigation, only one was closed when it allowed its license to expire.[50] In this instance, this clinic's owner, Dr. Arnold Bickham, moved his base of operations to an abortion clinic in Indiana. But by 1984, Dr. Bickham had returned to Chicago where he continues to perform abortions today.[51]

A second clinic investigated by the *Sun-Times* closed a little over a year later. The voluntary shutdown of the Chicago Loop Mediclinic was due primarily to financial insolvency. The owners allowed the state license for their clinic to expire, and under pressure from the state, agreed not to renew their abortion activities in Illinois.[52]

The other two abortion clinics, Biogenetics and Michigan Avenue Medical Center, branded as "abortion mills" by the *Sun-Times*, continue to operate under the same management, with many of the same "cold, mechanical" physicians.

Even if it could have been proven that any of the above clinics were operating at standards below those of the abortion industry in general, it is doubtful whether any state regulation could have been enforced to correct the perceived deficiencies. For example, when the Chicago Board of Health attempted to shut down another clinic where a number of serious complications and deaths had occurred, the owner appealed the decision to the Supreme Court and won. In another case, when it was discovered that an abortion clinic was operating without a state license, the owner was fined only $500 dollars. Three months later, this same operator was granted a license to resume his business.[53]

In the aftermath of the *Sun-Times* exposé, one of the clinic owners, Dr. Arnold Bickham, accused the reporters of malicious "innuendo." He charged that the series was "sensationalism . . . designed to sell newspapers and assist in building esteem for individual reporters who are muckrakers and exponents of yellow journalism at its very worst."[54] The view that the *Sun-Times* stories were exaggerated was shared by many respected members of the medical fraternity. For example, Dr. Clifton Reeder, the president of the Chicago Medical Society, saw "no great urgency" to the problems cited in the abortion series. According to Dr. Reeder, the charges against Chicago's abortion clinics had been "blown all out of proportion to reality."[55]

While we agree with the *Sun-Times* that the abortions provided in the four investigated clinics were indeed dangerous and dehumanizing, we must also agree that Dr. Bickham's accusations are largely correct. The "Abortion Profiteers" articles were sensationalized and biased. These articles were looking for scapegoats and depicted them in the darkest manner possible. The *Sun-Times* investigation discovered little—if anything—that was illegal, except for a few violations of sanitation codes. All they truly did was to give a close-up look at a very ugly business: abortion. They highlighted all the lurid aspects and human flaws typical of the business of providing mass abortion on demand. But these flaws are not unique to four Chicago clinics. They are common to any abortion clinic, and especially to large abortion clinics, which though highly profitable, are also busy and unwieldy.[56]

The *Sun-Times* abortion series was muckraking. But undercover investigators "raking" for scandal in any abortion facility would find the same unsavory "muck," the same callousness, the same greed, deception, and pain that were the grist which sold the *Sun-Times* series. It is "muck," but it is also very true and very common. What is unfortunate is that undercover investigators were placed in only four of Chicago's thirteen abortion clinics, only four of Illinois's twenty-four clinics, only four of the nation's four thousand abortion facilities. The *Sun-Times* series brought little or no reform to abortion practices in Chicago or Illinois. Occasional investigations by other reporters have proved equally ineffective in producing any lasting results, even though investigators consistently find the same abuses.

On April 21, 1991, CBS's "60 Minutes" did an exposé on the Hillview Abortion Clinic in Suitland, Maryland. The story was prompted by the case of Suzanne Logan who had an abortion at the clinic in 1989 and was given anesthesia by a clinic aide, not a doctor, or even a nurse. Suzanne suffered severe brain damage. She is almost completely paralyzed and unable to speak. The clinic did not have any functional emergency equipment or medicine to treat Suzanne at the time of the complications because abortion clinics are unregulated in Maryland. The owner of the clinic, Barbara Lofton, who frequently uses the unwarranted title of "Doctor," admitted that "accidents happen" and that a previous "accident" had even been fatal for a previous client. Despite numerous malpractice suits, the unlicensed clinic continues to perform abortions.[57]

Another recent investigation was sparked by *The Miami Herald*'s Sunday supplement *Tropic*, which on September 7, 1989, published an exposé on the shady Dadeland Medical Center. The list of abuses and horrors almost exactly paralleled those cited in the *Sun-Times* series from 1978. The story prompted the State Department of Health and Rehabilitation Services (HRS) to begin inspections of over fifty clinics during the next three months. Rampant abuses and health risks were discovered, resulting in the temporary closing of numerous clinics. U. S. District Court hearings, however, upheld an injunction against any HRS regulation of "laboratory services, housekeeping, and even sanitation regulation" on the basis that such regulations were an unconstitutional infringement on abortionists' rights to practice medicine.[58]

THE SELLING OF ABORTION

Like any other commercial business, the abortion industry has a specialized sales force and a carefully defined marketing strategy. The sales force is composed of abortion counselors who "help" women to make their abortion choice. The marketing strategy is to tell their clients as little as possible—and never anything negative—about their product. The sales and marketing divisions of the abortion industry were described in lurid detail in the *Chicago Sun-Times* abortion exposé. In that series, undercover reporters charged that at "Michigan Ave. abortion mills, women who are hired to counsel don't—they're paid to sell." And the selling of abortion, they observed, included "sophisticated pitches and deceptive promises."[59]

At one of the clinics investigated, slick brochures assured women that "From admission to recovery, patient ease and comfort are first considerations. She is encouraged to ask questions, share feelings or misgivings." But in actual practice, the same clinic gave its counselors these three guidelines: 1) "Don't tell [the] patient the abortion will hurt." 2) "Don't discuss [the abortion] procedure or the instruments to be used in any detail." 3) "Don't answer too many questions."[60]

The *Sun-Times* reporters criticized this type of "counseling" as superficial and deceptive. On both counts, the reporters were right. But this kind of counseling is not only common throughout the country, it is the accepted and recommended philosophy of the abortion industry. According to that counseling philosophy, the patient is to be "protected" from information that might discourage her or make her choice more difficult. Instead of "confusing" them with facts, women are to be eased *through* their abortion choice in a way that will minimize any doubts and regrets.

This philosophy of supportive counseling was developed at a 1971 conference for abortion providers held in Los Angeles. Some of the statements made during a special symposium devoted to the "proper" role of abortion counseling are particularly revealing. For example, one nurse told her colleagues that "whether rich or poor, few women really wanted an abortion."[61] Therefore, she suggested, it was important for counselors to avoid conveying any attitudes that would embarrass, humiliate, or frighten patients out of their reluctantly chosen abortion. Counselors were advised to be particularly careful about their choice of words. They were told never to refer to the procedure as "abortion," but instead to use euphemistic expressions. Another speaker, nurse Henrietta Blackmon, advised that counselors and nurses should be able and willing to describe the procedure, but should never describe the abortion instruments, since this might upset the client. Above all, she warned, counselors should be on guard to keep their own true feelings in check:

> If you say, "Suck out the baby," you may easily generate or increase trauma; say instead, "Empty the uterus," or "We will scrape the lin-

ing of the uterus," but never "We will scrape away the baby." These may seem very, very insignificant to us, but to the patient it can really imply that you are using a judgment, and quite often we are not aware of what we are saying. We have to be very, very sensitive, and very, very aware of what words we are using to describe the procedures used. Use the word *fetus:* This is a fetus; this is not a "baby."[62]

According to these experts, who were establishing the counseling standards to be used across the nation, an abortion counselor's only purpose is to act as "facilitator and participant" in the abortion process—a compassionate friend to help the aborting woman face the unknown and overcome her doubts. Counselors, they warned, were *not* to urge reevaluation of either the client's needs or her decision to abort; they were only to make it as easy as possible for the woman to carry out her decision. Any other form of counseling that challenged her decision, provided new information about risks or fetal development, or dwelled on options, would only increase doubts, anxiety, and guilt. Experience showed, they insisted, that women did not want to be talked out of their abortion decisions. Therefore, the role of the counselor was to provide emotional support, explain the clinic's routine, describe the procedure in a neutral manner, and "—[only] if the doctor approved—warn the patient of the possibility of future sterility." Finally, the counselor should reassure the patient that the decision to abort was good, ethical, and acceptable.[63]

Measured by the standards of respected experts, the counseling offered at the Michigan Avenue clinics was not improper. While their activities might be interpreted as "selling" abortions (and indeed that is what it is), abortion professionals defend such counseling on the grounds that it "protects" women and makes the abortion experience as "easy" as possible.

One factor that allows abortion counselors to get away with telling so little is that many women seeking abortions are vulnerable, frightened, and insecure. In one case, for example, a woman who was counseled in a group situation had several questions she wanted to ask, but she did not, saying, "I was afraid to ask them with all those people around. Maybe it was best I didn't know anyway."[64] Feeling frightened and dependent on others, women seeking abortion are generally at a loss for the assertiveness needed to insist on complete answers.

Second, many women do not know what questions they should ask, especially when it comes to complications. In general, the most that they are told is that "There are only slight risks to this procedure, like in any operation. It's nothing to worry about." The vagueness of this reassurance prevents women from asking questions such as: "Will dilation damage my cervix? Will a 'slight infection' reduce my ability to conceive in the future?"

But worst of all is the lack of counseling about fetal development; it *never* occurs. Information about the stage of development of the fetus to be aborted is available at any local library, but never at the local abortion clinic. To abortion counselors, discussion of fetal development is absolutely taboo. It will only upset their patients, they argue, and increase the guilt women face. Counselors are so concerned with "protecting" women from these facts that distortions and lies are an accepted method of easing the patient's concerns.

An example of such "reassuring" counseling is described by Julie Engel, who received an abortion when she was three months pregnant:

> Then I asked, "Is abortion a threat to future pregnancies?"
> "Women often have D&C's [dilation and curettage] to help them get pregnant," was the perfunctory answer.
> "Are there psychological problems?" I continued.
> "Hardly ever. Don't worry," I was told. . . .
> "What does a three-month-old fetus look like?"
> "Just a clump of cells," she answered matter-of-factly.[65]

In the years that followed, Julie Engel discovered that she was no longer able to conceive a wanted pregnancy. And then one day she saw some pictures of fetal development.

> When I saw that a three-month-old "clump of cells" had fingers and toes and was a tiny, perfectly formed baby, I became really hysterical. I'd been lied to and misled, and I'm sure thousands of other women are being just as poorly informed and badly served. To prove it, John [her husband] and I visited most every clinic in Cleveland. I pretended I was pregnant and asked for guidance. What we heard was incredible. One counselor told us the fetus did not begin to resemble a human being until seven months; another said five months, and so it went.[66]

Karen Yates, a counselor at Washington, DC's Southeast Crisis Pregnancy Center, serves a primarily black community. Yates has found that for most of the young women she serves, facts about fetal development—facts about exactly *what* they would be destroying by having an abortion—are often the "deciding factor" in a woman's abortion decision. But she also reports that 95 percent of the women she counsels were told by some pro-abortion advocate, their doctors, family planning counselors, or someone else that the fetus is just a "clump of cells," that it is not really alive. But when Yates and others fully explain the biological facts, the vast majority of women choose not to abort.[67]

Abortion counselors not only avoid the biological facts of fetal development, they also avoid all the moral dimensions of the abortion choice. Instead of helping women to explore their own views on the ethical question, "Do you believe abortion is a moral solution to your problem?" counselors focus attention on utilitarian questions such as, "Do you want to have a baby? Are you ready to be a parent?" In the long run, however, it is the answer to the ethical question which matters most. It is the question, "Did I do the *right* thing?" that aborted women must live with for the rest of their lives.

Examining this question is especially important since, as shown in previous chapters, the vast majority of women considering an abortion are uncertain about the morality of what they are doing. Abortion clinics, however, not only avoid such questions, they actively urge clients to suppress and deny their feelings whenever they have doubts. At one clinic, for example, when a woman voiced her concern that abortion might be killing, the counselor said, "Don't think of it as killing. Think of it as taking blood out of your uterus to get your periods going again."[68]

Any counseling that fails to resolve these moral concerns about abortion is leaving a time bomb of guilt and self-condemnation buried in the woman's psyche. But abortion clinics deny any responsibility for helping their clients explore their moral misgivings. Instead they emphasize discussion of personal desires rather than personal values. Their avoidance of "moral issues" not only makes the job of abortion counseling easier, it improves clinic profits. For according to one study, women who approach abortion as a moral choice are much more likely to keep their pregnancies, while those who approach abortion in terms of furthering their self-interests are more likely to abort.[69]

The desire to "protect" women from the biological facts and moral issues of abortion is all part of the paternalistic attitude of abortion providers, which automatically presumes that abortion is the "best" solution for women in trouble, especially if the women they serve are young and destitute. Instead of giving women all the available information and alternatives so that women can decide for themselves, counselors screen the information given so as to "guide" their clients to the "best" solution (and most profitable) which they, the counselors, have already picked out for them. This patronizing concern often becomes the doorway through which the counselor's unconscious biases influence his or her recommendations. Thus, a young black girl who would really like to keep her child but doesn't know how is likely to become a victim of a biased abortion equation because of her age, race, and income level. Recognizing that in our society the cards are stacked against this girl, the compassionate counselor sincerely believes that abortion is "best," despite the girl's "naive" desire to keep her baby.

Once counselors decide what is "best" for their clients, it is an easy matter to influence the clients' final decisions toward the predetermined outcome. Counseling, in such cases, downplays or even denies the availability of support resources and instead concentrates on the "tremendous burdens" involved in raising a child. Such counseling sessions encourage the women to believe that abortion is the only "safe and easy" solution and "the only practical thing to do." Explaining how she handles such cases, abortion counselor Betty Orr of Preterm in Cleveland says, "I ask them who is going to take care of the baby while they're in school. Where are they going to get money for clothes?"[70] Faced with antagonistic questions rather than offers of affirmation and support, frightened and vulnerable young women are easily convinced that abortion is their *only* choice—even when it is a choice contrary to their real desires.

When counseling teenage girls, many family planning and abortion counselors are so confident that *they* have the "best" solutions, they envision themselves as "better" parents than the girl's own natural parents. Seeing themselves as "substitute parents," they jealously guard their "right" to decide what is "best" for their troubled girls. Wanting no interference from the "outside," many clinics will go to great lengths to "protect" a young girl from family members who might encourage birth rather than abortion.[71]

One last factor common to abortion counseling throughout the country is the high priority placed on providing birth control advice. While abortion counseling is weak in describing the procedure and its risks, totally negligent in describing fetal development, and often paternalistic in the extreme, it is *always* thorough and detailed when it comes to recommending and selling birth control devices.

The emphasis on urging contraceptive protection has long been an established part of abortion counseling. The clear intention of such contraceptive counseling has always been to help clients avoid the need for repeat abortions.[72] But while the contraceptive push seems to be a sensible approach to preventing abortions, the recommendation seems odd coming from those who insist that abortion is "safe and easy." For if abortion is such a "good" solution, why do abortion counselors find it desirable to prevent repeat abortions? Do they think there is something wrong with abortion after all, despite all they say? The answer is yes. Despite what they tell their clients, abortion counselors do not really approve of abortion at all.

ABORTION COUNSELORS:
THE PEOPLE BEHIND THE RHETORIC

In *The Ambivalence of Abortion,* Linda Bird Francke interviewed a Planned Parenthood abortion counselor who was frustrated and angry at repeat aborters, saying:

> I have one kid here, seventeen, who's just had her third abortion. . . . I want to beat the s—t out of her. I want to put her through the d—n wall. "What's the matter with you," I say to her. Every time she thinks a relationship is going on the rocks, she gets pregnant. Then she has an abortion and starts up a new relationship. She swears every time she has an abortion she won't — again. I tell her —ing isn't the problem, protection is.[73]

The reason for this anger lies in the ambivalent feelings abortion counselors and staff have toward abortion. Working side by side with the employees at an abortion hospital in preparation for her book *In Necessity and Sorrow,* Dr. Magda Denes describes the workers as "dedicated and full of doubt, committed but uneasy."[74]

Like most of the women who come to them seeking abortions, abortion clinic workers are also uncertain about the morality of what they are doing. On a personal level, this uncertainty places a constant stress on the consciences of the workers. Furthermore, on a professional level, this stress is compounded by the requirement that they hide their uncertainties in order to "protect" their clients from additional doubts.

The tension between what they feel and how they must act is revealed in a number of interviews with abortion counselors. One counselor, for example, recognizes the high level of guilt aborting women face, saying:

> A lot of people say they're killing their baby. You get a lot of that. Some people afterwards get very upset and say, "I killed my baby." Or even before, they say, "My circumstances are such that I can't keep it, but I'm killing my baby."[75]

As a counselor, it is her job to alleviate and deny this guilt. But when asked about her own personal views, she too is ambivalent:

> Well, they are killing a baby. I mean, they are killing something that would develop into maturity, but under the circumstances, that's necessary and probably better for the baby. You have to realize that these children would be unwanted and a lot of times uncared for, so it's much better that they are not brought into the world. . . .[76]

Yet another abortion counselor, a college student who was previously aborted herself, unwillingly believes abortion is murder, saying:

> I see more of murder the further along they get. Although inside me I know it's murder from the beginning, because there is the fact that when it is conceived, it is a potential human being, potential person, potential life, potential organism, or whatever you want to call it. There's just so much terminology: is it a human, is it a person, is it a being, is it a life or organism or whatever? I believe that, yes, it is a potential life or being, person, but at the same time it is not independent of the mother and it's not able to live by itself. Until we can reach that point where we can really say that, yes, there is a unit out there that will maintain its life, it's really the mother that has the decision over the life. . . . Does that make sense?[77]

The first of these counselors rationalizes "killing a baby" as necessary to protect the child from a life of potential misery. The second counselor, on the other hand, rationalizes the "murder" of abortion by relying on the pro-abortion doublespeak which even she doesn't fully understand or have much faith in. In both cases, abortion is recognized as destructive and evil, but is excused because it is "necessary" for either the freedom of women or for the sake of the "unwanted" children. But as we will see, these rationalizations are extremely fragile. They are based in the blind *hope* that abortion has redeeming qualities, rather than in observation or follow-up of the patients they profess to have "helped."

Two distinct questions must be asked about counselors and other abortion clinic staff. First, what motivates them to work in an abortion clinic? And second, how do they cope with the stress of daily participation in the "evil necessity" of abortion?

The question of motivation has many answers. Many see their work at an abortion clinic simply as a job, an opportunity to make a living.[78] Others see it as an opportunity to help women or as their contribution to the cause of women's liberation. Still others see their abortion-related work simply as a temporary stop on the way to other career goals. As one counselor confided:

> You know, I mean it's gory, and it's really a sad situation to see the abortions and I have my own opinion about how I feel about abortion . . . [but to] me it's a job and it's the closest I could get to what I really wanted to do. . . . I want to be a nurse-midwife.[79]

While sympathetic to the motives of the abortion counselors she interviews, Dr. Denes is skeptical of their stability and qualifications: "All of them are single, young, exposed and extremely vulnerable themselves to the pitfalls that have brought the majority of patients to this hospital."⁸⁰ One wonders what these immature counselors can offer the frightened and vulnerable women they are supposed to "counsel." In fact, as even most abortion counselors admit, they are able to offer the women they serve nothing more than companionship. Rather than counseling patients to reach mature and thoughtful decisions, they are the blind leading the blind—able to offer comfort and encouragement but not guidance or information.

Furthermore, what abortion counselors lack in personal maturity is not compensated for by training. In fact, none of the counselors at Denes's hospital were professional mental health workers. They all received only on-the-job training, a common practice at most abortion facilities. But on-the-job training, at this one facility at least, was carefully limited so as to isolate the counselors from the graphic truth of abortion: "Not a single one among them has ever seen a D&C performed nor watched the expulsion of a fetus."⁸¹ Thus, what the counselors did not know could not be inadvertently revealed to the patients.

Besides those motivated to work in abortion clinics because of their desire for a job, their desire to "help people," or their desire to advance the cause of "freedom of choice," there is one more class of workers drawn to work at abortion clinics: aborted women themselves.

It is not uncommon for aborted women to return to clinics to work as counselors or in other capacities. Many clinics, in fact, prefer to hire aborted women since they are more likely to empathize with the situations that compel women to abort. But the willingness of aborted women to work in abortion clinics does not necessarily mean that they were satisfied with their own abortions or have come to terms with their own doubts and ambivalence. Instead, it means exactly the opposite.

Aborted women who work as counselors are almost invariably victims of a disturbing abortion experience themselves. On one level, they choose to work in clinics in the hope of preventing other women from experiencing the traumas they had faced and may still be facing. But on a deeper level, they return to the abortion clinic in the hope of easing the guilt and trauma they themselves are still experiencing.⁸²

For many women who have been deeply disturbed by their own abortion experiences, working as an abortion counselor is a way of hardening themselves to their own unforgettable experiences. By "returning to the scene of the crime," some women seek to reenact their own abortion decisions through the decisions of others. In this sense, the aborted counselor has a high stake in the final decision of her clients. By watching others choose abortion for the same reasons that she did, she is able to reaffirm the "rightness" of her own decision. In contrast, however, when an aborted counselor witnesses a client suddenly choose against abortion and boldly accept the challenges of an unplanned pregnancy, the counselor may become cynical, ashamed, and envious.[83]

Two WEBA women who had previously worked in counseling or hospital situations that brought them into contact with women seeking abortions have described how the immersion in abortion can be soothing to the troubled conscience. According to one, "I found that in talking to other women about abortion, their decisions to abort satisfied something in me. It made me feel better about what I had done. . . . [It] strengthened my own decisions to abort." Another woman found comfort in being surrounded by people constantly repeating pro-abortion rhetoric as justification for their work. "There's safety in numbers," she says. "I didn't feel really awful about my abortion as long as everyone where I worked was patting me on the back."[84]

This brings us to our second question: How do abortion clinic workers cope with the daily stress of participating in the "evil necessity" of abortion?

The first line of defense lies in the unity of purpose abortion workers share. Relying on "safety in numbers," they close ranks and reaffirm each other and the "good" that they do. Among them is an unwritten agreement never to openly question what they do, never to admit their doubts, and *never*, under any circumstances, to discuss the destruction of the fetuses over which they preside. Denes calls this collective defense mechanism a "conspiracy of denial."[85]

Denes is adamantly pro-choice, but as a clinical psychologist, she is keenly aware of the duplicity that keeps abortion workers from going insane:

> It seems that none who work here can witness the extinction of a segment of the future generation without guilt and fear. The word "murder" surfaces again and again, and it sticks on the tongue like a searing coal of fire that one knows will do further damage whether it is swallowed or spat. A struggle evolves between reason and conscience, between pragmatic morality and one's own commitment to all human seed. With the struggle there also evolves a shamefaced solution: "I do not decide for these women, I just do my job"; "I give them what they want"; "I only help out." As if disclaiming responsibility could make one free of it.[86]

The importance of denying the reality of abortion sheds additional light on why abortion clinics consistently oppose informed-consent requirements, especially requirements for discussing the relevant stage of fetal development. In refusing to provide informed consent, abortion providers are ostensibly "protecting" the woman seeking abortion from disturbing and "confusing" facts. But it may also be that abortion personnel are seeking to protect *themselves* from the same disturbing facts. The requirement to tell women the facts about fetal development, day after day, would destroy the wall of denial that holds clinics together. By focusing attention on the unborn, informed-consent requirements would not only compel women to consider the moral consequences of their acts, but would also force abortion counselors to face their *own* moral doubts about abortion.

After denial, the second line of defense for abortion workers is rationalization. Undoubtedly, the most common rationalization is the belief that despite all the blood and murder they witness, their work at the clinic somehow improves the lives of the trapped and vulnerable women they serve. By sacrificing one life, they hope, the quality of another's life is improved.[87]

Because their own sanity and "job satisfaction" rests on the belief that abortion is good and worthwhile, it is crucial for counselors to believe that the women they serve really do *need* the abortions and really do benefit from them. This is the source of the prejudgment by which counselors always believe that abortion is the "best" solution for their clients. But the lurking fear that maybe their clients' lives are not improved keeps counselors from looking too closely at their patients' situations, or from getting too involved in their lives. When the aborted woman walks out the clinic door, the staff wishes her the best, but they are loath to follow her progress or witness her struggles, her ambivalence, or her guilt. (This is also why post-abortion counseling is so very rarely offered by abortion clinics.)

For counselors who are secretly uncertain and ambivalent about abortion, it is far better to cling to the illusion of "helping others" than to test that belief against reality. To look too deeply at the post-abortion experience, to see the pain and heartache of aborted women, is to allow doubt into their own citadels of denial and rationalization. To risk learning that the lives of women are *not* improved by abortion, or are even *worsened*, is to risk destroying the illusion of all the "good" that they do. Their own self-images depend on maintaining that illusion of abortion's "necessity." They *want* to believe in it; they *must* believe in it, and they will ignore any evidence to the contrary. To do otherwise is to invite self-doubt and even self-loathing.

Wanting to believe that their work is "good," abortion counselors believe that abortion is not only an adequate solution for women with unplanned pregnancies, but that it is the "best" solution. Thus, abortion counselors tend to become biased against other alternatives. Abortion is a difficult and sad course for women in "trouble," they believe, but it is *absolutely necessary*. This bias was observed by Cynthia Martin, who studied a large number of abortion clinics for her doctoral dissertation on the psychology of abortion. According to Dr. Martin, abortion counselors are biased against the idea of "a teenager carrying a child to term" and "refuse to admit that having a child might be a healthier experience for a woman who would go through life blaming herself for the abortion that 'killed her baby.'"[88] Counselors refuse to admit that alternatives to abortion might be better, because to admit that any abortion over which they presided might have been unnecessary is to admit their own guilt in providing it.

Another common rationalization for abortion is the belief that aborting "unwanted" children saves them from miserable lives. But what is most disturbing about this excuse is that it is generally offered by those abortion clinic personnel who are most dissatisfied with their own lives. Many counselors and other abortion workers suffer from low self-esteem and are even self-destructive. It would seem that they find so little comfort in their own lives that they see themselves as doing a favor to others by preventing them from being born. Subconsciously wishing they had not been born themselves, they are quick to believe that abortion is a positive good that prevents other "unwanted" children of the world from being born.[89]

Obviously, denying their own doubts about the morality of abortion and maintaining the rationalization that abortion is a "positive" thing is a constant drain on abortion personnel. Even the strongest of counselors is likely to leave work each day feeling "emotionally beaten up."[90] Thus, in order to survive, abortion workers are forced to harden themselves and take on a depersonalized view of their work.[91] They see themselves and the women they serve as victims of a cold, cruel world—too weak to bring about change. One orderly, for example, admits to feeling that abortion is wrong but feels impotent to interfere, saying:

> I can't tell them [the abortionists], "Hey man, don't do that, that's not right." They want to make money, I need a job. I really don't care. I want to work. The patients come, they have the abortion, I need a job.[92]

This feeling of impotence becomes so great that even when witnessing a woman being forced into an abortion by her boyfriend, counselors will ignore the obvious and instead join the boyfriend in "guiding" the woman towards the unwanted abortion as the only "sane" choice.[93]

The constant stress faced by abortion workers often manifests itself in hostility. One lab technician, for example, feeling guilty about her own work with abortion, began to take it out on the patients: "I didn't get rude or nasty with the girls, but it was a form of hostility that could be sensed. I would have an attitude."[94]

Sometimes this frustration surfaces as petty fighting between staff members. Reading Denes's inside look at an abortion hospital, one finds frequent outbursts of extreme hostility between abortion personnel. One gets the impression of tense and explosive people, battle-fatigued warriors, driven forward only by the combined motives of duty and greed.[95]

To survive, abortion workers must become detached; and detachment invariably leads to callousness. This callousness may in turn lead to warped behavior and twisted humor. At one New York abortion hospital, a sign is hung for the amusement of the staff: "You rape them. We scrape them. No fetus can beat us."[96]

Charged with "protecting" women from the truth of what they are doing, abortion workers are sometimes forced to bear the guilt themselves. For example, one nurse describes the dilemmas she faced when assisting with second trimester saline abortions, saying:

> They always wanted to know the sex, but we lied and said it was too early to tell. It was better for the women to think of the fetus as an "it." Then we'd scoop up the fetuses and put them in a bucket of formaldehyde, just like Kentucky Fried Chicken. I couldn't take it any longer, and I quit.[97]

Another nurse, who assisted in over 1,000 saline abortions, eventually resigned from her grisly duty and became a pro-life activist. But even now, the guilt of participating in the "murder" of abortion haunts her:

> The other day I saw an abortion on TV and I had to run to the bathroom. The guilt of having assisted with abortions is so great 10 years later that I sometimes think I need therapy. The trouble is I don't know any therapists I could talk to about this.[98]

At almost every abortion clinic, "staff burnout is a major problem."[99] Studies have found a high incidence of negative psychological reactions among abortion providers, often including ghastly nightmares of giant fetuses seeking revenge.[100]

Like guards at a death camp, abortion workers are uneasy about all that they witness, but they force themselves to continue because it is their duty, their job. If they didn't do it, they rationalize, someone else would, and probably with less compassion than they. But according to Denes, even this excuse is a frail defense against the weight of the guilt they bear:

> Death is no easy companion. Not even in the veiled and necessary shape abortions lend it. Under pressure, the conspiracy of its denial cracks. In an astonishing turnabout I am sought out by the staff to be told by each what a hell of a business this has been. I am sought out to be told that one has to make a living but otherwise—otherwise, who *would* such burdens bear?[101]

THE ABORTIONISTS

Next to the aborted woman, it is the physician who is most directly involved in the actual "killing" act of abortion. In fact, whereas the woman's role requires only consent and passive "acceptance" of the abortion procedure, the abortionist is actively employed as the "executioner."[102]

Because most doctors are committed to saving lives, the vast majority of physicians (and obstetricians in particular) are unwilling to play the part of the "executioner" for elective abortions.[103] Rather than 20,000 doctors providing the nation's abortion needs, as was predicted by early abortion promoters, most of today's abortions are provided by only a few hundred "specialists" scattered in metropolitan areas around the country.[104]

According to Edward Eichner, director of medicine at a Cleveland abortion clinic, it is extremely difficult to maintain a staff of doctors willing to perform abortions. He notes that female physicians are especially hard to find and keep on the abortion clinic payroll. Women physicians who have experienced childbirth themselves, he believes, tend to have too much sympathy for the pregnancy and so are not emotionally suited to the rigors of performing repetitive abortions. But besides the moral unease related to performing abortions, Eichner reports, most physicians, male and female, simply find the work unchallenging: "The work is rote and repetitive. Suction abortion is just not stimulating from the point of view of medicine."[105] In other words, abortion is not only a morbid task filled with ethical overtones of murder and death; it is also deathly dull.

Another reason why physicians shy away from doing abortions is that the task of providing abortion on request is not really one of *medicine.* Except for the extremely rare cases when an abortion is necessary to save the life of the mother, abortions are purely "elective." They are a "service" provided for a fee. They do not advance the patient's health in any way; they only satisfy the client's immediate social needs. Thus, for a physician trained to save lives and improve health, abortion represents a prostitution of his knowledge and skills. In applying his surgical skills to nonsurgical, nontherapeutic tasks, he is simply selling his professional integrity to the highest bidders. It is no wonder, then, that studies of those physicians who do "sell" themselves in the lucrative abortion market report "untoward reactions which include dread, depression, anxiety, guilt and *identity crisis related to the role conflict of healer and abortionist*"[106] (italics added).

For those physicians who do choose to enter the abortion business, there is no easy solution to this identity crisis. According to one abortionist:

> You have to become a bit schizophrenic. In one room you encourage the patient that the slight irregularity of the fetal heart is not important, everything is going well, she is going to have a nice baby, and then you shut the door and go into the next room and assure another patient on whom you just did a saline abortion that it's fine if the heart is already irregular, she has nothing to worry about, she is *not* going to have a live baby. I mean you definitely have to make a 180-degree turn. . . .[107] (emphasis his own)

The solution for many abortionists is to simply avoid thinking about the ethical question of abortion. Some claim that they are only doing their jobs and that they are not qualified to "speculate" on morality, not even on their own morality.[108] Others avoid the ethical questions of abortion by focusing on its "practical" values. For example, Dr. Ronald Pion, an abortionist committed to his trade for the purpose of advancing world population control, argues that "we ought not to discuss the ethics of abortion but the ethics of procreation. . . . [W]e have pragmatic and utilitarian involvements to get on with."[109] Similarly, Dr. Edward Allred insists that abortion is necessary for "suppressing poverty, crime, and other problems of society."[110]

The desire to avoid any internal ethical review of their acts leads some abortionists to insist that the ethical question has already been "decided at law by the Supreme Court."[111] But in fact, the Court specifically avoided making any pronouncement on the morality of abortion. The illusion that it did, however, is a precious salve for uneasy consciences. As we have seen, the simplistic view that "if it is legal, it is moral" also plays a major influence in the decision-making of many women who choose abortion. Thus, since the law is a teacher, it is capable of influencing the moral views of both aborters and abortionists.

But while most abortionists try to avoid the moral issue of abortion, few are entirely successful. After interviewing nearly a dozen abortionists in the preparation of her book *In Necessity and Sorrow* Denes reports that "There wasn't a doctor who at one time or another in the questioning did not say, 'This is murder.'"[112]

Some abortionists readily admit their guilt feelings:

> I've tried not to make it a moral issue, but a social issue without moral overtones as much as possible. But I think from a straight moral point of view I probably would object to abortion. Because I love kids. From that point of view every fetus is a potential child, and morally I just really don't think that [abortion] should be done. . . . I suppose that if you want to go below the surface, and thinking about it, I do feel you'd be an abnormal person if you could really honestly say that abortion didn't bother you at all. It goes against all things which are natural. It's a termination of life, however you look at it. It just goes against the grain. It must. . . . [113]

Others are even more schizophrenic, admitting and denying guilt all in the same breath:

> In my own case I never had any psychological adverse reaction. Except an occasional feeling that one was destroying life. But in my own mind the issue had already been resolved that this is necessary because otherwise these poor girls are going to risk their own lives. . . .[114]

Yet another states:

> My feelings about doing abortions were very significant and it was a long period of time for me to work it out. I dare say any thinking sensitive individual can't not realize that he is ending life or potential life, you know. I certainly don't enjoy that. I have no conscious conflict over killing a fetus. There's certainly nothing enjoyable in the act, except providing a necessary something to a person to make their life or burden happier, or easier, or whatever. But there's got to be more to it.[115]

But while this last abortionist claims no "*conscious* conflict over killing a fetus," he later adds: "I think we're certainly living in a time of decreased human respect, of decreased human relationships, and of decreased sensitivity to killing off things."[116]

Sometimes, despite the best attempts to suppress and deny the moral issues at the heart of abortion, the reality of the act just cannot be ignored. One "complication" difficult to avoid, but seldom discussed, is always a rude shock for at least this one abortionist who reports:

> [O]n a number of occasions with the needle, I have harpooned the fetus. I can feel the fetus move at the end of the needle just like you have a fish hooked on a line. This gives me an unpleasant, unhappy feeling because I know that the fetus is alive and responding to the needle stab. . . . No one has ever mentioned this, but I've noticed it a number of times, you know that there is something alive in there that you're killing. . . .[117]

For many physicians, the weight of guilt is eased by setting arbitrary limits—refusing to abort advanced pregnancies. For example, one physician sets the limit at sixteen weeks of gestation, saying:

> I just decided it's not worth it to do it, because I have had such terribly strong feelings that it's turned me off. I feel that I am destroying life. I feel that I'm actually killing them. And that kind of feeling I don't like to live with. And I rationalize by saying to myself that from one week to sixteen weeks is to me the upper limits of what I would do. . . . Then after that time I leave it to others, more radical than myself, to do whatever they want to do.[118]

But setting upper limits is one thing; abiding by them is another. Faced with pressure from desperate clients and the prospect for additional revenues, some abortionists find their limits of fifteen and sixteen weeks being stretched later and later into the term.[119] Denial of responsibility soon leads to an inability to question what they do. One doctor specializing in second trimester saline abortions, for example, insists that doctors should not even ask what a woman's reasons are for wanting an abortion; he should just "follow orders," so to speak: "We'll just have to face it, that somebody has to do it. And, unfortunately, we are the executioners in this instance."[120]

For doctors, as well as women, the moral responsibility for what they do is passed about like a hot potato. Women, in the passive role of "accepting" abortion, perceive it as something done "to" them. Doctors try to excuse it as something "demanded" of them by their patients. And both say that they are only doing what is sanctioned by the law and society. Meanwhile, of course, the law and society disclaim responsibility, saying that abortion is solely a matter for the private consciences of the "woman and her physician."[121]

One abortionist who recognizes the guilt-passing that occurs believes that the type of abortion performed has a drastic influence on how the woman perceives the experience:

When we do D&C's it's under general anesthesia, so the patient comes in and the doctor does the dirty work. And then she wakes up, and it's his sin, and she's cured. But with a saline she's participating in this sin, because she's awake, she knows what's going on, she feels it coming out.[122]

The impact on the abortionist is also related to the type of procedure used. Some doctors prefer to do saline abortions during the second and third trimesters because once the instillation procedure is finished, they can leave the hospital and turn over the burden of delivering the dead fetus to the patient and nurses.[123] Others, more concerned with easing the emotional shock of the patient, take on the stressful and "grisly" task of dismembering the unborn child and manually removing the fetal parts themselves.[124]

Thus, it would seem, rather than avoiding guilt, at least some abortionists see themselves as *substitute* guilt bearers for the women they serve. In this "martyr's" role, physicians quickly adopt a superior and paternalistic attitude towards their clients. Even the most blatant lies become acceptable in order to "protect" their "girls" from the guilt-laden truths of abortion.[125] But the cost of these lies carries with it the risk that abortion will become overused and that too many patients will suffer from this "safe and easy" procedure. As one abortionist admits:

[W]hat they think are simple solutions are not as simple as they think. They can die, they can become sterile, and they can have many other complications. That unfortunately is the biggest evil of abortions.[126]

Like the other staff members in abortion clinics, abortionists are so busy trying to maintain their own psychic balance that they have little energy left over for worrying about the psychic welfare of their patients. They are so busy trying to remain distant and unimpassioned about what they do that they become distant and unimpassioned towards those they serve.

Dr. Consuelo Sague, a repentant former abortionist who is now vice-president of a pro-life group called Peaceful Solutions, believes that abortion deadens a physician's capacity for compassion.

Once a person becomes accustomed to inflicting pain, he becomes callous in other ways. One of my teachers, a very clever professor who performed many abortions, turned very cold in his attitude toward women. He didn't care about them at all. He was unaffected by their physical and emotional pain. He had an academic detachment from women and their feelings. Yes, I think doctors who do abortions become dehumanized. They have to.[127]

Another physician, a practicing abortionist, agrees, though he extends the charge of sexism towards all male gynecologists. According to Dr. Abraham Holtzman (a pseudonym), the Chief of Gynecological and Obstetrical Services at a major New York abortion hospital:

Basically every gynecologist doesn't like women, otherwise he couldn't work with them. He enjoys the position of mastery over them. The fact that he is the god, king, they do what he tells them, which is what he would always want women to do, because every man wants his women to be subservient to him. The patients are subservient to us, and when they rebel it's very simple: "Go to somebody else. Don't come back to me, if you're not going to take my advice." What better relationship can a man have with a woman?[128]

Does abortion make physicians callous, or does abortion *attract* physicians who are already callous? Dr. Bernard Nathanson, co-founder of the National Association for the Repeal of Abortion Laws and director of the nation's largest abortion clinic prior to 1973, reports that many of the physicians hired at the clinic experienced drastic personality changes: "I was seeing personality structures dissolve in front of me on a scale I had never seen before in a medical situation. Very few members of the staff seemed to remain fully intact through their experiences."[129] On the other hand, he also reports that the clinic employed several physicians who had already been doing illegal abortions for years. Among this "venal band of scoundrels" were physicians already used to being vicious, even sadistic with patients."[130] Nathanson himself, after presiding over 60,000 abortions, became "increasingly troubled by my own increasing certainty that I had in fact presided over 60,000 deaths."[131] This troubling notion eventually led Nathanson to become a leading activist in the national pro-life movement.

While it seems clear that the burnout rate for abortionists is high, it is equally clear that some abortionists are able to ply their trade for decades with few signs of wear, much less repentance. For these sturdy professionals, a hard and detached personality appears essential. Many perform thousands of abortions per year, and this task requires a "robot-like constitution."[132]

Yet it is possible that some abortionists may not be so unimpassioned about what they do. Instead, some may find a sense of satisfaction in wielding their power over life and death. Psychiatrists have observed that at least some abortionists are motivated by "psychological inadequacy" and "anti-social personalities" motivated by greed.[133] Elements of sadism, and even symbolic self-destruction, may be motivating factors for some abortionists.

A trained social worker at one abortion hospital is disquieted by the personalities of the abortionists with whom she works, saying that "there's really pathological things in their involvement with abortion. Like Dr. Rodrigo. He is very sarcastic and he really, you know, like goes after people."[134]

Examples of crude and callous behavior abound in the abortion literature, and not all of it is confined to the abortion "mills" of Chicago. For example, Denes reports witnessing an abortionist who seemed to enjoy inflicting guilt upon his patients. After failing to kill the fetus during the first saline induction, this particular physician attached a heart monitor to his patient's womb and filled the room with the amplified beat of the baby's heart.

> "That's it," he cries triumphantly, "that's it—the induction didn't work. Sturdy fellow you have in there, eh?" He gives a loud guffaw, and his broad obscene wink darkens the room.[135]

In reading through interviews with abortionists, few though they are, one is struck by how many of these physicians seem uncertain as to why they even entered medicine in the first place. Frequently they describe themselves as fleeing from family demands to enter another occupation. Others became doctors only because of family demands. Still others entered medicine simply for the money. All together, many abortionists seem cynical about their medical careers and even about their entire lifestyles. Dissatisfied with their own lives, they have little sympathy for the lives of the women they serve or for the unborn they profess to "save" from similar lives of empty "unwantedness." For many, it is clear that they are not devoted to the art of healing or even inspired by it. Instead, medicine, like abortion, is just a job—just a lucrative way to get by one day at a time.[136]

Consider, for example, one New York abortionist who admits to general feelings of guilt, yet describes himself as ruthless and cold when it suits his needs:

> I would make a good Mafia member, because I honor my friends and destroy my enemies. I never forget a slight, I never forget an encouragement. Those who helped me when I was younger and struggling up, I've lifted them up when they were going down. And those that stepped on me, I stepped on them and crushed them while I was going up.[137]

But despite such cold self-centeredness, it is difficult to believe that any abortionist is ever left unscathed. Having observed several abortionists from close range over a long period of time, psychiatrist Magda Denes sees scars everywhere: "No one is untouched. No one is untorn. Each, propelled by who he is, builds his own mythical world where this is all right, that is wrong, one thing is just, another a crime. Morality is a fluid notion."[138]

Perhaps the comments of Dr. William Rashbaum, chief of family planning services at Beth Israel Medical Center, are prototypical of the "average" abortionist's views. Speaking to reporters, Dr. Rashbaum admitted that there was a time in the midst of every abortion he performed when he was troubled by fantasies of the fetus hanging on to the walls of the uterus with tiny fingernails, resisting the abortion with all its strength.

> How, he was asked, had he managed [to do abortions] while enduring this fantasy? "Learned to live with it. Like people in concentration camps." Did he really mean that analogy? "I think it's apt—destruction of life. Look! I'm a person. I'm entitled to my feelings. And my feelings are: Who gives me or anybody the right to terminate a pregnancy? I'm entitled to that feeling but I also have no right to communicate it to the patient who desperately wants that abortion. I don't get paid for my feelings. I get paid for my skills. . . . I'll be frank. I began to do abortions in large numbers at the time of my divorce when I needed money. But I also believe in the woman's right to control her biological destiny. I spent a lot of years learning to deliver babies. Sure, it sometimes hurts to end life instead of bringing it into the world."[139]

Abortion means money. And for most, if not all abortionists, money is the primary motive for enduring the boredom, the guilt, and the indignity of performing mass abortions.[140] Compared to other "minor surgeries," the cost of abortion is amazingly high, yet to abortionists no price is too high for putting "aside his doctors oath. . . . The high fees may be paying no longer for the criminal risk [involved in doing an illegal abortion], but for the indignity."[141]

Finally, as psychiatrist Conrad Baars, notes: "Abortionists, whether performing their sinister work in hospitals or back alleys, get richer, but not happier or healthier . . . the emergence of feelings of guilt and depression cannot be suppressed forever."[142] It is an occupation with no joy, and therefore it is limited to those who are, or are willing to be, callous and mercenary. Truly compassionate doctors have no stomach for the "evil necessity" of abortion and certainly lack the stamina to provide the nation with 1.5 million abortions per year. Such a task takes professionals with that unsavory and "robot-like constitution" that the *Sun-Times* reporters deplored.

While it is clear that the characters who thrive in the abortion industry will never win humanitarian awards, it is also clear that these are the only types of characters that can survive the pressures of delivering mass-scale abortion on demand. There is no way to bring "compassionate" care to what is inherently a compassionless business—clinics held together by illusion, self-deceit, and lucrative profits. It is in the hands of these abortion professionals that the health and "counseling" of desperate, vulnerable women lie. But cold proficiency may not be enough. For as Magda Denes notes after her inside look at the fragile psyche of the abortion industry:

> Renown is no guarantee of skill. Skill is no safeguard against cruelty. Patients are vulnerable to the mental health of their helpers. The helpers should, therefore, be watched like potential enemies.[143]

SUMMARY

Abortion in America is not medicine; it is a commodity, delivered with businesslike proficiency. In order to facilitate the abortion trade, abortionists (with the blessing of the Supreme Court) have abandoned many of the medical standards originally established to protect needy people from unscrupulous health care. These professional codes of ethics were deemed too cumbersome for the business of supplying abortion on demand.

In attempting to make abortion services more efficient and profitable, abortion clinics place heavy reliance on low-skill, low-pay workers who are responsible for performing the "routine" tasks normally undertaken by health care professionals. Along with other cost-cutting measures, this dependency on non-medical personnel increases the health risks faced by aborting women in the event of an emergency or an unnoticed complication.

Like all business enterprises, the abortion industry has a special sales force: abortion counselors. Counselors act as "facilitators." Counselors are not supposed to *inform* clients, only to help clients make the choice for abortion with the least amount of pain and doubt. In fact, "proper" abortion counseling recognizes that women may become "confused" if presented with the facts and may be "irrationally" dissuaded from choosing an abortion in their own "best" interests. Abortion counselors, therefore, feel obligated to "protect" women from any information which might be "disturbing" or "discouraging." According to the Supreme Court, the right of counselors to withhold any information they feel might have a "chilling effect" on the abortion choice is an absolute right guaranteed by constitutional safeguards. Thus denied the full and complete information they need to make their *own* decisions, it is no wonder that so many aborted women feel betrayed and manipulated by their "counselors."

Though abortion is an extremely lucrative trade for clinics and doctors, it is not a pleasant trade. Staff turn-over rates are high, and most workers, counselors, and physicians in particular suffer from guilt and ambivalence about what they do. The dark side of their work is avoided by denial, rationalization, and impersonal attitudes. They avoid thinking about the moral overtones of their work, and they cling to the illusion that the lives of the women they serve are really *improved* because of their abortions. Any evidence to the contrary is ignored.

Pro-choice advocates who may hope to reform the abortion industry are only deceiving themselves. "Abuses" in the abortion industry are unavoidable and uncontrollable. The judicial interpretations which elevate abortion to the status of a constitutional right also forbid any regulation to make abortion a *safe* right. Furthermore, the nature of the business naturally attracts "cold, mechanical" profiteers. Compassionate physicians are either repelled by abortion, burn out after a short time, or are shaped into "cold, mechanical" profiteers themselves.

Abortion is a grueling, tough business; it is almost as tough on the providers as it is on aborted women.

EPILOGUE

Even to many of its defenders, abortion is at best a "necessary evil." It is not a right one exercises with pride. Unlike the proud civil rights gained by blacks—the right to attend all-white universities, the right to eat in any restaurant, the right to live in any suburb, the right to sit at either end of the bus, and so on—the abortion "right" is practiced with shame, not pride.

As we have seen repeated in story after story, women choose abortion because they feel there is "no other option." They abort because it is the "easy way out." They abort because they feel abandoned by their lovers, friends, and families. Without the support to do the right thing, they yield to doing the "easy thing." Or as one WEBA woman put it, "I made the decision to be weak." In today's society, it does not take courage to abort; it takes courage to stand up against all the pressures and inconveniences which push towards abortion. Thus, abortion is not a liberating experience; it is a deflating experience which involves a shameful yielding to despair.

In many ways, abortion is like suicide. A person who threatens suicide is actually crying out for help, and so are women who contemplate abortion. Both are in a state of despair; both are lonely; both feel faced by insurmountable odds. Granting the wish for suicide or abortion is not an aid to these desperate people. It is abandonment.

If we were to legalize suicide and create suicide clinics where counselors would ease people into and through their suicide decisions, there would be no shortage of desperate people willing to exercise their "freedom to choose." Suicidal persons would be promised a "quick, easy and painless" solution to their problems. They would be promised compassionate care and a release from their seemingly insurmountable burdens, their feelings of loneliness and pointlessness. And

149

so suicide rates would skyrocket, just as abortion rates have soared in the last ten years.

Like the suicide clinics described above (a real proposal recommended by right-to-die groups), abortion clinics exploit desperate people. They promise to satisfy the dark impulses of our despair. They appeal to our demand for instant solutions to all our problems. They pose as places of compassion, but are actually reaping huge profits through the harvest of the lonely, frightened, and hopeless people who are "unwanted" by society.

Women who face unplanned pregnancies do not need abortion. They need help and support so they can keep their commitments. They need to be applauded for their bravery against difficult circumstances so that their courage might last, their self-esteem might grow, and their integrity might remain firm. As it is, the social acceptability of abortion makes a woman feel that struggling with an unplanned, inconvenient pregnancy is a pointless task. The pride she feels in doing the right thing is taken away from her by those who insist that it is better to do the convenient and practical thing.

But as we have seen that abortion is almost invariably an act of despair on the part of desperate women, so too is the modern abortion system itself a sign of a society which has given in to despair. Abortion signifies an America with crumbling courage, an America which has lost hope in the great dream of justice for all. Abortion is accepted not because it is just, but because it gives the appearance of helping a few women at the expense of their as yet unseen children. Too cowardly, or too selfish to offer love to *both* the women and their children, "pro-choice" friends, family, and society at large offer women abortion as the "easy way out" which saves everyone from getting too involved with her problems. Abortion is a cover-up; it hides women's problems by eliminating their children and silencing the women themselves with shame. Abortion is a half-hearted solution urged by those who have only a half-hearted concern.

Professor of philosophy Donald DeMarco sees abortion as symptomatic of this surrender. He writes:

> Without courage, love tends to degenerate into sentimental kindness. . . . The inherent weakness of sentimental kindness is not its lack of benevolence but how it buckles in the face of difficulties. For most people, all that is required to feel kind is that nothing threaten them at that moment. But let a man who is merely kind enter a truly uncomfortable situation and his kindness may quickly give way to cruelty. As C. S. Lewis points out, such "kindness consents very readily to the removal of its object," for it is concerned not with whether

its object is good or bad, lives or dies, but only that it escapes suffering.[1]

Abortion has become an excuse for *not* offering real aid to pregnant women. Feminist author Paulette Joyer has complained that the abortion mentality is an "obstacle to true, progressive social reform." In this context, she writes:

> If every unintended pregnancy can be aborted, why should the government and private sector make any special considerations for the single parent? Or even the two parent family? Logically, only people who can provide for their children without reliance on concessions of others should have children. Logically, why talk about decent maternity and paternity leaves? Job protection? Flexible career options? Shared jobs? Low cost, high quality child care? . . . If every unintended pregnancy can be aborted, why should local governments feel any obligation to provide additional nutrition and health care to poor women who are pregnant? If it is known that a child will be born with a physical or mental handicap, but that that fetus can be aborted, why should there be any pressure to provide care and support to handicapped citizens and their families?[2]

The abortion solution is a financially cheap way for society to brush troubled women out of the way while claiming to have done them a service. Abortion is the "cheap love" offered by an uncaring society too busy with "more important" problems than the hardships faced by pregnant women. By promoting abortion, society can avoid addressing the real issues such as those listed by Joyer. By avoiding these issues, by denying women the collective support of the community, society is pressuring more and more women into accepting the abortion "solution."

The effort to stop abortion is not an attempt to deny women an option; it is a promise to provide them with better options. It is a promise to alleviate their despair, to prevent their exploitation.

SHOULD LAWS REFLECT MORALITY?

We have seen that the overwhelming majority of women oppose abortion for convenience.[3]

We have also seen that abortion is abusive of women and is an excuse by which they are abandoned to fend for themselves. But still many would argue that we should not "legislate morality." These people insist that anti-abortion laws violate the principle of separation of church and state.

In response to these arguments we might first note that "separation of church and state" is a convenient slogan for those who oppose certain moral or religious convictions, but it is not a principle incorporated in the Constitution. What the First Amendment forbids is the "establishment of religion" by Congress. The wisdom of this article was derived from experience with British abuses which attempted to force people to accept the Church of England as the official national denomination. The First Amendment, therefore, was designed to prevent the federal government from instituting such a national denomination or legislating religious doctrines.

But while the First Amendment would clearly forbid a national law requiring certain religious observances (such as a requirement to attend church on Sunday or to refrain from meat on Fridays), it was never intended to prevent the government from incorporating religious *values and morals* into its laws. Indeed, all the rights defended by the Constitution are derived from the founding fathers' common belief in God and the sanctity of human life. This view was stated most succinctly in the Declaration of Independence, which recognized the "self-evident truths" that "all men are created equal, that they are endowed by their Creator with certain inalienable Rights, that among these are Life, Liberty, and the pursuit of Happiness."

This was the philosophy upon which this nation was founded— that human rights are inalienably endowed by God, derived from His moral order. First among these is the right to life. It is also worth noting that the founding fathers saw all men as *"created* equal," not "born equal." Human dignity, they believed, is God-given at the moment of an individual's creation, at conception—not at birth, not after achieving certain abilities arbitrarily defined as "personhood."

The idea that rights are based on the moral order of God was not new at the time of the American Revolution. Ever since the first civilizations, a belief in a moral order was the basis for all laws which restricted human behavior and guaranteed human rights. Laws against murder, theft, and exhibitionism, for example, were based on the belief that such actions violated the rights and dignity of others.

All laws, since the beginning of time, impose values upon other people. Even traffic laws against speeding impose a value upon those who would like to speed. Every stoplight is an imposition on personal behavior. *Laws always attempt to legislate morality.* To separate morality from the law is to leave the law without purpose.

Pro-abortionists argue that since some people do not believe abortion is immoral, it is not right to prevent them from having abortions. But no law depends on everyone agreeing to it. Not all thieves, rapists and murderers believe they are committing immoral acts, and there are many prominent philosophers who would insist that since there is no

God nothing is objectively immoral. But even though there is never a perfect consensus on what is moral and what is immoral, it is the purpose of the law to address these issues.

Carried to its logical conclusion, the "freedom of choice" argument is an appeal for anarchy—freedom from any laws, any imposition of values or morality. If "freedom of choice" is made the highest of all laws, then no other laws are possible.

But pro-abortionists are anything but anarchists. While they oppose the anti-abortion "morality" which would legislate against abortion, they are at the same time seeking to impose their own values on society by insisting that there is a moral obligation to provide *free* abortions for the poor. The abortion debate, then, is not one of whether or not the law should be used to impose values upon the people. Instead, it is a debate about *whose* values are going to be imposed upon the rest.

Similarly, politicians who support pro-abortion laws saying, "Personally I don't believe abortion is right, but I refuse to impose my moral views on others," are at best cowards who are unwilling to stand by their own moral convictions, or at worst nothing more than hypocrites. When these same politicians vote to build defense systems, they are imposing their values on pacifists. When they vote to tax the rich for the sake of the poor, they are imposing their morality on those wealthy persons who don't care about the poor. Writing moral choices into the law is what their jobs are all about.

Above all, laws exist in recognition of the fact that there is a difference between what we *can* do and what we *ought* to do—especially in our relationships with other human beings. It is a means of educating and guiding the members of a society to respect and protect the rights and dignity of others. In large part, these laws are built up by tradition, formulated by trial and error. Thus, it is through the law that the people of one age attempt to teach their values and pass on their wisdom to their descendants.

Laws are also a mechanism by which people are encouraged to do what they know is right, even when it is difficult to do so. Without community support, it is all too easy to give in to despair, to violate one's own principles because it seems like no one cares what you do anyway. Besides condemning evil actions against the dignity of others, the law reminds us that right actions are noble actions. As philosopher and social activist Peter Maurin often reminded his followers, the goal of social justice is to "create a society where it would be easier for people to be good."[4]

In this sense, laws against abortion may seem restrictive to those who want abortions, but they are also an encouragement to those who are tempted by abortion but know that it is wrong. For those women who struggle against the pressures which force them toward abortion, the law is a backstop that reminds them that their sacrifices are worthwhile, that they are doing the *right* thing if not the convenient thing. Social acceptance of abortion, on the other hand, tells women that they are foolish *not* to abort an inconvenient pregnancy. The choice is one of deciding which of the two different moral viewpoints we want to encourage.

Studies into the psychology of morality reveal that the law is truly the teacher. One of the most significant results of these studies shows that existing laws and customs are *the most* important basis for deciding what is right or wrong for most adults in that culture.[5] Whether one wants "morality in the law" or not, most people look to law for moral guidance. Right now the law is teaching that abortion is a moral and presumably effective solution to unplanned pregnancies. As a result, millions of unborn children are being destroyed, an equal number of women are being physically and emotionally violated, and society's compassion for both women and their children is being eroded. Is this really the type of morality which we want our laws to teach?

TRANSFORMING EVIL TO GOOD

It has been the theme throughout this book that women are victims of abortion. It is the people who profit by abortion and those who advocate its use as an "easy," superficial solution to real problems who are the perpetrators of this crime.

In many ways, though, this last description includes us all, even those who vocally oppose abortion. Consciously or not, we have created a society where individuals are expected to solve their problems on their own, or at the very least to solve their problems in a way which poses the least inconvenience and expense on the rest of us. This attitude of abandoning the unfortunate to deal with their own problems, particularly if the "problems" are of their own making, was the fertile ground from which the abortion mentality sprang. For a society which conceals abandonment under the guise of promoting "individualism," the promotion of abortion as a solution for women "in trouble" was inevitable because abortion is cheap and easy—at least for those who don't have to have the abortions.

Abortion is a symbol of how we have abandoned our ideals of community, love of our neighbors, and care for the weak. To forbid abortion is to promise to strive for our ideals; to accept abortion is to bow down to the non-ethics of the utilitarian counting-house philosophy. Failing to help women cope with the problems of pregnancy is to push them toward the false solution of abortion. There is no neutral ground. If we do not choose life, we choose death.

But just as every scientific experiment yields knowledge, even if it fails, so does every social policy. In seeing failures we learn what to avoid; in seeing evil we learn how to seek good.

Having gone through this period of abortion on demand, and having witnessed its horrors, it is our hope that all of us have learned to look more closely at the needs of women faced with problem pregnancies. Perhaps having recognized the Pandora's box of abortion, we have even developed a greater commitment to help these women in more constructive, creative, and loving ways. This is the hope of the women who have formed WEBA, and the tens of thousands of other post-aborted women who have become pro-life activists: that through the deaths of their own children we might all learn a greater respect for life; that through their own sufferings we might all build the foundation for increased awareness and the motivation for change. These women and their children paid a horrible price, but if we use this experience as an impetus for change, their sacrifices may ultimately be redeemed.

As we have repeated time and again, this goal will not be achieved merely by banning abortions. Instead, such a ban must be only one step towards compassionately, and unjudgmentally, supporting pregnant women through inconvenient, unwanted, or otherwise difficult pregnancies. In the wombs of these women live new hopes and dreams, new friends and companions in life. To love these children, we must love their mothers; to care for these mothers, we must love their children. Mother and child are as one, and they cannot be separated without doing violence to both.

How to Find Help

Help for dealing with post-abortion problems and assistance with a crisis pregnancy is almost always available in or near your community. Often these organizations are listed in your local phone book. A number of national organizations also exist which can directly provide you with assistance or arrange for assistance through a local or regional organization.

The following is a brief list of some national organizations which are able to offer assistance. This list is by no means comprehensive. The author apologizes in advance to all the organizations which were omitted.

ASSISTANCE FOR CRISIS PREGNANCIES

Bethany Christian Services (616) 459-6273
Birthright, Inc. (800) 848-5683
Christian Action Council (703) 237-2100
Nurturing Network (800) TNN-4MOM

LEGAL AID AFTER ABORTION

American Rights Coalition (800) 634-2224
Legal Action For Women (800) 962-2319

POST-ABORTION COUNSELING

National Office of Post-Abortion Reconciliation & Healing
Support and Referral Line (800) 5WE-CARE
Open Arms (314) 449-7672
Post Abortion Counseling and Education (P.A.C.E.)
(703) 237-2100
Victims of Choice (707) 448-6015
Women Exploited By Abortion (214) 366-3600

APPENDIX

Survey Results

The survey discussed in Chapter One was distributed through WEBA chapters to 252 women in forty-two states. It consisted of two sections: background information and the actual survey questions. The instructions read as follows:

ABORTION EXPERIENCE QUESTIONNAIRE

This survey is being conducted to review the decision-making processes of women who have had abortions, and their subsequent satisfaction or dissatisfaction with their decisions. Please answer the questions as honestly as possible. If you wish to elaborate, please feel free to write further explanations or comments on separate sheets of paper. (If possible, please number your explanations according to the number of the question which prompted your comment.) Your written comments may be used in published results of this study. Names and addresses will not be used and will remain confidential unless written permission for use is requested and granted. If you know of anyone else who has had an abortion and may be willing to answer this survey, please make a photocopy of this form for them, or write to the survey address for an additional copy.

The first section of the survey requested the following background information:

Name:_____   Age: _____

Address: _____   Race or

City: _____   ethnic origin: _____

State:_____

Highest grade
completed: _____

Was your abortion □ legal, or □ illegal?

Name of clinic or hospital where abortion was performed:____

_____

City: _____   State: _____

Abortion referral or counseling agency (if any): _____

_____

City: _____   State: _____

How many weeks pregnant were you at the time? _____ wks.

How old were you at the time? _____ yrs.

Marital Status: □ single   □ married

□ engaged   □ divorced

How many children did you have at that time? _____

Income level at the time: □ less than $5,000 per year

(of your parent(s) or   □ $5,000 to $10,000

yourself and/or spouse)   □ $10,000 to $15,000

□ $15,000 to $20,000

□ over $20,000

Was the cost of your abortion subsidized by an outside source?

□ Yes   □ No

Source, if known:_____

_____

Tabulation of the background information yielded the following results:

AGE DISTRIBUTIONS

Age at time
of abortion:

<15 yrs	15–19	20–24	25–29	>30
3%	42%	33%	14%	8%

Average age at time of abortion: 21.2 yrs
Low age at time of abortion: 12 yrs
High age at time of abortion: 40 yrs

Age at time
of survey:

<20	20–24	25–29	30–34	>34
1%	11%	33%	35%	20%

Average age at time of survey: 31.2 yrs
Low age at time of survey: 16 yrs
High age at time of survey: 64 yrs
Average time since abortion: 10 yrs
  (Survey age - abortion age)
Greatest time since abortion: 36 yrs
Least time since abortion: 7 months

RACE OR ETHNIC ORIGIN

White — 87%
Other — 13%

LEGAL AND ILLEGAL ABORTIONS

Legal — 92%
Illegal — 8%

EDUCATION LEVEL

		Degree Equivalent				
No Answer	Under 12 yrs	High School (12 yrs)	Associate or Trade (13–14)	Bachelors (15–16)	Masters (17–18)	Ph.D. (>18)
5%	6%	39%	26%	19%	4%	1%

WEEKS PREGNANT AT TIME OF ABORTION

<5 wks	5–6	7–8	9–10	11–12	13–24	>24
2%	13%	23%	18%	24%	19%	0%

Average gestation at time of abortion: 10.2 wks
Low gestation at time of abortion: 4 wks
High gestation at time of abortion: 23 wks

MARITAL STATUS

Single:	65%	Married	17%
Engaged:	8%	Separated	11%

NUMBER OF CHILDREN

Number of Children	0	1	2	3	>3
	73%	14%	9%	4%	1%

INCOME LEVEL

Under $5,000 per year: 33%
$5,000 to $10,000:   25%
$10,000 to $15,000: 14%
$15,000 to $20,000:   7%
Over $20,000:   21%

Though the above figures tend to show that the women surveyed generally had low incomes at the time of their abortions, these numbers should be interpreted with caution. These figures are not necessarily indicative of the general incomes or social classes of these aborters. At the time of their abortions, most of these women were in their early twenties or late teens; many were college students. While some respondents elsewhere indicated that they were from middle- or upper-class families, they considered themselves independent at the time of their abortions (whether working or attending college) and so reported only their personal incomes. Thus, the income *potential* of many of these aborters may have been significantly higher than the above figures indicate. Moreover, these income levels are not adjusted for inflation.

SUBSIDY OF ABORTION

This question was meant to identify government subsidized abortions (i.e. through federal or state Medicare programs). Another frequent response, however, was that insurance (usually the insurance policy of the woman's parents or college insurance) covered the costs of the abortion. Responses such as "paid for by boyfriend" or "parents" were tallied as being abortions that were *not* subsidized.

Subsidized: 23%   Government subsidy: 64%

Insurance subsidy: 36%

Unsubsidized: 77%

Following the background questions was a list of fifty-eight questions which were to be answered on a scale of 0 to 5. According to the directions for this final section:

> Instructions: Unless otherwise indicated, most questions require answers on a scale where 1 = Not At All, ranging up to 5 = Very Much. Unsure is always indicated by circling 0.

In practice, most of the women did not answer any question which they felt was not applicable to their circumstances. If, for example, they had not consulted with their parents before their abortions, they simply did not circle a response to the question as to whether or not their parents influenced their decisions. Since computer tabulation of the results would have been overly complicated by unanswered questions, all unanswered questions were recorded as a "0" response. Therefore, all "0" responses include those respondents who were unsure of their response to a particular question, as well as those who were sure that the question was "Not Applicable" (N/A) to their particular circumstances.

In general, most answers clustered at the extremes of the 1 to 5 scale. Therefore, in the description of these survey results found in Chapter One, 1-2 responses were generally combined into a single percentage, as were 4-5 responses, and the middle response, 3, stood alone. The few exceptions to this rule were noted in the text.

The following is a complete listing of the questions asked, with answers recorded according to the *percentage* of respondents falling in each category.

	N/A or Unsure	Not at All				Very Much
	0	1	2	3	4	5
1. Were you satisfied with the abortion services you received?	10%	44%	8%	18%	10%	8%
2. Were you satisfied with your choice at the time?	8%	42%	14%	13%	10%	14%
3. Are you satisfied with your choice today?	3%	95%	0%	1%	0%	1%
4. Was the decision made for reasons of:						
mental health?	40%	34%	4%	6%	6%	11%
physical health?	41%	48%	2%	3%	1%	6%
financial limits?	32%	27%	5%	9%	5%	23%
social acceptance?	20%	12%	3%	7%	10%	47%
family size?	42%	48%	1%	2%	1%	6%
career goals?	41%	30%	4%	7%	5%	13%
long-term needs?	43%	22%	4%	7%	6%	18%
short-term needs?	41%	14%	2%	5%	9%	28%
other:—(See Chapter One)	54%	2%	0%	3%	2%	39%
5. Do you feel you were "forced" by outside circumstances to have an abortion?	4%	12%	10%	10%	10%	54%
6. Were you encouraged to have an abortion by:						
parents?	34%	35%	2%	6%	2%	21%
other family members?	41%	39%	3%	3%	2%	12%
husband?	54%	33%	1%	1%	2%	9%
boyfriend?	27%	27%	2%	4%	7%	33%
social worker?	52%	32%	2%	0%	4%	10%
abortion counselor?	39%	20%	2%	4%	8%	27%
doctor?	41%	27%	3%	6%	5%	18%
friends?	38%	28%	2%	7%	6%	18%
other:—(see Chapter One)	77%	5%	0%	2%	3%	13%
7. Would your choice have been different if any or all of the above had encouraged you differently?	8%	4%	2%	3%	7%	76%
8. Do you feel you were "forced" by others to have an abortion?	4%	23%	10%	10%	14%	39%
9. If abortion had not been legally available, would you have sought an illegal abortion?	16%	72%	3%	4%	2%	4%
10. Would you have attempted a self-induced abortion?	4%	87%	2%	2%	2%	3%
11. Did you feel rushed to have an abortion?	3%	8%	3%	5%	12%	69%

12. How long did you take to decide?

❏ 1–4 days,	❏ 1 wk.,	❏ 2–3 wks.,	❏ 4–6 wks.,	❏ longer
51%	24%	12%	6%	6%

	N/A or Unsure	Not at All				Very Much
13. Do you feel your decision was well thought out?	1%	74%	8%	9%	2%	6%
14. Do you feel you had all of the necessary information to make the decision?	2%	88%	5%	3%	1%	2%

15. Have you had more than one abortion? 47% Yes 76% No

How many?

1	2	3	>3
76%	20%	3%	2%

16. Would you ever have another abortion?	4%	95%	1%	0%	0%	0%

17. Were there any physical complications following the procedure? 47% Yes 44% No 9% Unsure

18. If so, were they severe or minor? (minor-1; severe-5)	47%	15%	6%	14%	4%	15%

Please list, if any:—(see Chapter One)

19. Was there any permanent damage? 18% Yes 47% No 35% Unsure

20. Have any subsequent pregnancies resulted in miscarriage or premature birth? 23% Yes 67% No 10% Unsure

If so, does your doctor attribute it to your previous abortion? 5% Yes 5% No 88% Unsure

21. Were there any negative psychological effects you attribute to your abortion? 94% Yes 2% No 4% Unsure

22. If so, were they minor or severe? (minor-1; severe-5)	6%	4%	3%	14%	19%	54%

23. Did they persist: ❏ 1–6 mos. ❏ 1-2 yrs ❏ over 3 years

8%	10%	82%

24. Do they still persist?	7%	25%	23%	19%	8%	18%
25. Was post-abortion counseling available through the clinic or referral agency?	16%	76%	4%	1%	1%	2%
26. Did you require professional counseling and/or treatment?	8%	45%	4%	6%	6%	31%

What other forms of counseling did you receive?—(see Chapter One)

27. Were you using a form of birth control when you conceived? 23% Yes 74% No 3% Unsure
If so, what type?—(see Chapter One)

	N/A or Unsure	Not at All				Very Much
28. Were you familiar with the available forms of birth control?	1%	7%	8%	15%	7%	63%
29. Knowing where your life is today, would you still have chosen abortion?	4%	94%	1%	0%	0%	1%
30. Did you discuss your decision with others?	1%	25%	28%	19%	10%	18%
31. When you went to the clinic or counselor, was your decision already firm?	5%	30%	9%	16%	10%	31%
32. Were you still looking for options?	9%	29%	9%	7%	8%	36%
33. Did the clinic, doctor, or counselor help you to explore your decision?	2%	84%	7%	3%	1%	3%
34. Do you feel their opinions were biased?	23%	6%	3%	3%	7%	59%

If so: ☐ for abortion, or ☐ against abortion
       79%   1%   20% n/a

	N/A or Unsure	Not at All				Very Much
35. Were you adequately informed about the procedure?	4%	49%	17%	15%	10%	6%
36. Were you given information about the biological nature of the fetus?	4%	90%	3%	2%	0%	2%
37. Were you well informed about the procedure and fetus through other sources *before* seeking an abortion?	1%	83%	7%	5%	0%	4%
38. Was your decision made in consultation with your doctor?	2%	70%	4%	5%	6%	14%
39. Were you encouraged to ask questions?	6%	64%	16%	8%	3%	2%
40. Were your questions thoroughly answered to your satisfaction?	19%	52%	12%	8%	4%	4%
41. Do you believe there was information you were not given, or were misinformed about?	8%	10%	1%	4%	4%	73%

If so, what?—(see Chapter One)

	N/A or Unsure	Not at All				Very Much
42. Were risks and dangers discussed?	7%	65%	16%	5%	4%	4%

43. What *was* your opinion about the nature of the fetus?
    4% no answer   26% human   30% non-human   40% other

	N/A or Unsure	Not at All				Very Much
What *is* your opinion about the nature of the fetus?						
3% no answer 97% human			0% non-human		0% other	
44. If counseling a friend who was in a situation such as yours, would you encourage her to choose an abortion?	1%	98%	0%	0%	0%	1%
45. Was your self-image improved or worsened by your decision? (worsened-1; improved-5)	2%	89%	4%	3%	1%	1%
46. Is your life today better or worse because of your decision? (worse-1; better-5)	21%	60%	6%	8%	1%	4%
47. Was the period of your pregnancy before the abortion emotionally traumatic?	4%	11%	6%	10%	11%	60%
48. Did you feel in control of your life when making your decision?	3%	65%	8%	9%	6%	10%
49. Did you feel your life was controlled by others?	4%	16%	8%	12%	14%	47%
50. Did the knowledge that abortion was legal influence your opinion about the morality of choosing abortion?	11%	12%	1%	6%	12%	58%
51. Did you consider carrying the pregnancy to full term?	5%	19%	12%	15%	12%	38%
52. Did you consider keeping the baby?	6%	23%	10%	13%	10%	49%
53. Did you consider adoption?	4%	62%	13%	7%	6%	8%
54. Under better circumstances, would you have kept the baby?	10%	1%	2%	3%	3%	81%
55. After your abortion, did you hope to have children at a later time?	6%	6%	1%	2%	1%	84%
56. Were there periods when you felt good or excited about your pregnancy?	9%	23%	8%	6%	10%	43%
57. What were your feelings about abortion prior to becoming pregnant? (negative-1; positive-5)	21%	33%	8%	20%	6%	12%
58. What are your feelings about abortion today? (negative-1; positive-5)	1%	98%	1%	0%	0%	0%

PLANNED PARENTHOOD GROUP

After the overall analysis, survey respondents who received counseling and/or their abortions at Planned Parenthood clinics were sorted out and tabulated separately, as discussed in Chapter One. A total of fifty-three respondents (21% of all respondents) fell into this subgroup. Their answers to the following questions were selected to provide a comparison of Planned Parenthood services to those of abortion providers as a whole.

		N/A or Unsure	Not at All				Very Much
1.	Were you satisfied with the abortion services you received?	11%	45%	11%	13%	8%	11%
6f.	Were you encouraged to have an abortion by (your) abortion counselor?	26%	10%	2%	2%	12%	48%
28.	Would your choice have been different if any or all of the above had encouraged you differently?	8%	0%	0%	0%	13%	80%
31.	When you went to the clinic or counselor, was your decision to abort already firm?	2%	36%	11%	23%	4%	25%
32.	Were you still looking for options?	11%	19%	6%	9%	9%	45%
33.	Did the clinic, doctor, or counselor help you to explore your decision?	2%	85%	13%	0%	0%	0%
34.	Do you feel their opinions were biased?	19%	4%	2%	4%	6%	66%

If so, □ for or □ against abortion?

89% for   0% against   11% no answer

		N/A or Unsure	Not at All				Very Much
35.	Were you adequately informed about the procedure?	2%	43%	15%	23%	11%	6%
36.	Were you given information about the biological nature of the fetus?	2%	85%	8%	4%	0%	2%
37.	Were you well informed about the procedure and fetus through other sources *before* seeking an abortion?	2%	81%	4%	6%	0%	8%
38.	Was your decision made in consultation with your doctor?	2%	89%	2%	2%	0%	6%
39.	Were you encouraged to ask questions?	4%	60%	19%	11%	4%	2%
40.	Were your questions thoroughly answered to your satisfaction?	17%	53%	11%	13%	2%	4%
41.	Do you believe there was information you were not given or were misinformed about?	4%	13%	0%	4%	6%	74%
42.	Were risks and dangers discussed?	6%	62%	19%	8%	4%	2%

NOTES

CHAPTER ONE: *A Survey of Women Who Aborted*

1. Howard and Joy Osofsky, eds., *The Abortion Experience* (New York: Harper and Row Publishers, Inc., 1973), pp. 500-501.
2. Linda Bird Francke, *The Ambivalence of Abortion* (New York: Random House, 1978), p. 29.
3. U. S. Department of Commerce, *Statistical Abstract of the United States 1984*, 104th Edition, 1983; and Illinois Department of Public Health, "Abortion Data Report to the General Assembly," July 19, 1982.
4. *Statistical Abstract*, p. 71.
5. *Ibid.*
6. *Ibid.*; and Elasah Drogin, *Margaret Sanger: Father of Modern Society* (Coarsegold, CA: CUL Publications, 1980), p. 31.
7. Germain Grisez, *Abortion: the Myths, the Realities, and the Arguments* (New York: Corpus Books, 1972), pp. 52-54.
8. Francke, *Ambivalence of Abortion*, p. 46.
9. *Ibid.*; and IDPH, "Abortion Data Report."
10. Mary K. Zimmerman, *Passage Through Abortion* (New York: Praeger Publishers, 1977), pp. 62-70; and James Tunstead Burtchaell, *Rachel Weeping* (Kansas City: Andrews and McMeel, Inc., 1982), p. 104.
11. The responses to this question were slightly distorted by the fact that 8 percent of the women surveyed actually did have illegal abortions prior to 1973. Some of these illegal aborters answered this question by saying they would have strongly considered an illegal abortion; others felt this hypothetical question was not applicable to them because abortion was illegal at the time and answered "Unsure."
12. Zimmerman, *Passage Through Abortion*, pp. 62-63.
13. Since 60 percent of those who sought counseling at Planned Parenthood were uncertain about their decision, as compared to about 50 percent of the total sample, it can be concluded that Planned Parenthood clinics are more likely to attract and counsel women who are ambivalent about their decision. This is especially likely since Planned Parenthood specializes in birth control programs targeted at teenagers and low-income women. Women from these groups are especially likely to want the baby, but feel unable to do so and are thus more likely to seek help in finding options through personal counseling. Self-affirmed women, on the other hand, are unlikely to seek any counseling from a family planning clinic, and instead they come to a firm decision on their own and go straight to the abortion clinic.
14. A causal link between abortion and cervical cancer has not yet been verified and is only now being investigated by medical researchers. This 4 percent rate, however, is many times higher than the national average, especially for young and middle-aged women.

15. Ann Saltenberger, *Every Woman Has a Right to Know the Dangers of Legal Abortion* (Glassboro, NJ: Air-Plus Enterprises, 1982), pp. 154-155.

CHAPTER THREE: *The Evidence from the Pro-choice Side*

1. Mary K. Zimmerman, *Passage Through Abortion* (New York: Praeger Publishers, 1977), p. 42.
2. *Ibid.*; and Linda Bird Francke, *The Ambivalence of Abortion* (New York: Random House, 1978), p. 82. Also see the testimonies of WEBA members Nancyjo Mann (Foreword) and Jackie Bakker (pp. 206-210) in David C. Reardon, *Aborted Women—Silent No More* (Chicago: Loyola University Press and Wheaton, IL: Crossway Books, 1987).
3. Zimmerman, *Passage Through Abortion*, p. 43. For an example of parental pressure on WEBA members, see the story of "Molly Graham" in Reardon, *Aborted Women—Silent No More*, pp. 302-304.
4. *Ibid.*, pp. 78-79.
5. *Ibid.*, p. 122.
6. *Ibid.*, p. 110
7. *Ibid.*, pp. 110-112.
8. *Ibid.*, p. 122.
9. *Ibid.*, p. 143.
10. *Ibid.*, pp. 146-147.
11. *Ibid.*, p. 193.
12. *Ibid.*, p. 139.
13. *Ibid.*, p. 129.
14. *Ibid.*, p. 139.
15. *Ibid.*, pp. 140-141.
16. *Ibid.*, pp. 189-190.
17. *Ibid.*, p. 69.
18. *Ibid.*, p. 193.
19. *Ibid.*, pp. 194-195.
20. *Ibid.*, pp. 55, 150.
21. *Ibid.*, p. 186.
22. *Ibid.*, p. 182.
23. Jane Doe, "There Just Wasn't Room in Our Lives Now for Another Baby," *New York Times*, May 14, 1976, Op-Ed section.
24. *Ibid.*
25. *Ibid.*
26. Francke, *The Ambivalence of Abortion*, pp. 245-255.
27. *Ibid.*, pp. 11, 18.
28. Francke's low grades for factual accuracy are discussed in James Tunstead Burtchaell, *Rachel Weeping* (Kansas City: Andrews and McMeel, Inc., 1982), pp. 53-55.
29. Francke, *The Ambivalence of Abortion*, p. 43.
30. *Ibid.*, pp. 50, 64, 71, 84, 100, 111, 168, 169, 175, 200, 203, 229.
31. *Ibid.*, pp. 49, 56, 61, 78, 85, 86, 89, 91, 95, 96, 99, 107, 110, 151, 153, 155, 166, 191, 192, 199, 205, 226, 235.
32. *Ibid.*, pp. 31, 49, 65.
33. *Ibid.*, p. 85.
34. *Ibid.*, pp. 84, 95.
35. *Ibid.*, p. 167.
36. *Ibid.*, p. 100.
37. *Ibid.*, pp. 55-56.
38. *Ibid.*, pp. 49-51, 53, 56-68, 61, 64, 66, 67, 71, 75, 77, 79, 84, 88-91, 94-100,

107-108, 110-112, 152, 155, 167-169, 171, 174, 188, 192-194, 198, 200, 203, 205, 227-228, 231, 235, 238.
39. *Ibid.*, p. 61.
40. *Ibid.*, p. 167.
41. *Ibid.*, pp. 74-75.
42. *Ibid.*, pp. 78-81.
43. *Ibid.*, p. 91.
44. *Ibid.*, p. 201.
45. *Ibid.*, p. 63.
46. *Ibid.*, p. 77.
47. *Ibid.*, p. 99.
48. *Ibid.*, pp. 101-103.
49. *Ibid.*, p. 96.
50. *Ibid.*, p. 93.
51. *Ibid.*, p. 64.
52. *Ibid.*, p. 65.
53. *Ibid.*, pp. 63-66.
54. *Ibid.*, pp. 105-106.
55. *Ibid.*, pp. 98, 103.
56. *Ibid.*, pp. 55-56.
57. Magda Denes, *In Necessity and Sorrow: Life and Death in an Abortion Hospital* (New York: Basic Books, 1976), p. xiv.
58. *Ibid.*, p. 94.
59. *Ibid.*, pp. 97-98.
60. *Ibid.*, p. 101.
61. *Ibid.*, p. 122.
62. *Ibid.*, p. xvii.
63. *Ibid.*, p. 6.
64. *Ibid.*, p. 14.
65. *Ibid.*, p. 50.
66. *Ibid.*, pp. 58-61.
67. *Ibid.*, p. 126.
68. *Ibid.*, pp. 222-223.
69. *Ibid.*, p. 240.
70. *Ibid.*, p. 246.
71. *Ibid.*, pp. 134-135.
72. *Ibid.*, p. 199.
73. *Ibid.*, p. 203.
74. *Ibid.*, p. 191.
75. *Ibid.*, p. xv.
76. *Ibid.*, p. 57.
77. *Ibid.*, pp. xv-xvi.
78. The Boston Women's Health Collective, Inc., *Our Bodies, Ourselves* (New York: Simon and Schuster, 1973), p. 234.
79. *Ibid.*
80. *Ibid.*, p. 236.
81. *Ibid.*
82. *Ibid.*, pp. 236-237.
83. *Ibid.*
84. Reprinted in "Mother Is the Other Victim of Abortion," *The National Right to Life News*, December 22, 1983, p. 10.
85. Interview by columnist Colman McCarthy, "A Psychological View of Abortion," *Washington Post*, March 7, 1971. In a follow-up interview, Dr.

Fogel repeated his remarks, adding, "There is no question about the emotional grief and mourning following an abortion. . . . Many [patients] come in—some are just mute, some hostile. Some burst out crying. . . . There is no question in my mind that we are disturbing a life process." Colman McCarthy column, "The Real Anguish of Abortions," *Washington Post*, February 5, 1989.

86. *Catholics United for Life Bulletin*, March 1982.
87. Reprinted quotes from Dr. Herbert Ratner, "A Baby on Her Mind," *Life and Family News* brochure.
88. See the moving testimony by Audra Stevens, "But Nobody Said Think," *Abortion and Social Justice*, Thomas W. Hilgers and Dennis J. Horan, eds. (New York: Sheed and Ward, 1972), p. 267. See also p. 187.
89. Donald Granberg, "The Abortion Activists," *Family Planning Perspectives*, July-August 1981, pp. 157-163.
90. *Ibid.*, p. 163.
91. *Ibid.*, p. 161.
92. *Encyclopedia of Associations*, 18th edition, 1984, pp. 906, 1105.
93. Granberg, "The Abortion Activists," p. 161; and *Encyclopedia of Associations*.
94. Francke, *Ambivalence of Abortion*, pp. 48-51. Also see, for example, WEBA member Karen Sullivan's story in Chapter Four.

CHAPTER FOUR: *Feminists Who Abort*

1. Linda Bird Francke, *The Ambivalence of Abortion* (New York: Random House, 1978), p. 5.
2. Thomas W. Strahan, *Major Articles and Books Concerning the Detrimental Effects of Abortion* (Charlottesville, VA: The Rutherford Institute, 1990), pp. 116-119. Strahan's annotated bibliography cites two major studies which found a statistically significant link between abortion and cervical cancer, and four studies finding a statistically significant link between abortion and breast cancer.

CHAPTER FIVE: *The Physical Risks of Abortion*

1. See for example the declaration of Esther Pratt that "The brutal consequences of illegal abortion—mutilation, blood poisoning and even death—have been almost nonexistent in the United States since January 22, 1973, when the Supreme Court ruled. . . . " in "Is An Acorn An Oak Tree?," *The Weekly*, Champaign-Urbana, Illinois, Vol. 4, No. 3, p. 1.
2. Lynn D. Wardle and Mary Anne Wood, *A Lawyer Looks at Abortion* (Provo, UT: Brigham Young University Press, 1982), p. 122.
3. Robert A. Destro, "Abortion and the Constitution: The Need for a Life-Protective Amendment," *California Law Review*, 1975, Vol. 63, p. 1303 (footnote 274).
4. John and Barbara Willke, *Handbook on Abortion* (Cincinnati: Hayes Publishing Company, 1979), pp. 78-80, 89. See also Pamela Zekman and Pamela Warrick, "The Abortion Profiteers," *Chicago Sun Times*, special reprint, December 3, 1978 (original publication November 12, 1978). Zekman and Warrick reveal how undercover investigators in abortion clinics found that clinic employees routinely checked off "no complications" before the abortion was even performed.
5. Ann Saltenberger, *Every Woman Has a Right to Know the Dangers of Legal Abortion* (Glassboro, NJ: Air-Plus Enterprises, 1982), p. 19.
6. *Ibid.*; Willke, *Handbook on Abortion*, pp. 78, 79; and Thomas Hilgers,

Dennis Horan, and David Mall, *New Perspectives on Human Abortion* (Frederick, MD: University Publications of America, 1981), pp. 145-150.

7. Margaret Wynn and Arthur Wynn, "Some Consequences of Induced Abortion to Children Born Subsequently," Foundation for Education and Research in Child Bearing, London, 1972, reprinted in *Marriage and Family Newsletter,* Vol. 4, Nos. 2-4, February, March, April 1973, Collegeville, MN, pp. 8, 9.

8. Willke, *Handbook on Abortion,* pp. 78, 80, 86.

9. Hilgers, et al., *New Perspectives on Human Abortion,* p. 147.

10. Wynn, "Some Consequences," p. 17.

11. D. A. Grimes and W. Cates, Jr., "Abortion: Methods and Complications," *Human Reproduction,* 2nd ed., pp. 796-813.

12. Willke, *Handbook on Abortion,* p. 29.

13. A 1971 German study of 1,234 abortions reported an "early complication" rate of 12.2 percent, cited in Wynn, "Some Consequences," p. 17. Another study of 2,498 vacuum abortions found 285 incidents of obvious post-abortion complications either immediately after the procedure or at an eight-week follow-up exam, yielding an "early complication" rate of 11.4 percent. (Edelman, Brenner, and Berger, "Abortion by Aspiration versus Curettage," *American Journal of Obstetrics and Gynecology,* June 15, 1974, Vol. 119, No. 4, p. 476.)

14. See Wardle and Wood, *A Lawyer Looks at Abortion,* pp. 112, 113, for statistics and a comparison of the morbidity and natural childbirth definitions.

15. Wynn, "Some Consequences," p. 20.

16. Saltenberger, *Every Woman,* general.

17. *Ibid.*

18. *Ibid.,* pp. 30-32.

19. *Ibid.*; Grimes and Cates, "Abortion: Methods and Complications."

20. Wardle and Wood, *A Lawyer Looks at Abortion,* p. 114.

21. See Saltenberger, *Every Woman,* in general; WEBA brochure "Before You Make the Decision."

22. Saltenberger, *Every Woman,* pp. 84, 180-181.

23. Wynn, "Some Consequences," p. 20.

24. Grimes and Cates, "Abortion: Methods and Complications," p. 810.

25. Willke, *Handbook on Abortion,* p. 31.

26. Thomas W. Hilgers and Dennis J. Horan, eds., *Abortion and Social Justice* (New York: Sheed and Ward, 1972), p. 292.

27. *Ibid.*

28. Saltenberger, *Every Woman,* p. 33.

29. Wardle and Wood, *A Lawyer Looks at Abortion,* p. 123.

30. See Saltenberger, *Every Woman,* p. 81.

31. *Ibid.,* p. 36.

32. *Ibid.* in general; Wardle and Wood, *A Lawyer Looks at Abortion,* p. 115.

33. Bernard Nathanson, M.D., with Richard Ostling, *Aborting America* (Garden City, NY: Doubleday, 1979), p. 276.

34. Liz Jeffries and Rick Edmonds, "Abortion: The Dreaded Complication," *The Philadelphia Inquirer,* August 2, 1981.

35. Thomas J. Marzen, "The Supreme Court on Abortion: Doctor Knows Best," *The National Right to Life News,* June 30, 1983, p. 15.

36. "The Doctor's Dilemma—When Abortion Gives Birth to Life," *Chicago Tribune,* August 15, 1982, section 12.

37. Jeffries and Edmonds, "Abortion: The Dreaded Complication."

38. See Linda Bird Franke, *The Ambivalence of Abortion* (New York: Random

House, 1978), p. 34, for an example of a physician's refusal to treat a live-born aborted fetus. He commented, "That's not a baby. That's an abortion."
39. Mike Masterson, "Baby Survives Abortion in Arkansas," *The National Right to Life News*, August 4, 1983, p. 6.
40. Jeffries and Edmonds, "Abortion: The Dreaded Complication."
41. *Ibid.*
42. Gretchen Kaiser, "Abortion Technique Injects Digitoxin into Baby's Heart," *The National Right to Life News*, September 13, 1984, p. 1. See also Saltenberger, *Every Woman*, p. 192.
43. See Dr. Thomas Hilgers, "The Medical Hazards of Legally Induced Abortion," in Hilgers and Horan, *Abortion and Social Justice*, p. 69. See also Saltenberger, *Every Woman*, p. 75.
44. Willke, *Handbook on Abortion*, pp. 53, 54.
45. See Saltenberger, *Every Woman*. See also "Ectopic Pregnancies Increasing," *The National Right to Life News*, August 16, 1984, p. 4 (from a health report printed in the *New York Times*).
46. Dr. and Mrs. J. C. Willke, *Abortion: Questions and Answers* (Cincinnati, OH: Hayes Publishing Company, 1985), p. 104, citing U.S. Dept. H.H.S., *Morbidity and Mortality Weekly Report*, April 20, 1984.
47. Hilgers and Horan, *Abortion and Social Justice*, p. 73.
48. Willke, *Abortion: Questions and Answers*, p. 103, citing the *British Journal of OB/GYN*, August 1976.
49. Wynn, "Some Consequences," p. 7.
50. Willke, *Abortion: Questions and Answers*, p. 91.
51. Willke, *Handbook on Abortion*, p. 92.
52. Saltenberger, *Every Woman*, p. 177.
53. Willke, *Handbook on Abortion*, p. 94.
54. Hilgers and Horan, *Abortion and Social Justice*, p. 70.
55. Wynn, "Some Consequences," p. 5; Willke, *Abortion: Questions and Answers*, pp. 105, 106.
56. Hilgers, et al., *New Perspectives on Human Abortion*, pp. 128-133.
57. Saltenberger, *Every Woman*, p. 182; Willke, *Abortion: Questions and Answers*, p. 109.
58. Willke, *Abortion: Questions and Answers*, p. 107.
59. Wynn, "Some Consequences," p. 18.
60. Willke, *Abortion: Questions and Answers*, p. 118.
61. *Ibid.*, p. 107; Wynn, "Some Consequences," p. 15.
62. *Science*, Vol. 215, p. 1589.
63. Willke, *Abortion: Questions and Answers*, pp. 97, 98.
64. *Ibid.*, p. 193.
65. Saltenberger, *Every Woman*, p. 27.
66. Zekman and Warrick, "The Abortion Profiteers."
67. See Willke, *Handbook on Abortion*, pp. 81, 82. See also Hilgers, "Medical Hazards of Abortion," *Abortion and Social Justice*, p. 61.
68. Destro, "Abortion and the Constitution," p. 1303 (footnote 274).
69. Willke, *Handbook on Abortion*, p. 78.
70. Saltenberger, *Every Woman*, p. 51.
71. Willke, *Handbook on Abortion*, p. 80.
72. *Ibid.* This 10 percent rate fits with the discrepancy in the reported mortality rates from the New York experience. See Hilgers, "Medical Hazards of Abortion," *Abortion and Social Justice*, and Willke, *Abortion: Questions and Answers*, pp. 98-99.
73. Saltenberger, *Every Woman*, p. 52.

74. Hilgers, et al., *New Perspectives on Human Abortion*, p. 82.
75. Andrew M. Kaunitz, M.D., et al., "Causes of Maternal Mortality in the United States," *Obstetrics and Gynecology*, May 1985, Vol. 65, No. 5, p. 607. It is noteworthy that this listing of abortion deaths excludes indirect deaths resulting from embolism, obstetric hemorrhage, obstetric infection, anesthesia complications, and deaths from ectopic or other pregnancies complicated as a result of a previous abortion. Deaths from these cases were listed under other maternal mortality categories even though they might more appropriately be under abortion-related deaths.
76. Saltenberger, *Every Woman*, p. 32.
77. *Ibid.*, p. 40.
78. Saltenberger, *Every Woman*, pamphlet edition.
79. Frances Frech, "Comparing the Figures," *The Human Life Review*, Fall 1982, Vol. 8, No. 4, p. 72.
80. Hilgers, "Medical Hazards of Abortion," *Abortion and Social Justice*, p. 63.
81. *Ibid.*, p. 61.
82. *Ibid.*
83. *Ibid.*
84. Hilgers, et al., *New Perspectives on Human Abortion*, pp. 82, 83.
85. Frech, "Comparing the Figures," p. 62.
86. Willke, *Handbook on Abortion*, p. 87.
87. *Ibid.*
88. Frech, "Comparing the Figures," pp. 69-72, and Hilgers, et al., *New Perspectives on Human Abortion*, pp. 69-91. Also, it should be noted that spontaneous miscarriage is the only natural phenomenon truly comparable to induced abortion. When this comparison is made, the maternal mortality rate for induced abortion is found to be two to five times greater than the maternal death rate for miscarriage during all stages of gestation. See Robert G. Marshall, "Spontaneous Abortion Deaths," *A.L.L. About Issues*, September 1985, Vol. 7, No. 9, p. 49.
89. "Is Abortion Safer Than Childbirth?", *The National Right to Life News*, February 3, 1983.
90. It is reported that there is only a 2 percent morbidity rate for childbirth (Wardle and Wood, *A Lawyer Looks at Abortion*, p. 112) as compared to abortion morbidity rates which are commonly reported to be in the 20 to 40 percent range.
91. Wynn, "Some Consequences," in general.

CHAPTER EIGHT: *Business Before Medicine*

1. David C. Reardon, *Aborted Women—Silent No More* (Chicago: Loyola University Press and Wheaton: Crossway Books, 1987), pp. 161-187 which examines abortion for "therapeutic" reasons.
2. Lynn D. Wardle and Mary Anne Wood, *A Lawyer Looks at Abortion* (Provo, UT: Brigham Young University Press, 1982), p. 159; John and Barbara Willke, *Handbook on Abortion* (Cincinnati: Hayes Publishing Co., 1979), p. 99; and *The Village Voice*, March 1, 1983.
3. Wardle and Wood, *A Lawyer Looks at Abortion*, pp. 120-125.
4. See the U. S. Supreme Court decisions *Akron v. Akron Center for Reproductive Health*, 1983, and *Thornburg v. ACOG*, 1986; also Willke, *Handbook on Abortion*, p. 99.
5. Willke, *Handbook on Abortion*, p. 99.
6. *Ibid.*, p. 98.

7. Pamela Zekman and Pamela Warrick, "The Abortion Profiteers," *Chicago Sun-Times*, December 3, 1978, pp. 21-22.
8. *Ibid.*, p. 12.
9. *Catholics United for Life Newsletter*, October 1981.
10. Zekman and Warrick, "Abortion Profiteers," p. 8.
11. Willke, *Handbook on Abortion*, p. 100.
12. Zekman and Warrick, "Abortion Profiteers"; Magda Denes, *In Necessity and Sorrow: Life and Death in an Abortion Hospital* (New York: Basic Books, 1976).
13. Zekman and Warrick, "Abortion Profiteers"; Ann Saltenberger, *Every Woman Has a Right to Know the Dangers of Legal Abortion* (Glassboro, NJ: Air-Plus Enterprises, 1982), pp. 170-171.
14. Willke, *Handbook on Abortion*, p. 100; Zekman and Warrick, "Abortion Profiteers," pp. 16-18.
15. Zekman and Warrick, "Abortion Profiteers," p. 19.
16. Saltenberger, *Every Woman*, p. 161.
17. Zekman and Warrick, "Abortion Profiteers," p. 15.
18. Willke, *Handbook on Abortion*, p. 99.
19. *Ibid.*, p. 100; Saltenberger, *Every Woman*, pp. 180-181; and Zekman and Warrick, "Abortion Profiteers."
20. Willke, *Handbook on Abortion*, p. 100.
21. Zekman and Warrick, "Abortion Profiteers," pp. 14-16.
22. *Ibid.*; Denes, *In Necessity and Sorrow*, p. 236.
23. Saltenberger, *Every Woman*, p. 170.
24. Zekman and Warrick, "Abortion Profiteers," p. 12.
25. *Ibid.*, p. 6; Bernard Nathanson, M.D., with Richard Ostling, *Aborting America* (Garden City, NY: Doubleday and Company, 1979), pp. 112-113.
26. Zekman and Warrick, "Abortion Profiteers," p. 3.
27. *Ibid.*, p. 9; Denes, *In Necessity and Sorrow*, p. 226.
28. Willke, *Handbook on Abortion*, p. 102.
29. *Ibid.*, p. 101; Zekman and Warrick, "Abortion Profiteers."
30. *Catholics United for Life Newsletter*, October 1981.
31. Donald DeMarco, "The Family at Bay," *The Human Life Review*, Vol. 8, No. 4, Fall 1982, pp. 44-54.
32. Zekman and Warrick, "Abortion Profiteers," p. 32.
33. Paul Marx, *The Death Peddlers: War on the Unborn* (Collegeville, MN: St. John's University Press, 1971), p. 124.
34. *Ibid.*, p. 142.
35. *Ibid.*
36. Wardle and Wood, *A Lawyer Looks at Abortion*, pp. 120-124; Thomas J. Marzen, "The Supreme Court on Abortion: Doctor Knows Best," *The National Right to Life News*, June 30, 1983, p. 15.
37. Willke, *Handbook on Abortion*, p. 101.
38. John Noonan, Jr., "The Akron Case," *The Human Life Review*, Vol. 9, No. 3, Summer 1983, p. 8.
39. Wardle and Wood, *A Lawyer Looks at Abortion*, p. 110.
40. Willke, *Handbook on Abortion*, pp. 102-103.
41. Zekman and Warrick, "Abortion Profiteers," pp. 11-15.
42. Denes, *In Necessity and Sorrow*, pp. 211-224, 236.
43. Zekman and Warrick, "Abortion Profiteers," pp. 12-13.
44. Mary Arnold, "Abortion Burnout," *Catholic Twin Circle*, August 5, 1984, pp. 3-4; Denes, *In Necessity and Sorrow*; and the stories of WEBA members Carol

St. Amour (4); Alice Gilmore (7); Donna Merrick (8) in Reardon, *Aborted Women—Silent No More.*

45. Thomas W. Hilgers and Dennis J. Horan, *Abortion and Social Justice*(New York: Sheed and Ward, 1972), pp. 69-70; Willke, *Handbook on Abortion*, p. 103.
46. Personal communication with the Illinois Department of Public Health (IDPH).
47. *Ibid.*
48. Personal communication with the Illinois Department of Registration and Education (IDRE), 1984.
49. Zekman and Warrick, "Abortion Profiteers," pp. 14-15, 31.
50. *Ibid.*, pp. 8, 41.
51. *Ibid.*, p. 43; and personal communication with IDRE.
52. Personal communication with IDPH.
53. Zekman and Warrick, "Abortion Profiteers," p. 8.
54. *Ibid.*, p. 45.
55. *Ibid.*, p. 10.
56. See for example the discussion regarding the abortion hospital studied in Denes, *In Necessity and Sorrow.*
57. "Feminists Furious Over CBS' Exposé of 'Safe, Legal Abortions,'" *IRLC News*, April/June 1991, p. 6.
58. Robert Bruce Spencer, "The Licensed Back Alley: Legal Abortion in Florida," *A.L.L. About Issues*, August/September 1990, 12 (8-9):16-19.
59. Zekman and Warrick, "Abortion Profiteers," pp. 2-3, 33.
60. *Ibid.*, p. 33.
61. Marx, *The Death Peddlers*, p. 19.
62. *Ibid.*, p. 21.
63. *Ibid.*, pp. 18-19.
64. Zekman and Warrick, "Abortion Profiteers," p. 33.
65. Milton Rockmore, "Are You Sorry You Had An Abortion?" *Good Housekeeping*, July 1977, Vol. 185, p. 120.
66. *Ibid.*
67. Debra Braun, "Nation's First Black Crisis Pregnancy Center Stresses Family Involvement," *The National Right to Life News*, January 12, 1984, p. 4.
68. Dr. Monte Harris Liebman and Jolie Siebold Zimmer, "The Psychological Sequelae of Abortion: Fact and Fallacy," in David Mall and Dr. Walter Watts, eds., *The Psychological Aspects of Abortion* (Washington, DC: University Publications of America, 1979), p. 133.
69. James Tunstead Burtchaell, *Rachel Weeping* (Kansas City: Andrews and McMeel, 1982), p. 80.
70. Linda Bird Francke, *The Ambivalence of Abortion* (New York: Random House, 1978), p. 179.
71. DeMarco, "The·Family At Bay," pp. 44-54; Thomas and Catherine Yassu, "The Abortionists Betray a Family," brochure printed by Sun Life, Thaxton, Virginia; and "Court OKs Abortion for Suicidal Minor," *Illinois Right to Life Committee News*, September/December 1986, p. 1.
72. See Marx, *The Death Peddlers*, pp. 19, 29-30.
73. Francke, *Ambivalence of Abortion*, p. 182.
74. Denes, *In Necessity and Sorrow*, p. 17.
75. *Ibid.*, pp. 76-77.
76. *Ibid.*
77. Burtchaell, *Rachel Weeping*, pp. 135-136.

78. See Denes, *In Necessity and Sorrow*, pp. 18, 156, and throughout several other interviews.
79. Burtchaell, *Rachel Weeping*, p. 136.
80. Denes, *In Necessity and Sorrow*, p. 32.
81. *Ibid.*, p. 8.
82. See the interviews with counselors who have been aborted in Francke, *Ambivalence of Abortion*, pp. 71-75, 86-89, 228-230. Also see the testimony of Karen Sullivan, Chapter Four.
83. See Denes, *In Necessity and Sorrow*, p. 134; Testimony of Deborah Hulebak in Chapter Four.
84. See the testimonies of WEBA members Karen Sullivan and Deborah Hulebak in Chapter Four.
85. Denes, *In Necessity and Sorrow*, p. 243.
86. *Ibid.*, pp. 89-90.
87. *Ibid.*, p. 245.
88. Dr. George Maloof, "The Consequences of Incest: Giving and Taking Life," *The Psychological Aspects of Abortion*, p. 92.
89. Denes, *In Necessity and Sorrow*, pp. 21, 39.
90. *Ibid.*, p. 80.
91. *Ibid.*, p. 18.
92. *Ibid.*, p. 156.
93. *Ibid.*, pp. 177-178.
94. *Ibid.*, p. 19.
95. *Ibid.*, p. 131.
96. Francke, *Ambivalence of Abortion*, p. 40; Denes, *In Necessity and Sorrow*, p. 246.
97. *Ibid.*, p. 34.
98. Mary Arnold, "Abortion Burnout," *Catholic Twin Circle*, August 5, 1984, pp. 3-4.
99. *Ibid.*, Denes, *In Necessity and Sorrow*, in general.
100. See Hilgers and Horan, *Abortion and Social Justice*, p. 77; and Francke, *Ambivalence of Abortion*, p. 33.
101. Denes, *In Necessity and Sorrow*, p. 243.
102. *Ibid.*, p. 69.
103. Burtchaell, *Rachel Weeping*, p. 220.
104. *Ibid.*, Nancy Koster, "Abortionists Incriminated by Their Own Statistics," *National Right to Life News*, September 27, 1984, p. 7.
105. Francke, *Ambivalence of Abortion*, p. 40; and Burtchaell, *Rachel Weeping*, p. 218.
106. Liebman and Zimmer, "Psychological Sequelae of Abortion," p. 128.
107. Denes, *In Necessity and Sorrow*, p. 67.
108. Burtchaell, *Rachel Weeping*, p. 210. See also the interview with abortionist Edward Allred in the film *A Matter of Choice* (New Liberty Pictures). When asked if there were any moral or ethical principles by which he justified abortion, Dr. Allred answered, "It's philosophical as much as anything. I don't choose to get into that aspect of it. I'm not much of a philosopher. I try not to delve into things like that too much."
109. Marx, *The Death Peddlers*, p. 125; "The New Ethic for Medicine and Society," *California Medicine*, (official journal of the California Medical Association), Vol. 113, No. 3, September 1970, pp. 67-68 (editorial).
110. See the interview with Dr. Allred in the film, *A Matter of Choice*.
111. Burtchaell, *Rachel Weeping*, p. 210.
112. John Powell, *Abortion: The Silent Holocaust* (Allen, TX: Tabor, 1981), p. 67.

113. Denes, *In Necessity and Sorrow*, pp. 146-147.
114. *Ibid.*, p. 141.
115. *Ibid.*, p. 64.
116. *Ibid.*, pp. 64-65.
117. *Ibid.*, p. 141.
118. *Ibid.*, p. 144.
119. *Ibid.*, p. 68.
120. *Ibid.*, p. 69.
121. Burtchaell, *Rachel Weeping*, p. 213; and see Robert S. Mendelsohn, *MalePractice: How Doctors Manipulate Women*, (Chicago: Contemporary Books, 1981), pp. 77-88 for additional examples of how physicians blame their own irresponsibility on the "demands" of their patients.
122. Denes, *In Necessity and Sorrow*, p. 140.
123. *Ibid.*, pp. 64, 147.
124. See the comments of Dr. Kerenyi in "The Doctor's Dilemma—When Abortion Gives Birth to Life," *Chicago Tribune*, August 15, 1982, Section 12.
125. Denes, *In Necessity and Sorrow*, p. 68.
126. *Ibid.*, p. 232.
127. Arnold, "Abortion Burnout," p. 4.
128. Denes, *In Necessity and Sorrow*, p. 227.
129. John T. Noonan, Jr., *A Private Choice: Abortion in America in the Seventies* (Toronto: Life Cycle Books, 1979), p. 170.
130. Nathanson, *Aborting America*, p. 110.
131. *Ibid.*, p. 164.
132. Germain Grisez, *Abortion: the Myths, the Realities, and the Arguments* (New York: Corpus Books, 1972), p. 51.
133. *Ibid.*; Howard Fisher, "Abortion—Pain or Pleasure?," *The Psychological Aspects of Abortion* (Washington D.C.: University Publications of America,1979), p. 50.
134. Denes, *In Necessity and Sorrow*, p. 79.
135. *Ibid.*, p. 134.
136. *Ibid.*, especially pp. 62, 225, 230. For an explanation of how the competition created by medical schools encourages the development and selection of compassionless doctors, see Mendelsohn, *MalePractice*, p. 89.
137. Denes, *In Necessity and Sorrow*, p. 145.
138. *Ibid.*, p. 239.
139. Burtchaell, *Rachel Weeping*, pp. 216-217.
140. Denes, *In Necessity and Sorrow*, p. 144.
141. Burtchaell, *Rachel Weeping*, p. 50.
142. Dr. Conrad Baars, "Psychic Causes and Consequences of the Abortion Mentality," *The Psychological Aspects of Abortion*, p. 121.
143. Denes, *In Necessity and Sorrow*, p. 240.

EPILOGUE
1. Hilgers, *et al.*, *New Perspectives on Human Abortion* (Frederick, MD: University Publications of America, 1981), p. 447.
2. Paulette Joyer, "Abortion Hasn't Helped Solve Women's Problems," *Sisterlife*, a publication of Feminists for Life of America, September 1984, p. 3.
3. Judith Blake, "The Supreme Court's Abortion Decisions and Public Opinion in the United States," *Population & Development Review* (March/June 1977); Raymond J. Adamek, "Abortion and Public Opinion in the United States," National Right to Life Education Trust Fund, 1982, p. 13; James Tunstead

Burtchaell, *Rachel Weeping* (Kansas City: Andrews and McMeel, Inc., 1982), p. 100.
4. Peter Maurin, *The Catholic Worker* (May 1976), p. 5.
5. Arthur Dyck, "Is Abortion Necessary to Solve Population Problems?," *Abortion and Social Justice*, p. 169.